San Antonio

The Story of an Enchanted City

San Antonio
The Story of an Enchanted City

Frank W. Jennings

San Antonio Express-News

1998

First Edition

10 9 8 7 6 5 4 3 2 1

Permissions
San Antonio Express-News
Post Office Box 2171
San Antonio, Texas 78297-2171

The paper in this book meets the minimum requirements of
the American National Standard for Permanence of Paper for
Printed Library materials, z39.48.1984.

Library of Congress Cataloging-in-Publication Data

Jennings, Frank W., 1917–
San Antonio : the story of an enchanted city / Frank W. Jennings.
— 1st ed.
p.   cm.
Includes bibliographical references and index.
ISBN 1-890346-02-0 (alk. paper) — ISBN 1-890346-03-9 (pbk. :
alk. paper)
1. San Antonio (Tex.) — History.   2. San Antonio (Tex.)
— Guidebooks.   I. Title.
F394.S21157J46   1998
976.4'351—dc21   98-5244
                                                                          CIP

Design by Layton Graphics
Cover art by Jane Digby

Dedicated to Isabelita

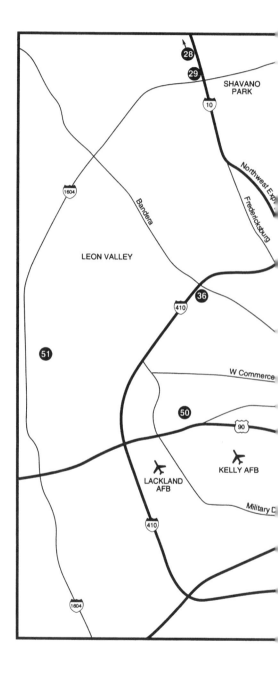

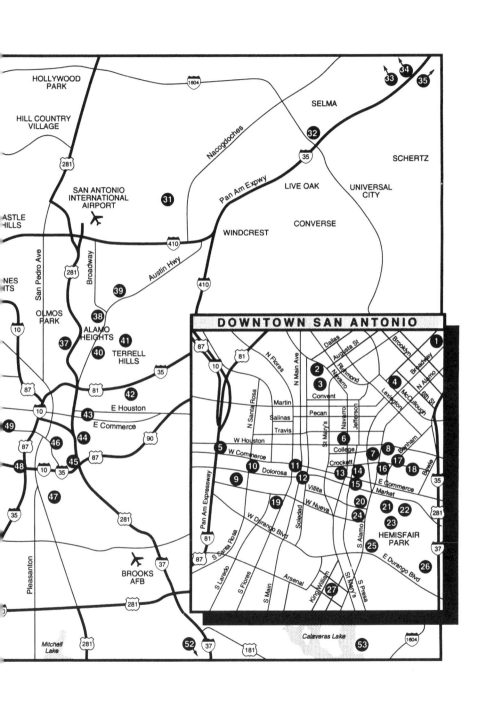

Primary rivers of early Texas region (Fred Himes illustration)

Contents

Foreword

Across the centuries, the greater community of San Antonio has attracted a legion of chroniclers, essayists, and writers. From Spanish colonial times to the present, the quality of the publications has varied, ranging from serious and scholarly to trivial and pedestrian. In the last quarter of the eighteenth century, Fray Juan Agustín Morfi, chaplain and chronicler of an inspection tour led by Commandant General Teodoro de Croix, produced the first *History of Texas, 1683-1779*, which Carlos E. Castañeda later translated and edited. In this chronicle Fray Morfi included discerning observations of frontier San Antonio.

In the twentieth century, beginning with the publication of *San Antonio—A Historical and Pictorial Guide*, by Charles W. Ramsdell, Jr., the checklist of books has become extensive. Among recent contributions, the authors who were not inclined to cover a broad sweep of San Antonio history concentrated on specialized aspects of the saga. Jesús F. de la Teja, in *San Antonio de Béxar*, examined only the Hispanic colonial roots and early development. T.R. Fehrenbach's *The San Antonio Story*, an excellent source teeming with colorful chronology, stopped at 1978, the year of its publication. Vernon G. Zunker's *A Dream Come True* focused on the life and times of Robert Hugman and the evolution of the San Antonio River Walk. Likewise, Jack Maguire, in *A Century of Fiesta in San Antonio*, discussed only the art of celebration, and Lewis Fisher's *Saving San Antonio* is a history of the preservation work of the San Antonio Conservation Society.

Other books—John L. Davis' *San Antonio: A Historical Portrait* and Cecilia Steinfeldt's *San Antonio Was*—are excellent photographic essays, replete with notes and bibliographies, but restricted in scope. The words of a remarkable teacher, Dr. Joseph W. Schmitz, S.M., co-founder of the San Antonio Historical

Association, are instructive for this purpose: "Each generation of historians must write its own history."

Frank W. Jennings energetically pursued a dream of writing an eclectic book about San Antonio, viewed from the perspective of an enchanted city. The result, after years of dedicated research, is a collage of sights, sounds, events, and emotions.

Native *San Antoninos* are naturally defensive about how strangers and newcomers perceive their city. Upon arrival, a sensitive spectator—as Frank Jennings initially discovered—becomes fascinated with the multiple layers of local history that have required at least three centuries to accumulate.

Inspired by successful publishing achievements in magazines and newspapers, Jennings, a gifted writer, conceived a thesis that focused on manifold contributions to local history by various ethnic groups. To his credit, in this discerning endeavor he cautiously avoided a folkloric, chronological approach in his composition. First, he acknowledged a cavalcade of ethnic groups whose human experiences fashioned the kaleidoscope of San Antonio. Next, he judiciously selected the principal groups—Native Americans, Hispanics, Mexicans, Germans, Texans (and *Tejanos*) who performed ascendant roles, with Anglo Americans and representatives of other cultures artfully integrated into the narrative whenever appropriate. Finally, the author flavored his treatise with a consistent aggregate of candor, creativity, curiosity, fairness, and sensitivity.

Although Colonel Jennings aimed this interesting and informative volume toward an inordinate number of visitors—casual tourists and serious observers—he also kept in mind the requirements of teachers, students, residents, and guides, most of whom patiently seek the cultural and historical enchantment of San Antonio, for a handy, insightful reference tool.

— Félix D. Almaráz, Jr., Ph.D.
Professor of History, The University of Texas at San Antonio, and past president, Texas State Historical Association

SAN ANTONIO

Coat of Arms, San Antonio

San Antonio's coat of arms was designed and approved about twenty-five years ago. A two-part shield is surmounted by a castle coronet, representing the municipality. On the left is the coat of arms of Saint Anthony of Padua, the son of a Portuguese nobleman. It was adapted from his father's. The T, or Tau cross, indicates that Anthony was a priest. The ermine tails dotting the lower left were on the coat of arms of the saint's father. On the right side of the shield, a red background, or field, represents the blood shed for Texas liberty. The star represents the Republic and State of Texas. The Battle of the Alamo is represented by the former mission church. The Latin Libertatis Cunabula *means "Cradle of Liberty."*

The coat of arms was designed by Thomas A. Wilson and illustrated by Ramón Vásquez y Sánchez, with the cooperation and approval of the Spanish government and appropriate organizations in both Texas and Spain. The City Council of San Antonio adopted the coat of arms on February 17, 1972. (Photo courtesy Institute of Texan Cultures)

Coat of Arms, Bexar County

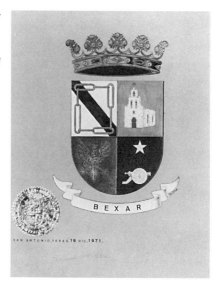

Divided into four quarters topped by a coronet, the coat of arms of Bexar County has been described by heraldic experts. Represented at the upper left are the arms of Don Alvaro de Zúñiga, Duke of Béxar in Spain, including the gold chains of Navarro, which in Spain corresponded to today's United States Medal of Honor. At upper right, Mission San Francisco de Espada represents the work of the Spanish missionaries. The eagle on the lower left represents both the Aztec eagle of Mexico and the American bald eagle. At lower right, the cannon represents the battles for independence of the Republic of Texas as well as the Texan support of the Confederacy in the Civil War. The coronet surmounting the quadrants of the shield represents a duke of Spain.

The coat of arms was designed by Thomas A. Wilson and illustrated by Ramón Vásquez y Sánchez, with the cooperation and approval of the Spanish government and appropriate organizations in both Texas and Spain. The Bexar County Commissioner's Court adopted the coat of arms for the county of Bexar on December 22, 1971. (Photo courtesy Institute of Texan Cultures)

Preface

*San Antonio speaks for itself, and much of its charm is in the
way it embodies its past.*
                                        —Larry McMurtry, 1968

*Every city lucky enough to be on a river ought to take as its
model San Antonio.*
                                 —Charles Kuralt, with CBS in 1990

*I rank [San Antonio] as one of the liveliest and most delight-
ful cities in the country. And romantic.*
                          —James T. Yenckel, *Washington Post*, 1992

The story of San Antonio is the story of a unique mixture of
people—American Indians, Hispanics, Germans, Anglo Americans and others—who have lived together in Texas for more than
a century and a half around four plazas, and who carried on commerce, freighting, agriculture, cattle-raising, petroleum production, military training, and scientific research. Here in South
Central Texas they thrived at the edge of the rolling green slopes
of the Hill Country by the verdant banks of three life-giving
streams.

The town's ten years as the oldest and largest community in
one of the world's independent republics of the 1800s—maturing
between two other burgeoning republics—left a permanent mark
on San Antonians as it did on all Texans. Together, they've shared
"the Texas experience." The dean of Texas historians, T. R.
Fehrenbach, has described this experience. He says: "What other
part of these United States, starting as twenty-three rural
counties, fought a foreign power to a standstill, won *de facto*

independence on the battlefield, established a republic that was recognized by Britain, France, Holland, Belgium and the United States and put its Lone Star flag on the high seas? All by its lonesome—remember, there were thirteen original colonies."

That unparalleled experience imprinted every Texan—including Tejanos and all other ethnic groups—with a distinct pride and self-satisfaction in being a living part of the Lone Star state. As a result, non-Texans are often justifiably piqued by what appears to be the uncalled-for smugness—sometimes even boastfulness—of Texans.

To learn what happened in San Antonio under Spain and later Mexico, to examine the reasons for that profound Texas act at the Alamo—to see how life was lived among the town's amazing variety of immigrants before and after the Civil War, and before the first passenger train arrived in 1877—is to learn a great deal about the history of all Texas.

San Antonio's people have preserved the traditions of both the non-Hispanics and the descendants of Spaniards and Mexicans—both the Texians and the Tejanos. Visitors marvel at the city's Hispanicity, while they revel in the joyful presence of the "Old West" customs formed in its years on the Chisholm Trail and its venerable ranching traditions.

The festive spirit and hospitality of its residents have become legendary. Yet in the early days, they fought numerous bloody battles in and around the town—mostly against attackers. Nowhere in the United States—from the 1700s to the mid-1800s—were there more skirmishes, attacks, coups, executions, massacres, surrenders, and full-scale battles. The scene of one of these, the Alamo, is known worldwide as a symbol of noble self-sacrifice.

The residents of San Antonio and their predecessors have molded a city of lofty spires and soul-stirring domes that has been acclaimed widely as one of the most charming in the United States. Its tree-vaulted River Walk, winding gently on both sides of the narrow stream—its watercraft cruising quietly past umbrella-topped tables in the shadows of lovely buildings—has made it "the Venice of America."

Significant examples of its architecture of the 1700s and 1800s have been remarkably preserved or restored in nostalgic settings. In no other part of the nation are there so many ancient Spanish mission churches in a city's environs.

The city's other-worldly appearance and unique culture have combined for many decades to evoke lyrical remarks from world travelers and visitors from "the States." The significance of a pervasive and unparalleled military imprint on San Antonio's unique character for 280 years has never been adequately analyzed or appreciated. Yet it has markedly affected the city's culture.

Today, you can witness the scenes and sites of a thousand stories yet to be finally told. And, if you wish, you can join the fun-loving folk of this enchanted city in one of their distinctive celebrations or cultural entertainments held in every week of the year.

A City To Return To

Some amazing findings about the attitudes of visitors to San Antonio were recorded by a private survey organization— McNabb, DeSoto, Salter & Co., headquartered in Las Vegas and Houston—when its staff members questioned more than 15,000 visitors to San Antonio between June 1994 and May 1995. Among those they interviewed, 46 percent were residents of Texas outside San Antonio, and 54 percent were non-Texas residents.

Why had they decided to visit San Antonio? On a scale of 1 to 10, their replies were "River Walk," 8.2; "Lots of things to see and do," 7.4; "Friendliness of the people," 7.2; and "International flavor of the city," 6.8.

The most extraordinary finding was the response of visitors to questions about their overall experiences in San Antonio—87 percent said theirs was "above average" or "excellent." And, virtually unprecedented for this kind of survey, 99 percent of the respondents said they would return for another visit.

A survey published in the July 1992 *Texas Highways* magazine showed that among the thousands of readers who responded, San Antonio was their favorite vacation destination in Texas. They also voted for San Antonio as "Texas' Friendliest City."

Readers of *Condé Nast Traveler* magazine have rated San Antonio among the top ten favorite destinations in the world for travelers since 1992, based on culture, restaurants, ambience, and attitude of the people. Santa Fe and San Francisco join San Antonio on the list of favorite destinations in the United States. Each of these Spanish-named cities of the West has a distinctive culture based on its unique history. Of the three, San Antonio is largest, and throughout its formative years has had the most diverse historic and ethnic influences.

The Alamo is the third most visited historical site in the United States, according to the National Park Service—right after the Statue of Liberty and the Liberty Bell. Yet in San Antonio the River Walk is visited by even more people than the Alamo. Visitors, including San Antonians, return to the river more often because of its great variety of attractions throughout the year.

Why have so many visitors to this city, beginning in the 1700s, found it so memorable—so charming, so enchanting? That's the question I've addressed. As a researcher, I've combed through the products of historians, journalists, pamphleteers, diarists, artists, photographers, and many other recorders of the past to find some of their most interesting writings and illustrations. I've tied stories of historical events to places you can easily find and visit. The book's maps as well as the city's excellent public transportation system will help you get there.

In examining the many treasures of the past that we enjoy in the late 1900s, we must pay tribute to Adina De Zavala, the first great advocate of historic preservation in Texas, beginning in 1889, and to the San Antonio Conservation Society—made up of more than 3,000 women—which, since 1924, has been devoted to rescuing the rarest treasures of the Enchanted City from the grasping hands of Progress. Moreover, the Society continually maintains sixteen historic properties—fourteen buildings and museum space for the Bolivar Hall Exhibit, plus the Hertzberg Clock, now at Houston Street and North St. Mary's, which since 1878 has been a landmark for generations of San Antonians.

Because the people of a great city have to do more than preserve the essential elements of their heritage, members of the Greater San Antonio Chamber of Commerce should be credited for promoting numerous economic stimulators since 1894. Many of San Antonio's amenities as a livable and convenient large, modern city—and its stature as a center for military bases, tourism, medical research, and international commerce—are results of the chamber's efforts.

As with any city in the United States, San Antonio has its share of poverty and crime and the other debilities of modern America. I have not covered these social problems in this book, although the city's poverty rate is notably high. City officials are working on a variety of programs to make improvements.

In 1993, San Antonio was rated Number 1 among the nation's top fifty cities for its fiscal management policies by Chicago-based *City & State*. At the same time, it was rated first among the nation's seventy-five largest metropolitan areas for its environmental quality. The World Resources Institute in Washington rated it at the top of its Green Metro Index for air and water quality and control of toxic emissions.

While San Antonio clearly is no Utopia—and no city on earth is—it is loved above all other cities by the great majority of its residents. Moreover, it is favored by millions who visit it. Because of the city's extraordinary attractiveness, tourism is its second largest and fastest-growing industry.

Texans from all over the state love what many call "the Alamo City." "All Texans have roots in San Antonio," said Texan Liz Carpenter—veteran Washington newspaper correspondent, later associated for half a century with President Lyndon B. Johnson and Lady Bird Johnson. "San Antonio," she said, "is a town where all the people know how to live."

From anecdotes in this book, you can acquaint yourself with some of the people who lived in the city's most formative years, helping to create its distinctive character. A book such as this must confine itself primarily to (1) the earliest inhabitants, the American Indians; (2) those who came next, the Hispanics, and (3) the Germans, who, in the mid-1800s, began making their distinctive mark on the growing town. I have given the Anglo Americans less concentrated coverage, both because of space limitations and because their culture is more familiar to most readers.

You can learn here also of San Antonio's natural history, its favorable geography and ecology, and the exciting events that have taken place, even before the 1600s, along its several streams. This also is the story of San Antonio's plazas, so filled with life over the centuries—and even today—and of dozens of attractions in all parts of the city for the visitor to enjoy. Among the book's anecdotes are stories about the city's ancient domed cathedral and its five stone Spanish mission churches, one of which became the Alamo. It tells briefly the story of the Alamo, "the Cradle of Liberty," and of the many battles fought in and around San Antonio.

You can learn more about the five military bases that have, through their effect on the daily lives of many thousands of people—active and retired, military and civilian employees—helped mold the character of San Antonio, and elevated its stature in management, medicine, science, technology, and cosmopolitan attitude.

On pages 331-336 is a useful list of vital San Antonio facts, and statistics about the city and county. In the Chronofacts, you can see where San Antonio's people, and the events that involved them, fit into the context of Texas history.

One of the best descriptions of San Antonio since poet Sidney Lanier's classic characterization in 1872 was the following by San Antonio poet Wendy Barker in 1994:

San Antonio is a coming-together place, geologically, climatologically, culturally; it's a nexus of natives and non-natives. People are drawn here by the complexity of cultures, a complexity that lacks the negative aspects of a Boston or Bay area. There's a kind of peace.

San Antonio might rightly be called "the enchantress," who has captivated the hearts of Texans and others who've experienced her charms. But more appropriately, San Antonio is a place "deep in the heart of Texas."

Italo Calvino wrote in a book titled *Invisible Cities*, about "cities of the mind, cities of the memory, the cities that once visited do not go away, but stay, labyrinthine and omnipresent."

Magically, San Antonio remains unavoidably visible as it casts its spell on the eyes and hearts of all who visit or stay. Labyrinthine and omnipresent, it is a city of the mind, a city of the memory. So let's explore this enchanted and enchanting place that, once visited, does not go away.

Sidney Lanier's "San Quillmas"

The classic comment about San Antonio was written by the eminent poet and musician Sidney Lanier in 1872:

> If peculiarities were quills, San Antonio de Bexar would be a rare porcupine. Over all the round of aspects in which a thoughtful mind may view a city, it bristles with striking idiosyncracies and *bizarre* contrasts. Its history, population, climate, location, architecture, soil, water, customs, costumes, horses, cattle, all attract the stranger's attention, either by force of instrinsic singularity or of odd juxtapositions.

It was from this quotation about "peculiarities and quills" that some latter-day San Antonians—including veteran radio personality Logan Stewart—began calling the city "San Quillmas"— relying on the listener to understand that, in Spanish, *más* means "more."

How San Antonians Say It

(A Glossary)

Acequias (ah-SAY-key-ahs): Ditches—once the city's water system for drinking, washing, and irrigating.

Ayuntamiento (Ah-yoon-tah-me-EN-to): Town council; municipal government.

Baile (BYE-leh): Dance; ball.

Barbacoa (bar-ba-COH-ah): Barbequed pieces of meat from cooked head of cow or hog. Eaten with tortillas and spicy salsa. Traditionally prepared for sale on Saturdays and Sundays on San Antonio's West Side.

Bexar (BEAR or BAYER): Early name of city—now county's name. Spanish speakers pronounce it "BEH-har." Historical documents show the place spelled both Béxar and Béjar.

Cabrito (kah-BREE-toe): Young goat, roasted.

Cibolo (SIB-a-low): Means bison or buffalo. Spanish say "SEE-bo-lo." Early Anglos said "Sea Willow."

Cinco de Mayo (SEEN-co-deh MY-oh): May 5, the day of a vital military victory in Mexico over invading French troops in 1862.

Coahuila (koh-a-WEE-la): Province in Mexico once joined with Texas as a state called Coahuila and Texas.

Conjunto (kone-HOON-toh): Group music featuring accordion, twelve-string guitar, and often electric bass and drums. Has roots in Mexican rhythms and German folk dance music.

Diez y Seis de Septiembre (Dee-AY-see SEH-ees-deh sep-TYEM-breh): Sixteenth of September. Often called just "Diez y Seis." Mexican "Fourth of July."

Ejido (Eh-HEE-doe): Common lands allotted by Crown.

Guacamole (walk-ah-MO-lay): Mashed avocados, mixed with seasonings such as onions, cilantro, and chiles. In Spain or Mexico City it is pronounced "gwa-cah-MO-lay."

Guenther (GINN-ther; GENN-ther; GUN-ther, GUN-ter): Pioneer German family. Name of Guenther House Museum and other enterprises.

Jacal (hah-KAHL): Hut used in absence of adobe house in San Antonio. Made from sticks embedded in ground, attached, and spaces filled with mud. Roof of branches and reeds.

La Villita (lah vee-YEE-tah): The little village once lived in by families of the Spanish Alamo soldiers and later by German newcomers, which was restored from 1939 to 1968.

Menger (MING-er): Rhymes with "linger." Historic San Antonio hotel.

Menudo (meh-NOO-doh): Stew of tripe, pig's feet, and hominy.

Nacogdoches (Nak-a-DOH-chez): Caddoan Indian tribe in far East Texas, where Spaniards established Mission Nuestra Señora de Guadalupe de los Nacogdoches in 1716 near site of present-day city.

Natchitoches (NAK-eh-tosh): Caddoan Indian tribe and name of Louisiana town near early Spanish mission and presidio of Los Adaes.

NIOSA (Nee-OH-sah): "A Night In Old San Antonio." A four-evening multinationally oriented celebration sponsored annually by the San Antonio Conservation Society.

Oaxaca (Wah-HAH-kah): A state and city in southeast Mexico.

Raspa (RAHS-pa): Shaved ice, flavored with various syrups, sold from carts in plazas.

San Antonio (San-an-TONE-ee-oh): "San" and "An" rhyme with "fan." Some oldtimers say (San TONE-yuh). Purists never say "San Antone"—but the many who do are not alone. Residents are "San Antonians."

San Jacinto (San Ja-SENT-oh): A river named for St. Hyacinth, not far from today's Houston, near which Texans won independence from Mexico in a battle on April 21, 1836. Pronounce the "J" in "ja" as in "judge."

Tejano/Tejana (Teh-HAH-noh/Teh-HAH-nah): Texan of Spanish or Mexican descent. San Antonio's Hispanics are not in total agreement on what to call themselves. Some prefer "Latino" and "Latina"; some say "Hispanic." A few like "Chicano." Historians, especially, prefer "Tejano." "Tejana" is the feminine form.

Tejas (TEH-hahs): Caddoan Indian groups of East Texas used this word generally to refer to the allied tribes of their confederacy. It usually meant "friends" or "allies," and to the first Spanish explorers sounded like tejas, tayshas, texias, techan, or teysas. In their exploration reports they wrote about the territory of the Tejas. In Spanish, the "j" and the "x" were sometimes used interchangeably.

San Antonio's Official Flag

The official flag of San Antonio—featuring a large white star surrounding the outlines of the Alamo and separating a blue field on the left and a red field on the right—was designed by William H. Herring, Deputy Commander of the Department of Texas of the United War Veterans, and presented to the city by the United World Veterans Council in 1935. It was approved on July 8, 1976, by the City Council under Mayor Lila Cockrell. Sixteen years later, at the request of the Dixie Flag Manufacturing Company, the words "San Antonio Texas" were removed from the flag by a resolution of the City Council under Mayor Nelson Wolff on August 27, 1992.

1

Great Crossroads of the Southwest

San Antonio was destined to become a city many centuries before it was founded as a *villa* by the Spanish crown in 1718. The climate, soil, and abundance of spring water nurtured vegetation and attracted animals and other creatures, and altogether these riches of nature made the area a perfect hunting, fishing, and camping site for the Native Americans, the first people to enjoy the benefits of what we call South Texas.

The Spanish government—which claimed the territory from 1519 to 1821—saw the location as an ideal way station on the route between the interior of colonial Mexico and the Spanish presidios and missions on the border opposite French Louisiana.

From the first days of settlement in the early 1700s—through the period when the bloodlines of the mission Indians were

1

blended into part of the populace, during the century and a half of bloody fighting in and around the city with Apache and Comanche warriors, until the days when settlers came to begin ranching and farming in the environs of San Antonio—the Indians were significantly affecting the spasmodic growth of the city and uniquely honing the spirit of its people.

The almost constantly warring Plains Indians, as well as those who melded peaceably into the population, affected the personality of the townfolk and the pioneers in outlying ranches. So did the people with recent European roots who lived in nearby villages, whose lives have been linked closely over the years with the lives of the people of San Antonio.

El Camino Real, the interwoven route of former ancient Indian trails (also known as the King's Highway and the Old San Antonio Road), was followed before 1700 by Spanish governors of Texas as a direct roadway from Monclova, Coahuila, through San Antonio to the missions in East Texas. In the 1700s and early 1800s, three major trails of the Caminos Reales came from the south and west, below the Rio Grande, and converged in *Plaza de Armas* (Military Plaza) and *Plaza de las Islas* (Main Plaza) in the center of old San Antonio to become a single road headed north and east.

There is a marker in Military Plaza known as the Zero Milestone, placed there on March 27, 1924. It marks the point at which the Old Spanish Trail—linking Florida and the settlements to the west, including San Diego and other western settlements—was crossed by El Camino Real. Beside the Court House across from Main Plaza, a red sandstone monument bears two markers, one commemorating the Jefferson Davis Memorial Highway and the other the American Legion Memorial Highway. When these markers were placed in 1936, they were said to be the only ones in the United States indicating the junction of two memorial highways. Jefferson Davis Memorial Highway once extended from Washington, D.C., to San Diego, California, and American Legion Memorial Highway extended south from the Red River above Wichita Falls, Texas, to the Rio Grande at Hidalgo.

From its beginning in the 1700s, San Antonio de Béxar was vital to the Spanish and Mexican presence in Texas. It was the seat of government of the Texas territory from 1773 to 1827, when the capital was transferred to Saltillo in Mexico. Under both Spain and Mexico and during much of its history, it was the largest city in Texas.

The experience of building a nation began with Texans from Northern Mexico, who were mostly of Spanish and Spanish-Indian origins—but over the years, more and more of the settlers came from Europe and the United States. In the 1820s, empresarios such as Stephen F. Austin, Green C. DeWitt, and Martín de León were given permission by Spanish and Mexican authorities to establish in Texas their colonies of new settlers. At one time—in

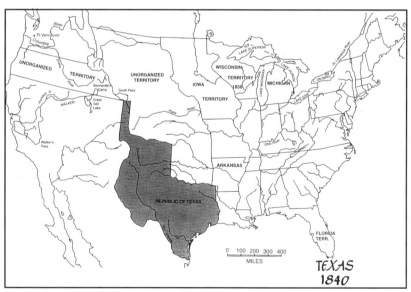

The Congress of Texas claimed in an act of December 19, 1836, that the southern and western boundary of the new republic was the Rio Grande from mouth to source and thence a line running northward to the forty-second parallel in today's Wyoming. The claim was based on the Treaty of Velasco, signed on May 14, 1836, by Gen. Antonio López de Santa Anna (who at the time was also president of Mexico) when he was a prisoner after the Battle of San Jacinto.

1834, for example—there were only a few towns in all of Mexican-governed Texas, and they kept in close contact although some were hundreds of miles apart. The largest at that time in the District of Béxar were San Antonio de Béxar (2,400), Goliad (700), San Patricio (600), and Victoria (304). San Felipe, Stephen F. Austin's colony of Americans in the District of Brazoria on the Brazos River, had 2,500 people. Nacogdoches in East Texas had a population of 3,500.

Bexar County, in which San Antonio is located, once included Santa Fe, now in New Mexico. The county, then stretching all the way west to the Rio Grande, was established after Texas won its independence from Mexico in 1836. From then until 1850, Texas claimed territory west of San Antonio to the Rio Grande, as far west as Albuquerque, and northward in a slender, panhandle-shaped section that extended to the stream's sources all the way through Colorado into today's Wyoming. This was a big "backyard" for Béxar—and in the minds of Texans it embraced both San Antonio and Santa Fe.

In 1860, when the partitioning of Bexar County began, 128 counties were created from the original area. Today, Bexar County covers 1,248 square miles, a few more than the state of Rhode Island. Yet so populous is the City of San Antonio that 78.9 percent of the county's residents live in the city. It is, in fact, the eighth largest in population among cities in the United States (an estimated 1,144,800). In the Metropolitan Statistical Areas of the nation, it is twenty-ninth in population (an estimated 1,537,900); thus it enjoys big-city amenities without big-city congestion.

The Mixed Heritage

The story of how San Antonio developed its charmed and charming life covers three enchanting centuries. It is a story of the amazing events that took place along the banks of the town's several waterways—the San Pedro, the Salado, the Olmos, the San Antonio, and the *acequias*, those ancient ditches lacing the early town with water for drinking, washing, and irrigating.

It is a story of the most Indian-besieged town in United States history, and the military headquarters and supply center for more than a dozen U.S. Army forts across West Texas that were out-posts in a major campaign theater of the Indian Wars fought throughout the Western United States for fifty years.

This is a story of continual self-renewal, of a river that became for the city a new stream of life, of the unusual shapes and mate-rials of houses, public buildings, and the four major plazas that captured the fancies of visitors. As these features changed over the years, they remained strangely different from the rest of Texas and from the architectural and landscaping mix in any other coun-try.

The fascinated tourists, authors, and health-seekers from the East and North who have come to San Antonio, especially since the mid-1800s, have affected the city's image of itself and thereby have influenced the actions of its leaders to preserve and amplify the charms that have made so many visitors exclaim in wonder-ment. Many have found in the venerable San Fernando Cathedral on Main Plaza, with its distinctive domed sanctuary, and the four stone missions south of San Antonio—mostly in ruins in the 1800s—the thrill of imagining briefly a world of long ago, an ancient European or Arabic world of mysticism and medieval beauty.

All that—plus the emotional experience of seeing the world-famed symbol of self-sacrifice, the Alamo—has cast on the city the enduring spell of an intriguing history.

Since the battle of the Alamo in 1836, when 189 Texians and Tejanos gave their lives in their war for independence from Mexico, Texans across the state have had a special feeling in their hearts for San Antonio. They love the city, even though to some Texans it is culturally a kind of distant relative.

> The event and the place of history imbedded deepest in the heart of Texans are the Fall of the Alamo and the Spanish mission by that name in San Antonio. Lord Macaulay said that every urbane man has two cities, his own and Paris. Every true Texan has two prides: his home town and the Alamo.
>
> *J. Frank Dobie*

The Strength of the Mexican Culture

In Main Plaza, three flags fly on towering poles. The United States flag is flanked left and right by the flags of Mexico and Texas. The Texas of the 1990s has been independent of Mexico for "only" 162 years, and from Spain only about 180 years, so San Antonio's roots in Latin America are even deeper than they may seem.

After the revolution in Mexico in 1910, more and more non-Anglos, more and more Mexicans, came to San Antonio. The city is a part of a cultural movement from Spain to the Americas—South, Central, and North—that has been expanding, year after year, across all the Southern states marked by long Hispanic-tinged histories. In San Antonio today, one of every two residents is Hispanic—55.6 percent of the population.

With the passage of time, the population of San Antonio consisted of the earliest inhabitants—the natives we call Indians—followed by the Spanish or Spanish-Indian *mestizos* from Mexico plus Spanish Canary Islanders—and then came the Irish, French, English, Scots, Germans, Poles, Hungarians, Czechs, Italians, Belgians, Greeks, Chinese, Syrians, Lebanese, Filipinos, and migrants

---

"A City in Granada"

In "Notes on Texas," by an anonymous author and published as a book titled *Texas in 1837* after editing by Andrew Forest Muir, the writer said: "As we ascended an eminence which commanded a prospect of the valley of the river, the far-famed San Antonio de Béxar, like a city of white marble, broke upon the view. The traveler, who has been for several days making his toilsome way through an unsettled country where there is nothing for the eye to rest upon but the extended plain or occasional groves of oak, when he comes to this spot and sees a city suddenly spread out before him is not prepared to realize the prospect. There is something in the fresh and beautiful appearance of the valley, covered with works of art, that reminds one of Washington Irving's description of the green valleys of Granada."

San Antonio Under Seven Flags

Spain	1519 to 1685
France	1685 to 1690
Spain	1690 to 4/1/1813
Republican Army of the North	4/1/1813 to 8/18/1813
Spain	8/18/1813 to 1821
Mexico	1821 to 1836
Republic of Texas	1836 to 1845
United States	1845 to 1861
Confederate States	1861 to 1865
United States	1865 to present

of all origins from the United States and other lands on the globe. Jews formed a significant group, marked by religion more than country of origin. A number of Africans were also among the early residents of San Antonio. Some were free men and women, but the City Directory of 1860 listed 592 as slaves in the town's population of 8,235. In 1876, eleven years after the Civil War, African-Americans represented the fourth-largest ethnic grouping in the city of 17,214. According to the City Directory of 1877-1878, the "Africans" (2,075) followed in number the "American, English, Irish" group (5,475), the "Germans, including Alsatians" (5,640), and the "Mexicans" (3,750).

Despite its cosmopolitan character, San Antonio has maintained an aura of Hispanicity unlike any other city in the state. This is not to say that the rest of Texas was not profoundly affected by the Hispanic culture from its earliest days, but historic stone structures in and near San Antonio are constant reminders of its past, beginning in the 1700s. The Texans of the new republic that was formed in 1836 after they defeated Santa Anna's Mexican army at San Jacinto adopted for themselves an enormously significant portion of the Hispanic culture that had come from Spain through Mexico.

This Spanish culture, gestating in Mexico for 200 years before being brought to what is now Texas, had become intermixed with the great native cultures of Mexico, such as those of the Mayans, Toltecs, and Aztecs. And this Spanish-Mexican amalgam contributed improved ways of living—through better agriculture, food preparation, and life appreciation—that were not originally Spanish.

This part of the cultural mix that Texans embraced was reflected in their approach to raising cattle and sheep, to ranching, to a legal system, style of dress, use of horses, architecture, favorite foods, celebrations and decorations, music and other art, as well as their use of the Spanish language to identify the things they lived with, and to name their towns and the physical features of their republic and state.

The Geographical Advantages

From its earliest days as a town, San Antonio has been the recipient of unusual praise and bemused wonderment at its distinctive attractions from visitors both eminent and humble.

The well-traveled chronicler Father Juan Agustín Morfi wrote in his *Memorias* in 1778, "I do not hesitate to say that in all New Spain there is not a more beautiful, more suitable, and more inviting place in which to establish and maintain a great city than that occupied by the villa of San Fernando and presidio San Antonio de Béxar."

More than 200 years later in 1990, a *Smithsonian Guide to Historic America* said: "San Antonio is the only major city in the state that existed before Texas won its independence from Mexico in 1836. Its many layers of history and purpose give it a unique character as much European as American, seemingly less 'Texan' to the casual observer, but on closer observation encompassing all that made Texas what it is."

An appreciative view of the Enchanted City has prevailed for more than two centuries and is shared by experienced travelers around the world. Why, from the 1800s until today, have more songs been written—in both English and Spanish—referring to San Antonio, "San Antone," or "the City of the Alamo" than to any other city in America?

Why has San Antonio been described over the centuries as "unique," "peculiar," "charming," "picturesque," "quaint," "foreign," "enchanting"? What makes this city so strikingly different?

The answer is not simple, for it is a curious mixture of elements that have merged in a fascinating way. It is more than the Alamo and the River Walk and the Spanish Franciscan missions. San Antonio is a city of the American West—still a cattle ranching center with stockyards, cowboys, rodeos, and plenty of country music dance halls.

Always a crossroads, its main source of revenue for many years was trade carried on by wagon trains between San Antonio and Mexico and San Antonio and New Orleans—the city founded by the French the same year the Spanish settled San Antonio.

Historian Walter Prescott Webb described the early-day Texas cattle kingdom as shaped like a diamond, with the points at San Antonio, Matagorda Bay, Brownsville, and Laredo. After the Civil War, San Antonio was a major intersection for the famous Chisholm Trail and other trails over which cattle were driven north from South Central Texas to rail points and pastures in the North, even as far as Montana.

Agribusiness is still a major base for the city's economy, but it also is a city with the nation's longest and most pervasive military presence. Its first military forces came in 1718, and today five military bases are in the city environs.

Although San Antonio was the largest city in Texas until sometime in the 1920s, the census of 1930 saw it drop behind Houston and Dallas, partly because it was slower to modernize. San Antonio had no railroad until 1877, when the Galveston, Harrisburg and San Antonio Railway arrived with its line from New Orleans to San Francisco.

Perhaps San Antonio's relative backwardness slowed an otherwise pell-mell growth. Perhaps its isolation from the newly burgeoning national commerce helped preserve many of its old buildings until the voices of its conservationists could be heard and heeded. In any event, the city's slower growth helped it age

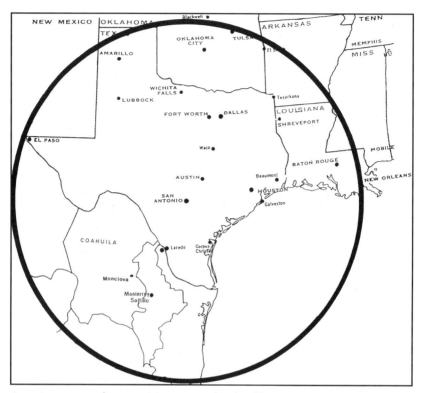

San Antonio is closer to Monterrey, the third-largest city in Mexico (population about three million), than to El Paso, Texas. It is closer, in fact, to New Orleans and to Oklahoma City than to El Paso. Road-mile distance from San Antonio to El Paso is 552; to New Orleans, 546; to Oklahoma City, 469; and to Monterrey, 297. (Fred Himes illustration)

more gracefully—helped it restore and maintain many of its historic landmarks and revive and cultivate old customs and traditions. Today it is the second-largest city in Texas, but the two other leading Texas cities are more than a century younger than San Antonio—and the Texas capital, Austin, elected its first mayor in 1840, 122 years after San Antonio was founded. The city of Houston, the state's largest, was not established until 1836-37, and Dallas got its first post office in 1844.

The cities of Dallas-Fort Worth, Houston, and San Antonio today form a triangle that is "the core area of Texas," according to cultural geographer D. W. Meinig in his book, *Imperial Texas*. In that triangle, he says, is "the seat of political and economic power, the focus of circulation, the area of most concentrated development and most characteristic culture patterns." The rest of Texas, says Meinig, is bound to that core.

In 1993, for the first time in United States history, Amtrak's Sunset Limited route allowed passengers to travel coast to coast—from Miami through San Antonio to Los Angeles—without changing trains. By rail, San Antonio is a leisurely 29 hours, 25 minutes from Los Angeles and 39 hours, 35 minutes from Miami.

The city's geographical nearness to Mexico is significant to its future economy. San Antonio is the major juncture for both interstate highways and rail lines leading to Mexico's major cities. It is the gateway to Mexico City, Monterrey, and Guadalajara. It has been called "a kind of Hong Kong to Mexico's China." Dallas is no closer to San Antonio than is Monterrey, a great industrial city and Mexico's third largest with a population of about three million.

Referring to South Texas, San Antonio's mayor in 1992, Nelson Wolff, said that "more than half of all trade with Mexico to and from the United States and Canada flows through our region." The North American Free Trade Agreement (NAFTA), which went into effect on January 1, 1994, destined the city to become a new kind of crossroads, with trade corridors linked to Mexico and Canada, and the East and West coasts. Already host to virtually every domestic airline except the Hawaiian and Alaskan carriers, San Antonio sees the phasing down of Kelly Air Force Base as an opportunity for conversion of its military facilities for gigantic cargo planes to civilian usage, with the potential of an aerial crossroads for global trade.

The Ambiance for Tourists

Here it waits . . . the Enchanted City. Its quiet river winds beneath great green trees; its ancient mission churches and symbolic shrine of patriotic sacrifice endure amid Old West dance halls, championship rodeos, Tejano music, colorful fiestas, historically preserved buildings, unparalleled military presence, unusual ethnic mixtures, exotic cuisines, an amazing variety of entertainment, advanced medical and technological institutions, and famously friendly residents.

No wonder, then, that it has become one of the favorite destinations of American and international visitors.

American Tourists Would Worship This City, in Europe

Richard Harding Davis wrote in 1892: "San Antonio is the oldest of Texan cities and possesses historical and picturesque showplaces which in any other country but our own would be visited by innumerable American tourists prepared to fall down and worship.

"The citizens of San Antonio do not, as a rule, appreciate the historical values of their city, they are rather tired of them. They would prefer that you should look at the new Post Office and the City Hall, and ride the cable road [the electric streetcar]. But the missions which lie just outside the city are what will bring the Eastern man or woman to San Antonio, and not the new waterworks."

2

Riches of the Land

To understand why San Antonio has come to be so often described as "unique" or "distinctly charming," one must turn back the pages of history. Look closely at "the lay of the land"— at San Antonio's location on the North American continent and on our planet.

Archaeologists found the story's beginning when they dug into the ancient campsites in the Olmos Basin north of the city and around the springs at the head of the San Antonio River. They found artifacts there that tell a great deal about the earliest inhabitants. And around San Pedro Springs, Salado Creek, and in Olmos Basin amateur collectors have discovered many of the ancient peoples' stone implements and weapons.

From the first years of the settling of Texas and into the early 1900s, the people, with the animals needed to carry them and their supplies, traveled across the land from one watering hole or spring to the next and from river to river. San Antonio's amply flowing springs made it a natural campsite for a restful stay, long or short—and a meeting place for anyone wishing to trade what he had for something he wanted. Trails led in all directions from its hub.

Inside North Loop 410 and east of U.S. 281, archaeologists have probed the edges of the spring-fed Olmos Creek and dug beside places where it flows south into the river below San Antonio Springs. A 1,940-foot-long dam topped by a 24-foot-wide roadway was constructed there in 1926. The creek has its source in northern Bexar County, and its watershed lies between the Salado Creek drainage to the northeast and Leon Creek to the southwest. It drains a basin covering some 34 square miles.

Archaeologists have examined the area around the Blue Hole of San Antonio Springs where the waters once gushed up through a narrow passage from deep in the cavity-pocked limestone aquifer to become a river. These days, the springs flow amply only in

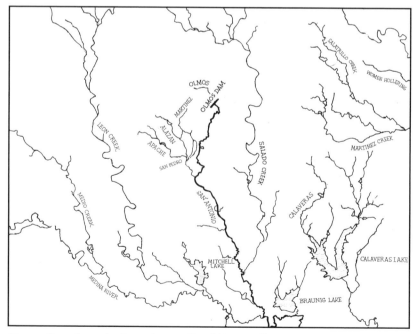

Upper San Antonio River basin (Fred Himes illustration)

years with unusually heavy rains. At one time, there were about 100 springs in this area.

Scientists tell us that the place we call San Antonio has attracted people for thousands of years. The stone tools and weapons, pottery, and other signs of human living, including the bones and shells of some of the animals and remnants of plants and nuts the natives ate, recount a fascinating story as interpreted by archaeologists and anthropologists. Hunters, fishermen, and gatherers were the earliest inhabitants of the Olmos Basin and the surrounding area, beginning some ten thousand years ago. They made use of what nature produced and were rewarded with the abundance of plant and animal food around the many springs.

Scholars at the Center for Archaeological Research of the University of Texas at San Antonio say that San Antonio lies near the intersection of several important biotic provinces where there are differing life conditions. As a result, the area has had an extraordinary variety of plants, mammals, and birds—so many that this area of Texas is, they say, "the biological hub of the northern half of this hemisphere." Even the two primary flight paths of the monarch butterfly, migrating to Mexico each spring from north central and northeast Canada, converge to a single line at San Antonio.

The water that flows from San Pedro and San Antonio springs is about as pure as most of nature's waters could be. The springs flow under artesian pressure from the limestone formations of the Edwards Plateau that make a kind of brittle "sponge," with millions of small pockets and many large caverns holding the water. The aquifer is refilled by rain and rivers, and by ponds and lakes where runoffs have been dammed.

The Edwards Aquifer stretches across all or part of eleven counties in the green, tree-covered Hill Country north of San Antonio. The many springs in the area rise to the surface by way of faults in the rock. The primary fault—the break in the Earth's crust through which the San Pedro and San Antonio springs once flowed voluminously, as well as Barton Springs in Austin, San Marcos Springs in San Marcos, and Comal Springs in New

What David C. Orchard Found in Olmos Basin

A giant ceremonial oak tree in Olmos Basin is a living monument to the Indians who roamed there centuries ago. Just a little more than seventy years ago, it still was being used by visiting Indians, but only a handful of San Antonians know the location of this sacred place.

In the 1920s, amateur archaeologist and collector C. David Orchard spent a great deal of time gathering artifacts in the Olmos Basin. He wrote several articles in Texas scientific journals and gave interviews about his findings. He told how, early in April 1924, he was camping near a spring beside the site for the Olmos Dam when he saw five Indians come by. Four of them, he guessed, were older than 50; the other was about 16. He offered them coffee; they accepted and then went to a very large live oak tree that rose above the rest in a motte near the center of and just south of the dam.

The Indians, who told Orchard they were from Ponca City, Oklahoma, and were "following the buffalo road," then began a ceremony involving smoking one cigarette among them, making a small fire, then extinguishing it with oak leaves, and pounding four nails in a burl of the large tree. Orchard later learned more about the ceremony from an old Tejano in the area whom he sometimes consulted and from two later visits by the Indians. He said that almost every April or May the Indians came there to collect the beans from Texas mountain laurel and *chiltipiquin* (a native hot pepper), and to conduct a ceremony. They said they were headed west from Olmos Basin to the Del Rio area to collect peyote buttons, which come from the mescal cactus and are hallucinogenic. Their whole journey, said the young Indian, included stops at four places on the "sacred road."

The mescal beans, which are the seeds of the mountain laurel (*Sophora secundiflora*), are hallucinogenic if taken carefully, and deadly if overused. One bean can kill. For thousands of years, they have been consumed by some groups of Indians in purification and other ceremonies.

Braunfels—is the Balcones Escarpment. This great cliff can be seen all the way from Del Rio in the south to the Red River far to the north. It is about 1,000 feet high near Del Rio, and its walls thrust up about 300 feet as it breaks to the northeast from San Antonio to Austin.

Blue Skies and Blue Northers

Its relatively mild climate makes the San Antonio area quite livable all year around. An exception is what is called a norther or "blue norther"—a sudden, drastic drop in temperature from a fast-moving cold front with strong northerly winds. The cold usually lasts only a few days, and some northers really are blue. Climatologists at Texas A&M University say that some arctic air masses are so cold they lack water vapor. The blue end of the visible light spectrum is thus scattered, giving a blue cast to the sky but one of extraordinary intensity. The norther can come with almost no warning. On December 21, 1990, for example, the temperature in San Antonio dropped from 82° at 1:15 P.M. to 26° at midnight. The wind chill was 4 degrees.

On the other hand, in the more than 100 years of weather records in San Antonio, there has never been a white Christmas. The average Christmas day is sunny or partly cloudy, with the high in the sixties. Once in a while, the Christmas temperature has even reached the seventies or higher. But it can be hot in San Antonio, too—at times above 100°. The daily average maximum temperature in August is 97.1°, while the minimum in that month is 75°. The average annual temperature is 70.8°F.

These high temperatures are not surprising if you know that San Antonio is approximately in the same latitude (near the 30th parallel) as Cairo, Egypt; Basra, Iraq; and Kerman, Iran. Bexar County's altitude, which runs from 486 to 1,892 feet, makes summers somewhat more tolerable in some locations than others— but almost universal air conditioning has made Texas living much more pleasant.

The sun shines on San Antonio an average 65 percent of the daylight hours during the year, and the annual growing season is

265 days. In the early morning hours the relative humidity is above 89 percent most of the year, but it drops to nearly 50 percent in the late afternoon. The city's climate has been described by meteorologists as modified subtropical—which means tropical-maritime during the summer and continental during the winter months. Normally, the annual rainfall is about 28 inches; however, in May 1992, rainfall had already reached 29 inches, measured from January. The total for the year was 46.49 inches, fourth wettest in history, but this was offset by abnormally dry years that followed—especially the drought of 1995 and 1996.

San Antonio was always known for its celebrated "healthful climate." Journalist and pioneer sheep-rancher George Wilkins Kendall said of San Antonio in 1843, "If a man wants to die there, he must go somewhere else."

Nationally known writers such as Sidney Lanier, O. Henry, Alex Sweet, and Richard Harding Davis spread the word about the city's popularity with "consumptives," persons suffering from tuberculosis who sought cures in San Antonio. In the 1890s, boosters could with some degree of honesty depict San Antonio as "the most famous health resort in America."

Thriving Flora and Fauna

Certainly the area's salubrious climate favored both animal and plant life. In 1691, when the Spanish governor of Texas explored the San Antonio region, a missionary priest keeping records for the expedition wrote that on the day they reached the area (June 13), "there were so many buffaloes that the horses stampeded and 40 ran away." The missionary recorded that a couple of days later, when they had traveled east for a day, they halted at a creek. "There were a great many buffaloes," he wrote, "and in the lagoons there were alligators and fish in abundance."

An expedition led by Domingo Ramón and guided by the French frontiersman and trader Louis Juchereau de St. Denis came to the San Pedro Creek-San Antonio River area on May 14, 1716. They found, according to the diarist Father Espinosa, "very tall nopals, poplars, elms, grapevines, black mulberry trees, laurels, strawberry vines and genuine fan-palms. There is a great deal of flax and wild hemp, an abundance of maiden-hair fern and many medicinal herbs. Merely in that part of its grove which we penetrated, seven streams of water meet. These, together with others concealed by the brushwood, form at a little distance its copious waters, which are clear, crystal and sweet. In these are found catfish, sea fish, *piltonte, catan* and alligators. Undoubtedly there are also various other kinds of fish that are most savory."

Captain Domingo Ramón noted in his diary on the 14th:

On this day I marched to the northeast seven leagues [about 18 miles] through mesquite brush with plenty of pasturage. Crossing two dry creeks we reached a water spring, which we named San Pedro. There was sufficient water here for a city of one-quarter league, and the scenery along the San Antonio River is very beautiful, for there are pecan trees, grape vines, willows, elms and other timbers. We crossed said stream; the water, which was not very deep, reached to our stirrups. We went up the river looking for a camping place and found a very fine location. There were beautiful shade trees and good pasturage as we explored the head of the river. Here we found . . . hemp nine feet high and flax two feet high. Fish was caught in abundance for everyone . . .

In the early 1800s, it was said that in Texas there was not a creek "a half a yard deep" where fish were not to be found. At that time, great herds of wild horses and wild cattle roamed the plains in south central Texas. J. Frank Dobie has told in his popular books, *The Mustangs* and *The Longhorns*, how horses came to Texas by way of North Africa, Spain, and Mexico, and how, along with the longhorn cattle, they were brought by Francisco Vázquez de Coronado to America in the 1500s.

Besides these imported animals—gone wild—as well as the buffalo herds that sometimes grazed to the south, there were many bears, cougars, wild cats, wolves, coyotes, deer, antelope, wild pigs and javelinas, wild turkeys, ducks, and other creatures of the countryside. Travelers, especially when they forded creeks and rivers, were wary of alligators. Some were said to be as long as fourteen feet. There were plenty of snakes, including rattlers. The settlers generally avoided them, although some found them good to eat at times, and some claimed their fat provided a fine gun oil.

Armadillos were another story. They did not show up in San Antonio until 1879. At least, that is when the first one was brought into town on a wagonload of wood by a woodcutter who had discovered it in Atascosa County, about thirty miles south. The woodcutter took the armadillo around town, offering it for sale for $50, while hundreds gathered wherever he stopped for their first view of the migrant creature with South American progenitors. Reporting on this, the *Express* wrote in its January 23, 1879, issue that "the specimen brought to this city yesterday was the first ever found in Western Texas, so far as we know of."

For some reason, known perhaps to persons fortunate enough to understand the Texas mystique, Texans took the armadillo to their hearts, and this slow-moving, shell-covered, burrowing mammal became one of their most beloved icons. On October 3, 1981, the governor of Texas proclaimed the nine-banded armadillo "a symbol of Texas" and a recognized mascot of the state. Granted, the proclamation was made by Senator Jack Hogg, acting officially as "Governor for a Day"—but it has never been rescinded.

Game by the Wagonload

Conservation of wildlife was unheard of in San Antonio in the 1800s. The prevailing attitude was reflected in a newspaper item on November 27, 1899: "Frank Sommers, Gus Heyer, Arthur Guenther, Harry Wurzbach and Emmanuel Seffel loaded an ambulance with provisions and cooking utensils and left on a 10-day hunting trip to Hondo Canyon." The reader would be sure that on their return, the hunting party's ambulance would be loaded with great numbers of game. (An ambulance was a large, horse-drawn passenger carriage, equipped with good springs for easier riding, and having a permanent top plus rolled canvas sides that could be unfurled.)

The uncontrolled shooting of game in San Antonio's early days was common. Wildlife was plentiful. With such abundance, it is not surprising that virtually no one gave any thought to conservation—that there were no game laws.

The *Express* reported on December 10, 1873, about a sale in Military Plaza of sixty-three wagonloads of produce, wild game, buffalo meat, wild turkeys, and deer. Three years later, a report stated that three San Antonio businessmen returned from a hunt on the Hondo with twenty-two deer, one bear, and hundreds of wild turkeys.

According to Vinton L. James, a San Antonio writer who was born at 123 West Commerce Street in 1858, wild turkeys were sold on the streets of the city for 15 or 20 cents in 1878. Quail were so numerous that the dirt roads in the afternoons "were alive with the birds dusting themselves." James, an enthusiastic hunter himself, was an early exponent of laws to control hunting. He wrote in 1938 of the "game hogs and market hunters" who, in earlier days, would go to the coast by railroad on a weekend and sometimes kill as many 700 ducks and geese, "and brag about it." This custom, he said, brought "the merciless slaughter of God's most beautiful creatures."

As to other kinds of birds—birds treasured for their beauty and songs and insect-control—the San Antonio area was favored by nature to have many. Texas is said to be by far the most species-rich state in the nation for birds, owing to its geographic location, and Bexar County has a significant number of the 566 kinds of birds in Texas. The Great Texas Bird Trail, now nearly completed, will include more than 200 sites stretching from the Big Thicket National Preserve in East Texas all the way to the Las Palomas Wildlife Management Area near Harlingen. Rockport is the key site in the Central Texas Coast section of the trail.

There are displays of many Texas birds, animals, and other wildlife at the Witte Memorial Museum and at the Buckhorn Hall of Horns, Fins, and Feathers at the former Lone Star Brewery, and of course the San Antonio Zoological Gardens and Aquarium offers close views of live specimens. At the San Antonio Botanical Center, varieties of plant life can be seen all year round, and there are birds there as well as at the new 4,700-acre Government Canyon State Park, now under development, and the Emilie and Albert Friedrich Park, a wilderness park on Interstate 10 near Camp Bullis that has nature trails, indigenous plant life, and rare birds.

Friedrich Park, consisting of about 250 acres of virgin Texas Hill Country belonging to the City of San Antonio, is a sanctuary for two endangered species of bird—the golden-cheeked warbler and the black-capped vireo. It also has seven rare or unusual plants, including the devil's shoestring (an endemic bear grass), and three endemic reptiles or amphibians. A nature-lover's retreat, it draws birders from around the world.

The green Hill Country comes to the edge of San Antonio. The hills are covered with live oak, Spanish oak, ashe juniper (locally called cedar), and tall native grasses. The land is among twelve sites selected by an international coalition, The Nature Conservancy of Arlington, Virginia, as one of the "Last Great Places." The organization is working with the Texas Nature Conservancy, headquartered in San Antonio, to help preserve the natural environment as development occurs. It uses private funds to buy land and protect critical areas and coordinates the efforts of interested public as well as private organizations.

The Conservancy defines the Hill Country as an 18,000-square-mile crescent the size of Vermont and New Hampshire combined. It takes in all of Bandera, Kerr, and Real counties plus parts of twenty-three others, including Bexar. It is the largest of the international Conservancy's dozen sites. The Hill Country's interlocking ecosystem includes the Edwards Aquifer, canyons, springs, rivers, ridges, mesas, and caves.

3

The Streams of Life

The crooked streets of downtown San Antonio—and a few other old San Antonio roads—were laid out along the streams that curled south from the San Antonio and San Pedro springs and along the irrigation ditches or *acequias* that branched off from those two main channels. The springs of the place—San Pedro Springs and San Antonio Springs—are the reason the first mission and the first presidio were established in this convenient stopping point between Presidio del Río Grande (Villa Guerrero in Coahuila, Mexico) and the missions and presidios in the vicinity of Nacogdoches near the Louisiana border.

Even today, Nacogdoches Road is one of the principal thoroughfares in San Antonio—part of what was once the Camino Real running from south of the Rio Grande to East Texas.

The life-sustaining waters from the two great springs north of town enabled the Villa de San Antonio de Béxar and the Villa de

San Fernando de Béxar to become, eventually, the city of San Antonio in Bexar County. A third stream, Salado Creek, was within the original boundaries of the San Fernando municipality laid out in 1731, and its waters supplied the mission ranches and farms on the east side of San Antonio.

All these streams help drain the San Antonio River Basin, an area of 4,100-square miles in South Central Texas that crosses parts of ten counties from Bandera to Goliad. Described in physiographic terms, the river basin includes the Edwards Plateau of the Great Plains province and the Western Gulf Plain of the Coastal Plain province.

In the city area of San Antonio, Martínez Creek, Alazán Creek, and Apache Creek flow from the northwest into San Pedro Creek, which later flows south into the river. To the northeast, Olmos Creek and Salado Creek also flow south to the San Antonio River. Spring-fed Leon Creek, which was one of the original boundary markers west of San Antonio in 1731, now flows sluggishly except when it rains.

The Medina River, farther to the west, flows into the San Antonio River about 14 miles south of the city. Cíbolo Creek, to the east, joins the river farther south as it flows toward the Gulf of Mexico.

From the campus of the University of the Incarnate Word at 670 feet above sea level, the San Antonio River winds through the city, then flows some 180 miles south through the coastal plain until it joins the Guadalupe River a few miles before it enters San Antonio Bay. At its mouth, the river is cut off from the Gulf of Mexico by Matagorda Island.

To know the stories of these three streams that flow through the city—San Pedro Creek, Salado Creek, and the San Antonio River that is fed near its springs by Olmos Creek—plus the tales associated with the ancient *acequias* is to learn about some of the most fascinating episodes in the history of San Antonio. Because of the geographical nearness of these streams, most of the stories of happenings along their banks are intermingled, so in telling the story of one, references to others often impinge.

For example, the founding and naming of San Antonio in the 1600s and 1700s is a story of two great springs and two historic streams. Although the San Antonio River is one of the most notable features of the city, the original settlement was not named for the river. On the contrary, the river was named years later for the place where San Antonio had been founded.

How the City Got Its Name

San Antonio was named in 1691 by an expedition led by Domingo Terán de los Ríos, the first governor of the Province of Tejas. The Tejas were an indigenous group living in East Texas that early Spaniards called by the natives' own word meaning "friends." A diarist with the expedition, Father Damián Massanet, wrote about first coming upon San Antonio en route to East Texas:

> On this day [June 13] we found at this place the *ranchería* of the Indians of the Payaya nation. This is a very large nation and the country where they live is very fine. I called this place San Antonio de Padua, because it was his day. In the language of the Indians it is called *Yanaguana*. . . .
> I ordered a large cross set up [on the 14th], and in front of it built an arbor of cottonwood trees, where the altar was placed. All the priests said Mass. High Mass was attended by Governor Don Domingo Terán de los Ríos, Captain Don Francisco Martínez, and the rest of the soldiers. . . . The Indians were present during these ceremonies. . . . Then I distributed among them rosaries, pocket knives, cutlery, beads and tobacco. I gave a horse to the captain [the Payaya chief].

About eighteen years later, on April 13, 1709, another expedition came through the area, and diarist Father Isidro Félix de Espinosa said that, because the river had never been named, he would call it "San Antonio de Padua." Perhaps in saying that the river had never been named, he interpreted the reports of Father Massanet and Governor Terán to say that only the place or campsite beside an *arroyo* had been named San Antonio.

San Antonio de Padua, for whom the city was named, was born in Lisbon, Portugal, in 1195 of a noble family. He was a Catholic priest and follower of St. Francis of Assisi, spending time in Portugal, France, and Italy. In the latter, he became famous as a preacher who drew large crowds. He also was unusually scholarly. Not many years after he died in Padua on June 13, 1231, he was declared a saint by Pope Gregory IX, who had known him.

In Texas, "the place of San Antonio" was named on June 13, the feast day of Saint Anthony. The tall bronze statue of Saint Anthony beside the river between the Chamber of Commerce building and the San Antonio Marriott Riverwalk was a gift from Portugal. Its inscription reads: "San Antonio, for whom the city and river are named." The sculpture was done by Leopold de Almedida in 1950. (Photo by author)

On the Ramón-St. Denis expedition in 1716, Father Espinosa, making the second of his four expeditions through the region, noted that the San Pedro Springs made a good site for a mission. As to the nearby river, he wrote that it was "very desirable [for settlement] and favorable for its pleasantness, location, abundance of water and multitude of fish."

Two years later, an expedition led by Don Martín de Alarcón, governor of the province of Tejas, reached the same area. A diarist of the group, Father Francisco Celíz, wrote that "in this place of San Antonio is a spring of water which is about three-fourths of a league from the principal river. In this location, in the very spot on which the villa of Béjar was founded, it is easy to secure water, but nowhere else."

He was referring to San Pedro Springs and to the ease of securing water for irrigation. The Spaniards sometimes referred to small streams in the wilderness as "irrigation ditches," because they could foresee their use for that purpose.

On the first of May 1718, Father Antonio Olivares dedicated the mission of San Antonio de Valero, founded by the governor "about three-fourths of a league down the creek." Then, "on the 5th of May," wrote the diarist, "the governor, in the name of his Majesty, took possession of the place called San Antonio, establishing himself in it, and fixing the royal standard with the requisite solemnity, the father chaplain having previously celebrated Mass, and it was given the name of Villa de Béjar. This site is henceforth destined for the civil settlement and the soldiers who are to guard it, as well as the site for the mission. . . ."

Here, near San Pedro Springs, was the first site of the mission church, a simple hut, that later was moved twice—finally ending up in the area we now call Alamo Plaza. It was later rebuilt in stone as the church of Mission San Antonio de Valero.

The Marqués de Valero, viceroy of New Spain at the time, was the second son of the tenth Duke of Béxar, and both Mission San Antonio de Valero and the villa and presidio of Béxar were named for him.

Historians credit Father Olivares with the founding of San Antonio, because of his many requests to the Spanish government to make a settlement in the area and of his establishing Mission San Antonio de Valero near San Pedro Springs. Earlier, the Franciscan missionary had been with Father Espinosa on the expedition of 1709, led by Captain Pedro de Aguirre, commander of the presidio of the Río Grande del Norte.

And the Payaya chief who had been given a horse in 1691, twenty-seven years before, when "this place called San Antonio" was named, was on San Pedro Creek on May 1, 1718, to witness the founding of the first of the two institutions of the village.

San Pedro Creek

From San Pedro Springs, in what is now San Pedro Park north of downtown, San Pedro Creek flows 4.9 miles south through the city until it joins the San Antonio River near Mission Concepción. Now a mere trickle except in years when heavy rains raise the underground water level, for centuries it streamed copiously out of a fault in the earth at the edge of the Edwards Aquifer.

Not only is San Pedro Creek the most historic in Texas, it is one of the most historic creeks in the United States. The significant events that have occurred along this stream for nearly three centuries are far greater in variety and duration than, for example, events that took place at that historic creek in Virginia called Bull Run.

Next to Boston Common, San Pedro Park is the oldest public park in the United States. It lies within a larger area designated the village *ejido*, or community land, by a royal grant of 1729. The historic site of the springs is behind the San Pedro branch of the Public Library at 1315 San Pedro, across the street from San Antonio College. A bandstand that was moved from Alamo Plaza around the turn of the century covers a former "bear pit." In his description of San Antonio's peculiarities, the poet Sidney Lanier pointed to the "bear-pit in which are an emerald-eyed blind cinnamon-bear, a large black bear, a wolf and a coyote, and other attractions." But he also was charmed by the "spreading water oaks, rustic pleasure buildings, promenades along smooth shaded avenues, between concentric artificial lakes, a race course, an aviary and a fine Mexican lion."

In the park there is also a fortress-like stone building, with a tower and what appear to be rifle slots in the walls. Its origin is a mystery, though archaeologists say the stonework is definitely of the German artisan period. We do know that during the war with Mexico in the mid-1840s, the area was a campground and training center for hundreds of U.S. military volunteers. J. J. Duerler, a born landscape artist, lived on the grounds for years. Beginning in 1852, he leased the park and created ponds, small lakes, islands, and covered waterways, providing a recreational center as well as a variety of commercial entertainments. The park was the site of the city's first agricultural fair in 1854, was briefly a camp for camel trains in 1856 and for war prisoners of the Confederate Army in 1860-61. It was the site for large political gatherings, as when Gen. Sam Houston spoke there more than once around 1860. San Antonio's first municipal zoo opened there in 1910.

The history of San Antonio began along the banks of San Pedro Creek near its springs, when the first settlers, the Indians, found its environment especially favorable for hunting and gathering. They camped there off and on for centuries before the Spaniards came.

According to some historians, in 1534, four Spanish survivors of a shipwreck on Galveston Island—Álvar Nuñez Cabeza de Vaca, Andrés Dorantes de Carranza, Alonso del Castillo Maldonado, and a Moor called Estevan—arrived at a friendly Indian campsite near San Pedro Springs. Experts disagree about whether their route took them through the Indian campsite at San Pedro Springs, but it is possible. If so, as one historian has speculated, San Antonio was the site of the oldest identifiable village within the present limits of the United States.

In 1722, four years after the presidio and mission of Villa de San Antonio de Béxar were established, the presidio was moved down the creek to a more defensible location near the San Antonio River's horseshoe bend. The mission was moved east of the river. Then, in 1731, settlers from the Spanish Canary Islands came to establish a municipality beside the creek.

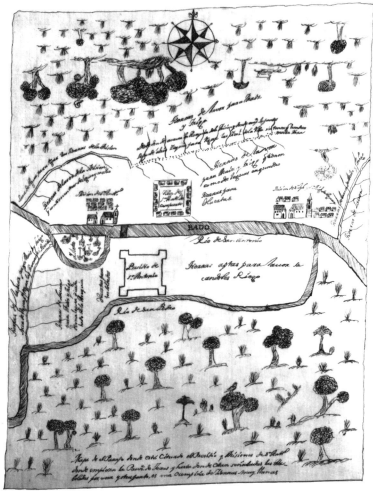

In 1730, the Marqués de San Miguel de Aguayo drew this map for Viceroy Marqués de Casafuerte. Some historians have noted errors in the map, when comparing it to certain current sites. The river, of course, is not depicted correctly. However, recent studies by archaeologists show that at the time the map was drawn, most features shown are not too far off. After the Canary Islanders arrived in 1731, both their villa and the presidio for its protection were established across the river from the walled Mission San Antonio de Valero—and a church was built in the villa, which at first was called San Fernando de Béxar. (Map courtesy Institute of Texan Cultures, from Archivo General y Público México, Provincias Internas)

In the 1720s, an acequia was begun to run nearly parallel to the creek. It soon flowed south from San Pedro Springs, passing between the front of the San Fernando church and Main Plaza. For many years it flowed to the river, at one time passing through the grounds of the United States Arsenal (which today houses the corporate headquarters for H-E-B Food Stores on South Main). San Pedro Acequia—known later as the Main Ditch—and San Pedro Creek were for many years the primary sources of water for the people and animals of San Antonio de Béxar.

Much of the commercial and military life of San Antonio was conducted in Military Plaza behind the San Fernando church (later to become a cathedral). The Spanish Governor's Palace, the *Comandancia*, was there. During certain periods in San Antonio history after 1772, a Spaniard governed all of Texas from his presidio in the plaza on this creek. The two streams from San Pedro Springs ran west of the plaza and east of the church.

This area, skirted by San Pedro Creek and San Pedro Acequia, was the very center of San Antonio, within a stone's throw of today's City Hall and Bexar County Courthouse. The presidio and the church were there—two vital building blocks used by Spain in settling the New World.

The area comprising Main Plaza, San Fernando Cathedral, Military Plaza, the Spanish Governor's Palace, and points west is still exotic and intriguing for many visitors to San Antonio. More than any other place in the city, this area—first nurtured by the waters from San Pedro Springs—is filled with astonishing, fascinating, and significant history.

Here, along San Pedro Creek and near Main and Military plazas, were historic battles with and among Indians, Spaniards, Mexicans, Texians, and Tejanos. Visitors with names written large now in history books—Moses Austin, Stephen F. Austin, Sam Houston, and scores of others—walked these streets long before they were paved. Here was the first Texas election, here the first municipal government in Texas. Here occurred celebrations, parades, bullfights, cowboy shenanigans, vaudeville theater, shootouts, hangings, public dances, Apache and Comanche attacks, and solemn treaty ceremonies. Soldiers, trail drivers, freighters, gamblers, outlaws, and exemplary citizens walked these streets.

This area was the stage for some of the most heroic, exciting, exotic, and even bizarre events in Texas history. It can be said that the first "rodeo" and first "Wild West Show" in the United States—with riding and shooting contests and demonstrations among Texas Rangers, Tejano *vaqueros,* and Comanche Indians— were held in the fields just west of San Pedro Creek in 1844. Eyewitness John C. Duval, recognized as the first Anglo "man of letters" in Texas, wrote about it in his book, *The Young Explorers.*

After San Pedro Creek flows south through Military Plaza, it moves past the historic stockyards before entering the San Antonio River. A key part of the South Central Texas cattle industry, the great heart of San Antonio's early commerce, comes clearly into view at the stockyards south of downtown where San Pedro Creek is fed by Apache and Alazán creeks. In the 1890s, San Antonio was Texas' largest horse and mule market.

Union Stockyards of San Antonio was founded in 1889 on San Marcos Street by a group of South Texas ranchers and trail drivers. In this area also was the intersection of all the railroads of San Antonio.

The San Antonio River

Frederick Law Olmsted is internationally famous as the landscape architect who laid out New York's Central Park and the Boston parks system, and designed the grounds of the U.S. Capitol, the Stanford University campus, and the Chicago World's Columbian Exposition of 1893. After he visited San Antonio in 1854, Olmsted wrote of the river's source, north of the city:

> The San Antonio Spring may be classed as of the first water among the gems of the natural world. The whole river gushes up in one sparkling burst from the earth. It has all the beautiful accompaniments of a smaller spring, moss, pebbles, seclusion, sparkling sunbeams, and dense over-

Bullfighting was popular in San Antonio for more than a century and a half. When Spanish Texas held celebrations in 1747 to honor its new monarch, Ferdinand VI, the people of San Antonio enjoyed a week of festivities sponsored by the town council, the cabildo. Among the various entertainments, bullfights (corridas de toros) were held for four days. In the 1800s, the arena was just southwest of San Pedro Park, but because of harassment by Indians it was moved closer in, near Franklin Square (now under the confluence of highways I-10 and I-35, northwest of downtown). Occasionally, matadors came from Spain and Mexico, but most bullring stars were local. At the San Antonio International Fair in 1903, patrons were bitterly disappointed to find the "bullfights" were staged with no horses, no metal swords, and no bloodshed.

hanging luxuriant foliage. The effect is overpowering. It is beyond your possible conceptions of a spring. You cannot believe your eyes, and almost shrink from sudden metamorphosis by invaded nymphdom.

Avoca

"The Head of the River" or "Blue Hole," like the river itself, has always had a fairy-tale aura about it. A town that never materialized was laid out there in 1830 by several entrepreneurs headed by Andrew Berry from Lexington, Kentucky. Its name, Avoca, was inspired by the song, "Sweet Vale of Avoca," written by Irish poet and lyricist Thomas Moore about a valley and river in Wicklow County, Ireland.

A plat of the townsite was drawn up, lots laid out, and glowing descriptions of plans for the metropolis were published in brochures distributed widely in the United States and abroad. The area extolled included the head of the river, although the city of San Antonio had never relinquished its ownership of the springs until it sold the property to city alderman (later mayor)

The Sniper's Tree and Others

About 300 bald cypress saplings were planted along the river in 1900, but some are much older. "The Milam Cypress," more than 200 years old, is said to be the tree from which Ben Milam was killed by a Mexican sniper as he stood in the yard of the Veramendi House on Soledad Street during the Battle of Béxar in 1835. You can see the twin-trunked giant if you stand on Commerce Street where the river crosses under it near Soledad Street at Main Plaza. Looking north, you'll see the legendary tree to your right, near the Holiday Inn's riverfront. Other native trees along the river are chinquapin oak, cedar elm, pecan, lacy oak, burr oak, Mexican buckeye, Mexican sycamore, and Texas mountain laurel. Desert and other palms, crape myrtles, and banana trees have been added, along with other trees including papaya.

JAN. 15, 1859.]   FRANK LESLIE'S ILLUSTRATED NEWSPAPER

This drawing from Frank Leslie's Illustrated Newspaper of January 15, 1859, is captioned, "Primitive Bathing Near San Antonio—From a Sketch by Our Correspondent." Several writers of books dealing with their visits to San Antonio in the 1800s were startled by the unabashed and innocent cavorting by residents in the river. When Dr. Ferdinand Roemer, a German scientist, traveled in Texas from November 1845 to May 1847, he wrote after visiting San Antonio that "it was quite a startling spectacle to see here just above the bridge in the heart of the city, a number of Mexican women and girls bathing entirely naked. Unconcerned about our presence, they continued their exercises while laughing and chattering, showing themselves perfect masters of the art of swimming. . . . My companion informed me that this spectacle was repeated daily and that both sexes of the Mexican population were fond of bathing." Other San Antonians bathed more discreetly, carrying their soap and towels; later they built canvas-draped enclosures in the river for private bathing.

The advertisement above was published in William Corner's San Antonio de Béxar *in 1890. (Courtesy Mary Ann Noonan Guerra)*

J. R. Sweet on November 8, 1852. Some of the published guides described Avoca as if the town actually existed.

But settlers did not swarm to buy the town lots from Avoca's visionary developers, and the land became the property of W. E. Howth, who sold twelve lots to Larkin D. Smith on June 27, 1832. In 1839, Smith acquired more land there for ranching. Eventually, some of the Avoca land was bought by residential developers of the Chamberlain Investment Company of Denver, and it began in 1890 to sprout into the city of Alamo Heights, now appearing to visitors as a pleasant neighborhood of San Antonio.

Allotting the Water

In 1830, San Antonio's city fathers decreed that only the water from San Pedro Ditch was to be used for drinking and cooking, while San Pedro Creek and the San Antonio River were to be used for bathing and for laundry. Besides water for human beings and animals to drink, and for cooking, bathing, laundering and irrigating, swimming, fishing, and boating, the San Antonio River provided power for grist mills to grind corn and wheat into meal and flour.

San Antonio's first city directory described the river in 1877: "From the head of the river to the city direct is less than three miles, while by the windings of the stream, it is over thirteen. In this distance there is a fall of almost forty feet, affording unlimited water power for propelling machinery." Eventually, there were as many as ten mills along the banks of the river—their large waterwheels kept moving by the swift current.

In 1890, the *Express* newspaper reported that "the San Antonio River is spanned by seven massive iron bridges, and four more of these will be built during 1890. Three have already been contracted for. There are 128 bridges over thirty feet in length in the city, and probably 300 of lesser dimensions." Many of these, of course, were small footbridges. Today, there are sixteen pedestrian and vehicle bridges crossing the river within the downtown area and twenty-seven more on the river between Brackenridge Park and Loop 410 south of the city.

In drier years, the water you see flowing in the San Antonio River has been pumped from artesian wells—at the rate of five million gallons a day. River water that in wetter years is forced to the surface naturally from artesian springs is pumped, when necessary, from wells in Brackenridge Park not far from the original springs at the head of the river. In 1991, 1992, and 1993, the pumps were not required.

Today, ninety-one high-volume artesian wells provide water to meet the needs of the city's populace. Wells from water lodged in countless honeycombed pockets and caverns of limestone in the Edwards Aquifer are the sources of virtually all the water for San Antonio's domestic and industrial uses. Few, if any, cities in the world the size of San Antonio get their water only from underground.

Currently, dozens of businesses, industries, schools, country clubs, communities, and military bases in the area also have their own artesian wells yielding millions of gallons of water yearly. The water's temperature as it comes from underground is a constant 23°C. (73.4°F.). The temperature of the river along the River Walk varies between 21° and 27°C. It averages around 77°F.

The River Walk

The river's long history of unpredictable, raging floods—especially in 1819 and twice in 1913—made the inundation of September 9-10, 1921, the deciding blow for downtown merchants. To many of these businessmen, the potentially dangerous river that flowed beside the streets of the city had to be eliminated. The flood of July 5, 1819, had been even worse than the 1921 inundation—a solid, overflowing stream roaring south, spread east and west from the walls of the former mission San Antonio de Valero all the way to San Pedro Creek. The La Villita area suddenly became popular with town folk as its elevation overlooked the flood.

The 1921 flood, loosed by a cloudburst in the Olmos basin north of the city, took forty-nine lives, left fourteen missing, and caused more than $8 million in property damage. In the two catastrophic days, rainfall in the Olmos Creek watershed ranged from seventeen inches in the upper area to about eleven inches near San Pedro Avenue. It inundated parts of downtown San Antonio with eight to nine feet of water, even reaching the mezzanine of the Gunter Hotel on Houston Street at St. Mary's. It was only one of fifteen deadly floods that had, with little warning, menaced and mauled San Antonians from time to time since 1819.

San Antonio leaders believed that the threatening river could be tamed by filling in and covering the large river bend that curved through the downtown, and building a bypass channel to allow the main stream to flow directly south, avoiding the big loop.

The concept of the River Walk emerged from a wave of protest among discerning preservationists to newspaper reports of flood control actions being recommended to the city government. It was variously reported that an engineering firm had recommended (1) building Olmos Dam to establish a retention basin, (2) straightening and widening the river in certain locations, (3) constructing a concrete channel from Seventh Street (now Brooklyn) to Nueva, and (4) filling in the "River Bend" of the river, now part of the River Walk. Most distressing was the rumor that a "well-defined movement headed by at least three real estate promoters" planned to close the River Bend in order to reclaim it for speculative land purposes.

The San Antonio Conservation Society and the City Federation of Women's Clubs led the battle to save the River Bend. The Conservation Society had been formed earlier that year on March 22, 1924, in a fruitless effort to help save the old Market House on Market Street from destruction as part of the flood-control project. (The Doric columns fronting the Greek-style Market House were salvaged by the Conservation Society and stored in Brackenridge Park for later use, but when an effort was made to emplace them at the new San Pedro Playhouse constructed in 1929 for the San Antonio Little Theater, they were too broken to be usable and had to be duplicated from new stones, using old photographs as guides.)

Emily Edwards, one of the founders of the Conservation Society, wrote and produced a puppet show, "The Goose That Laid

Emily Edwards, at the Golden Jubilee luncheon of the San Antonio Conservation Society in March 1974. A half century earlier, in September 1924, Miss Edwards, the first president of the San Antonio Conservation Society, presented to Mayor John Tobin and four commissioners a little play that she had written. Calling it "The Goose That Laid The Golden Egg," she dramatized the need to preserve the San Antonio River (the "goose") as a great historic legacy and source of economic benefit. With the help of several friends, she put on a show at City Hall in which several helpers manipulated handmade puppets, which Emily, an accomplished artist, had authentically dressed, sculptured, and painted to resemble key San Antonians. Three actors, Lucretia and Margaret Van Horn and Miss Edwards, played both male and female roles as they spoke their pieces. Here, with one of a number of the play's stage directions, are a few essential lines from the script:

> *And as they go on telling*
> *Wherever tales are told,*
> *San Antonio's little river*
> *Is our legacy of gold.*
> *And so strangers come to see you*
> *(SHE TURNS TO GOOSE)*
> *And learn to love you, too,*
> *And leave behind with us*
> *Their gifts all shining new.*

(Photo courtesy San Antonio Conservation Society)

the Golden Egg," which she and her colleagues presented to a meeting of the city commissioners on September 28, 1924. Her dramatization succeeded in persuading the commissioners and Mayor John Tobin that they should not kill "the goose," so the city government postponed action on filling in the Bend, and the river flowed on.

It was nearly five years later, on June 28, 1929, that a new mayor, C. M. Chambers, and two city commissioners met with a group of civic leaders and property owners to hear a presentation by architect Robert H. H. Hugman on his plans for beautifying the San Antonio River. This history-making meeting had been arranged by the president of the San Antonio Conservation Society, Mrs. Lane Taylor.

Hugman titled his presentation "The Shops of Aragón and Romula." He said he wanted to preserve the historical character of the river—yet to transform its banks in a way reminiscent of narrow, winding streets of the old cities of Spain. He wanted it "barred to vehicular traffic yet holding the best shops, clubs, banks and cafes; prosperous, yet alluring with its shadowed doorways and quaint atmosphere." He emphasized the need always to maintain a public park atmosphere and a balance and mix among recreational offerings, living areas, and business enterprises.

The project was begun during the Depression, on March 27, 1939, and completed on March 14, 1941. It provided much-needed employment for many San Antonians. The chief engineer, Edwin P. Arneson, became ill and died in the early stages of the construction. It is for him that the outdoor Arneson River Theater is named. The project was financed by bonds underwritten by property owners living in the district and by the Works Progress Administration of the United States government.

Maury Maverick, U.S. Representative from 1935 to 1939 and mayor from 1939 to 1941, played the key role in obtaining Federal financing for the project, but it took many others to make it happen, including Jack White, a hotel entrepreneur and later mayor, and business leader David Straus. Through the efforts of Straus, the River Walk District and the River Walk Advisory Commission were created in 1962.

The transformation of the river did not approach what we see today until the 1960s—indeed, until after San Antonio had lengthened and improved it in 1968, the year the city celebrated with an international fair the 250th anniversary of its founding.

The main channel of the River Walk winds about $2\frac{1}{2}$ miles south from Lexington Street to the King William Historic District. The horseshoe-shaped River Loop, including its two extensions—from the Hilton Palacio del Rio Hotel to the Convention Center, then to Rivercenter Mall—is about a one-mile walk. The river is only $2\frac{1}{2}$ to four feet deep in the restaurant area of the River Walk—but it may run $4\frac{1}{2}$ to six feet deep elsewhere, and in the flood channel eleven to eighteen feet. Its width varies from eighteen to twenty-five feet in the restaurant area; in places it is twenty-five to fifty feet wide.

Today, the River Walk is maintained and improved by the city's River Walk Commission and by the Paseo del Rio Association. Its park-like borders are maintained by the Superintendent of River Operations of the city's Department of Parks and Recreation.

Deep under the river runs an enormous flood-diversion tunnel 130 to 154 feet beneath the city, block after block. That is deep—a distance about half the length of a football field. The cavernous space inside the tunnel is twice as high as a San Antonio VIA streetcar and as wide as two streetcars. Its inside diameter is twenty-four feet four inches.

North of downtown, the intake structure is near the Brackenridge Park golf course where the river swings toward Josephine Street. South of the city, some three miles from the tunnel's entrance, the floodwaters will flow into the San Antonio River from an outlet near Lone Star Boulevard. An almost identical gigantic flood diversion tunnel, more than a mile long, has been carved out of the limestone under San Pedro Creek. By adding five large pumps to the inlet of the river's flood control tunnel, the city is preparing to treat waste water so it approaches drinking water standards and to make it available for use when needed in the downtown river and Salado Creek and for irrigation of parks, golf courses, and cemeteries.

The River Walk now is the Number One tourist attraction in Texas. It is the stage for entertainment and pageants held intermittently throughout the year. Some 100,000 people ring in the Christmas season on the evening after Thanksgiving with the spectacular river parade of the Holiday River Festival. More than two dozen decorated barge-floats pass down a two-mile stretch under overhanging trees twinkling with 50,000 lights.

Some travel experts believe that this event and those in the days that follow make it a premier holiday period rivaling the

---

How Long is the River Walk?

If you take a stroll somewhere along (1) the Main Channel or (2) the River Loop or (3) the River Loop Extension, the distance you cover will depend, of course, on where you begin and end your walk. Gate 3 (the North Floodgate) is where the River Loop meets the Main Channel near Commerce Street. Gate 4 (the South Floodgate) is near St. Mary's and Market streets, where the River Loop again meets the Main Channel. The River Loop Extension runs from the pedestrian bridge at the Hilton Palacio del Rio Hotel to the Convention Center and then over the New Extension to Rivercenter Mall. Here are some distances to consider:

	Feet	Miles
Lexington St. to Houston St. (East Side)	3,327	0.63
Houston St. to Gate 3 (West Side)	609	0.12
Gate 3 to Gate 4 (River Loop, East Side)	4,180	0.79
River Loop Extension—(North Side)	1,533	0.29
River Loop Extension—(South Side)	1,446	0.27
River Loop New Extension—(West Side)	477	0.09
River Loop New Extension—(East Side)	514	0.09
Gate 4 to Nueva St. (East Side)	616	0.12
Nueva St. to Durango Blvd. (East Side)	1,438	0.27
Durango Blvd. to Arsenal St. (East Side)	1,029	0.20
Arsenal St. to Pedestrian Bridge (East Side)	1,006	0.19
Pedestrian Bridge to Guenther St. (West Side)	450	0.08
	16,625	3.14

Congressman Maury Maverick points out the new San Antonio Post Office to Franklin D. Roosevelt during the president's visit to San Antonio in June 1936. Grandson of two prominent pioneers, Samuel A. and Mary Maverick, Maury served San Antonio and Texas as mayor from mid-1939 to mid-1941 and U. S. Congressman from 1935 to 1939. He was chairman of the government's Smaller War Plants Corporation during World War II. La Villita and the River Walk are reminders of his vision and political skills in achieving major projects. Maverick is remembered also for bringing back the "chili queens," at least for a time, to San Antonio's unique evening ambiance in the plazas, and for using his influence with Eleanor and Franklin D. Roosevelt to obtain two housing developments in what was called the Mexican Quarter, west of San Pedro Creek, as well as Wheatley Courts, Lincoln Heights Courts for African-Americans, and Victoria Courts. (San Antonio Express-News photo)

April Fiesta because of the ethereal river canopy of dazzling and colorful lights, the traditional holiday ceremonies, the music, the exciting cultural mixture of people, and the generally pleasant wintertime weather.

Six million people stroll along parts of these river banks each year, many coming down the steps twenty feet from street level to enjoy the sight of fifty species of trees and countless flowering and tropical plants growing beside the winding River Walk. In 1995, a hiking route that follows a portion of the River Walk was named the second most enjoyable walk in the United States by the American Volkssport Association. (The top walk on the AVA list is at West Point on the Hudson River in New York.)

Salado Creek

San Antonio's Salado Creek—running from north to south on the eastern edge of the city—has a history almost as eventful as does San Pedro Creek. It has seen some of the most active Indian camp sites in the San Antonio area, as well as buffalo hunts, ancient Spanish expeditions, Texas Rangers, cattle ranches of the missions and early Tejanos, bloody battles between the first inhabitants and the former Europeans and others who entered Indian territory, battles between U.S. landseekers and Spaniards, and—when Mexico ruled Texas—battles between Texians and the government forces of Mexico.

Overlooking nearby Salado Creek at an altitude of 760 feet above sea level is St. Mary's Hall, a private girls' school. On its

Graham Greene's Ivory Tower

The San Antonio River is wound cunningly through the town like a pattern on a valentine (does it make a heart?) with little waterfalls and ferny banks. . . . You have the sensation in San Antonio by day of the world's being deliciously excluded. . . This—during the day—was the perfect ivory tower. The horror and the beauty of human life were both absent.

—*Graham Greene*, 1938

Literally, A Historic Bridge

Judge J. M. Rodríguez, born in 1829, recalled in his memoirs that when he was a boy, the bridge across Commerce Street consisted of two or three large mesquite trees with their forks in the river. Later, more stable bridges at Commerce Street fascinated writers such as the musician and poet Sidney Lanier, who said in 1873 that "any stranger may be safely defied to cross this bridge without becoming meditative." O. Henry, who spent time in the city in the 1880s and 1890s, wrote in *A Fog in San Antone*, a short story about a tubercular man, of "a little iron bridge, one of the score or more in the heart of the city, under which the small, tortuous river flows." And in 1895, Stephen Crane, famous for writing *The Red Badge of Courage*, jumped into the river there to save a young girl from drowning.

---

grounds many weapons, tools, hearths, and other stone artifacts dating back to 6000 and 3300 B.C. have been found by archaeologists. Salado Creek runs through Fort Sam Houston, one of San Antonio's most history-making institutions since the 1870s.

The Battle of Rosillo Crossing (1813); the Battle at Concepción (1835) under forces led initially by Stephen F. Austin; the Battle of Salado (1842); and the Dawson Massacre (1842)—all included action along the banks of Salado Creek.

In June 1861, an ill-fated military expedition was formed on Salado Creek. Led by Confederate Brig. Gen. Henry H. Sibley, formerly a U.S. Army officer, the Texas Mounted Volunteers rode slowly west by way of Fort Bliss at El Paso, hoping to take New Mexico away from the Union. Sibley's brigade of more than 2,000 men turned toward the northwest, reached Santa Fe in March 1862, and took over the town. But on March 28, at nearby Glorieta Pass, his forces were defeated by New Mexico militia, trained regulars, and Colorado volunteers, and he was forced to retreat. The Texas Confederates lost thirty-two dead, forty-three wounded, and seventy-one prisoners. (On April 25, 1993, thirty of the dead

San Antonio Nights

Away from the literate river
where Stephen Crane leapt
to save a pretty face
and O. Henry absorbed
the living
and the dying,
where I can still hear
Lanier's flute.
Away from the holy ground
where heroic ashes still burn
the nostrils,
where history has a meaning
but time does not.
Insulated
by the dark rain
my heart flutters to a child's cry —
still to listen, to identify,
to search my own house
and go beyond
into the streets
searching for a face
to match the pain.
                —Bryce Milligan, from *Daysleepers & Other Poems*

who had been interred in a mass grave beside the Santa Fe Trail
were reburied with honors at the Santa Fe National Cemetery.
Admirers tossed bluebonnets and yellow roses onto the Texans'
graves.)

   As early as 1731, Salado Creek was recorded as the northern
boundary of the surveyed pasturelands of San Antonio (then called
San Fernando). It drains an area of 223 square miles—drawing
from a long, relatively narrow watershed thirty-five miles long
and six miles wide, beginning in the Edwards Recharge Zone of
the Edwards Plateau. Camp Bullis Military Reservation is in this

Photos at left: One of the fleet of cruisers provided by Yanaguana Cruise Services for the River Walk. The San Antonio Parks and Recreation Department is responsible for the operation and maintenance of the River Walk, and the nonprofit Paseo del Rio Association is dedicated to its promotion and preservation. Throughout the year, Association members produce a variety of special events, including the annual River Walk Holiday Parade, Scout Canoe Race, and Great Country River Festival. You can experience an extraordinary spectacle in late November with the Lighting Ceremony and the River Walk Holiday Parade, when the trees and bridges are illuminated by some 50,000 Christmas lights and Santa Claus arrives with the floating river parade in a crescendo of joyful music. (Photos courtesy Yanaguana Cruises, Inc., and San Antonio Express-News)

area off Interstate 10, north of Charles Anderson Loop (1604), which circles the city. The creek meanders down from an altitude of 1,450 feet to about 458 feet, where it enters the San Antonio River not far south of Brooks Air Force Base.

At this point, the creek has skirted the community of Shavano Park in the north, passed the International Airport, Fort Sam Houston, housing developments, and the Joe and Harry Freeman Coliseum. It then has flowed on through the recreation places of Willow Springs Municipal Golf Course, Martin Luther King Park, Southside Lions Park, and the Pecan Valley Golf Club.

Southeast of San Antonio, below the traffic exchange of Highways 37 and 410, Salado Creek joins with historic Rosillo Creek, then flows into the San Antonio River just south of Mission San Francisco de la Espada.

Certainly an entire book could be written to tell of the people who have lived and died along Salado Creek—and of those who directly affected the way these people lived or died: the Indians, the mission fathers, the Spanish officials, the leaders from Mexico, the vaqueros, the settlers, the Tejano and Anglo cattle ranchers, the Texas Rangers. Its history involved the soldiers of Spain, Mexico, the United States, and the Confederacy, America's earliest military aviators as well as the entrepreneurs, the merchants, the politicians, the predators. All these people helped change the burgeoning city, with its growing populace and proliferating concrete streets and highways and buildings, erasing forever the early ranches and quiet old communities.

The Acequias

No other Texas city—in fact, no other city in the United States—has such a long history of interlaced waterways used for drinking, washing, irrigating, and waterpower. The wandering, man-made streams that followed the contours of the land sustained the farms of both the missions and the early settlers. And in the 1800s, they became another reason why visitors found San Antonio quaint and charming.

Originating in San Pedro Creek and the San Antonio River, these ditches, large and small, branched out through the town from two main canals or *acequias*. It was these narrow streams that often determined the curves in the meandering streets we see today—while nurturing and defining lines of trees and colorful flower and vegetable gardens throughout the little town. George Wilkins Kendall, the noted New Orleans newspaperman who visited San Antonio in the 1840s, told how the "rich and fertile bottoms of the river are intersected in almost every direction by irrigating ditches, which carry the limpid waters."

The secret of building *acequias*, using gravity and surveying techniques, came to San Antonio by way of Spain and the Spanish Canary Islands. From the Romans as well as the Moors of North Africa, the Spaniards had learned and practiced for many centuries the art of making water flow to where it was needed. The Moors—the Moslem Arabs who had come from North Africa in the eighth century to conquer and rule a large part of Iberia until the late 1400s—had developed the skills for deploying water after living for centuries in dry lands extending far to the east beyond Iraq. This kind of irrigation had originated in ancient Mesopotamia. "*Acequia*" comes from the Arabic word for irrigation ditch, "*assaqiyah*."

The Canary Islanders, who came to San Antonio in 1731, significantly influenced the control and distribution of water. The system of allotting water rights for irrigation was complex, and the town council controlled it. By the 1780s, land conveyances in San Antonio began to mention water rights in specific time units. Conveyances also referred to *"labores"*—a *labor* being a grant of land reserved for agriculture. Landowners were granted specific *dulas*, an Arabic-rooted word meaning days of water.

One conveyance, for example, described a certain woman's grant thus: "The days of water are, the first of *dulas*, one on the 9th and one on the 21st, as is the custom observed in the said *labor*. Each *dula* of water consists of twenty-four hours and in this form I grant her the three *dulas*."

A federal government report prepared in 1898 stated:

> The irrigation ditches at San Antonio are historically the most interesting in the state, for here are found the earliest systems and structures, which have been in use for more than a century. . . .
>
> The old missions, now in ruins [in 1897], were rendered habitable by these ditches, and the lands adjacent were the garden spot of the frontier, making possible the growth of the city which now is the center of civilization and trade of the Southwest. These ditches are now almost completely concealed by the ancient trees and the luxuriant verdure that line the banks, and through the lapse of time they have assumed the character of natural drainage channels, so that it is almost impossible to believe that they were artificial works.

Edwin P. Arneson did considerable research on waterways of Texas. He described the technique used when the *acequias* of the San Antonio missions were dug by the mission Indians under the supervision of the missionaries, assisted by soldiers from the presidio, and said that "those who laid out the *acequias* appear to have been slaves to the grade contour, for in many places no reasons are clear today why the location should not have cut through a ridge instead of going the long way round a hill." He believed

Fred Himes illustration

that "for the leveling and ascertaining the grades of canals, the monks used a frame in the shape of an equilateral triangle, with a plumb line hanging from the apex. The grade of the Espada ditch is reported by A. Y. Walton as having been 18 inches to the mile."

Arneson described how the Moorish waterwheels used in the canals for irrigation added an exotic touch to the San Antonio scene. "They were of the undershot kind and had trough-like buckets fixed at intervals around the periphery. The energy of the water flowing in the acequia was utilized to turn these wheels, and so to lift water for irrigating plots of ground lying higher than the canal itself."

Originally, there were seven *acequias*: Two served the town, which was on the west side of the San Antonio River, and five served the missions—until the missions were finally secularized (inactivated) in 1824.

Judge J. M. Rodríguez wrote in his memoirs that "all the farming that was done was by irrigation within the city limits or immediately outside of it and the ditches supplied the water. The irrigated fields were along what is now South Flores Street, running between the San Pedro Creek and the San Antonio River. There were also irrigated fields along what is now River Avenue [Broadway] between the main ditch and the San Antonio River, and as a rule the community raised enough produce from them to supply the necessities of life and to keep up the garrison."

The San Pedro Acequia, also known as the Main Ditch, was begun in the 1720s and later supplied water to the Villa de San Fernando. About two feet deep and six feet wide, it ran from San Pedro Springs, south between Main Plaza and the church of San Fernando, and on down to rejoin the creek before it entered the river near Mission Concepción. A small section of it has been restored near the Bexar County Justice Center, across from San Fernando Cathedral, where it can be seen today.

The other waterway serving the early settlers was the Upper Labor Acequia. This was built in 1777-78 for the use primarily of the military families and others who had preceded the Canary Islanders as settlers. Until then, they had been denied the water rights enjoyed by the Canary Islanders, who controlled the municipal government. This one ran from near the head of the San Antonio River to near the head of San Pedro Creek and irrigated about 600 acres. Some of its remains can be seen today in Brackenridge Park.

The explanation for why North St. Mary's Street is so crooked goes back to the days when it was called Rock Quarry Road and ran for some distance beside the Upper Labor Ditch. The rock quarry was where the Zoo is today in Brackenridge Park. A branch of the ditch ran from near Rock Quarry Road toward Madison Square (between Lexington and Richmond avenues near Camden Street), irrigating lands from there to the San Antonio River.

Another diversion of the Upper Labor Ditch was the Alazán Ditch, which carried the Upper Labor's water north up San Pedro Avenue and around San Pedro Springs to the west, turned in a southerly direction to irrigate lands west of San Pedro Creek, and then joined Alazán Creek. The route into the city of the International and Great Northern Railway followed this branch of the Upper Labor Ditch in 1881.

The five *acequias* serving the missions—the Alamo Madre, San José, San Juan, Espada, and Concepción—were begun in the early 1700s and took their water from the river. The canal at Concepción was also called *Pajalache Acequia*, probably for the preponderance of Pajalache and other Pajalat Indians at that mission.

In what is now downtown San Antonio, the river was partly diverted to Mission Concepción by a dam (*presa*) about five feet high near the bridge on Presa Street next to the Hertzberg Circus Collection Library. It was the largest of the old *acequias*—and historic reports tell us the padres used a boat which they poled for transportation and maintenance of the canal as it flowed down today's South St. Mary's Street toward the mission. In 1869, the dam and canal were abandoned, partly because they backed up water in the city during floods.

The other mission acequia, within the city after the settlement expanded across the river from Main Plaza, was the Alamo Madre Ditch. It was the earliest of all the *acequias* excavated by the mission Indians and it brought water from near the headwaters of the river down several miles south into Mission San Antonio de Valero—today's Alamo—eventually returning to the river.

A number of lateral ditches branched off the Alamo Madre. One served the little village beside the Alamo—La Villita. At one time, the ditch flowed through the Menger Hotel courtyard. There is still a little ditch today behind the Alamo.

The Irish Flats, the section of San Antonio settled in the 1840s by Irish teamsters and sutlers with the U.S. Army, was served by the Alamo Madre Ditch. Although a number of prominent San Antonians of Irish descent had lived in the city since the 1830s, the newcomers settled in an area from Alamo Plaza north to Sixth Street and from Broadway east to the Alamo Madre Ditch.

In the early days of San Antonio, the inhabitants of the Villa de San Fernando and the missionaries vied for water rights. The problem was how much and by whom water should be drawn from the river for irrigation ditches. The missions had the right to use the San Antonio River, while the townspeople were to use San Pedro Creek.

In October 1733, the governor of Texas, Juan Antonio de Bustillo, authorized the settlers to draw water from the San Antonio River "at whatever point may be convenient for them to do so, from the site of the present settlement to its source," and to draw an equal amount from the Arroyo de San Pedro, "and no more." It was understood that, if in the future the volume of river water should be diminished so the missions were not getting their just share, their prior rights would be exercised in preference to those of the town.

Most of the irrigation canals serving the missions fell into disuse in the 1790s after the missions began to be secularized, but they left a legacy that can still be seen. Lifeblood of the missions, the *acequias* had enabled the missionaries and their Indian wards to raise cattle, sheep, goats, horses, mules, donkeys, corn, beans, cotton, melons, pumpkins, sweet potatoes, chilies, fruits (especially peaches), sugar cane, and grapes. Wheat was transported to Mission San José as late as the 1790s to be ground into flour at the handmade, water-powered mill there.

In the city, all the major ditches had laterals for distributing water into fields or to institutions or private homes. A hollow log called a *canoa*, made usually of cypress, was used to carry the water across small ditches. For larger ditches, well-built aqueducts of stone and mortar were used. In some places, cuttings of cactus were planted thickly so their thorns would keep livestock from the water.

The Town Ditches

A piped city water system did not reach most houses for many years. Even in the early 1890s, people were opposing the public water company that had been started in 1877—preferring water from the *acequias* or springs, or the vendors who used horse- and donkey-drawn carts to carry barrels of water.

Keeping the ditches clean was a constant problem. The San Antonio city ordinances, revised in 1899, abolished the office of ditch commissioner but transferred his duties to the new super-intendent of street cleaning and sanitation. His function, for which he was paid $100 monthly, was to control the collection and dis-position of garbage, the sweeping and sprinkling of the streets, and "the cleaning of the ditches and the river, together with the distribution of water for the purpose of irrigation, and the collec-tion of rents therefor. . . ."

The ordinance stated that the superintendent "shall see that the banks, locks, gates, abutments and aqueducts of the ditches are constantly kept in a condition to prevent overflow of the pub-lic streets, plazas, lanes and alleys of private property. . . ." The ordinance required that "when a private irrigating ditch crosses any of the public streets, it shall be the duty of all persons irrigat-ing from such a ditch to construct and keep in repair, at their own expense, good, substantial bridges across such public street."

In 1887, a reporter for the *Express* wrote:

Ten years ago the river, San Pedro Creek, and the irriga-tion ditches which the good old missionary fathers pro-vided for us over a century and a half ago, were our only water works. The ditches were all uncovered, and the involuntary baths on dark nights were so common as not to excite special comment.

The annual ditch cleaning was then as much dreaded by the good housewife as the annual house cleaning is by the sterner sex, for it meant shutting off the water supply for several days.

There is still a relic of the days of the *acequias* in a park-like setting near Mission San Francisco de la Espada. This is the Espada Aqueduct that carries water to the mission in a narrow ditch over the double-arched masonry aqueduct from Espada Dam on the river.

The dam across the San Antonio River—perhaps more than 250 years old—can be seen today in Espada Park. It elevates the water level five or six feet to a point from which it flows into the acequia. The aqueduct over which the acequia flows is the only structure of this kind in the United States. Engineer Edward Arneson observed that the middle pier is nearly as wide as the span of an arch, which is almost twelve feet, and its thickness suggested the old Roman rule of making piers one-third of the arch span.

Like the mission, the aqueduct was begun during the 1731-45 time period. Built some two and a half centuries ago, it is the oldest operational aqueduct in the United States, still irrigating gardens and farms in the area—still running after all these years!

The First Swimming Pools in Texas

Swimming pools for fun and cleanliness, and chicken soup for the sick, were offered by the Franciscan friars to their wards at Mission San José in 1768. Official reports from the missionaries south of San Antonio to their superiors in Mexico told of two swimming pools they had made beside the river—one for the Indians and one for the soldiers. But when Indians fell ill, they disliked the chicken soup or mutton broth they were given. They called it "dirty water" and disdained its lack of something to chew on.

4

Indians: The First Families

An extraordinary mixture of people has made San Antonio distinctive. The story of their influence begins with an examination of the area's very first inhabitants—those we call Indians or Native Americans—who, coming by way of Asia, were the earliest immigrants to this continent; they were followed by the Hispanics and other immigrants from Europe, the United States, and, eventually, other continents.

By the time of the 1860 United States census, most San Antonio Indians had been absorbed into the populace and were not listed separately. At that time, the census showed that 47.1 percent of San Antonians were "foreigners." These were listed as 1,477 Germans, 1,220 Mexicans, 310 Irish, 232 French, sixty-eight

English, and 294 "others." The "others," from twenty-two countries, included 117 Poles, fifty-seven Swiss, sixteen Russians, thirteen Italians, and twelve Danes. With a population of 8,235, San
Antonio was the largest town in Texas.

During the rest of the 1800s and into the early 1900s, other
newcomers came in sufficient numbers to make lasting marks on
the city's life.

Yanaguana

The first families of San Antonio—the American Indians—called
their campground *Yanaguana*. This Payaya word meant "refreshing waters," according to the respected mission historian Father
Marion A. Habig—although some anthropologists question the
translation. But until all the facts are in, "refreshing waters" serves
well as the sense of the word *Yanaguana*. Certainly the springs
that give rise to San Pedro Creek and the San Antonio River
always have been considered "refreshing waters."

In the 1600s and 1700s, Spanish explorers found a number of
groups of Indians camping around San Pedro Springs and the
springs that give rise to the San Antonio River. Like everyone
else who lives in the Americas today—North, South, or Central—
ancestors of the first Indians had come from another continent.
The most generally accepted theory is that they crossed to North
America over a once-existing land bridge from Siberia on the continent of Asia sometime between 10,000 and 40,000 years ago.
These first inhabitants moved south through present-day Alaska,
Canada, the United States, and Central and South America.
Referred to as Paleo-Indians by today's archaeologists and anthro-
pologists, the original pioneers spread over the three continents,
reaching the southernmost tip of South America by about 9000
B.C.

Paleo-Indians lived in the Olmos Basin north of today's San
Antonio and in the vicinity of springs that give rise to San Pedro
Creek and the San Antonio River. They also lived along Salado
Creek.

The Mission Indians

San Antonio's experience with the Indians was mixed. On one hand, the mission Indians were, for the most part, more tractable and peaceful than the nomadic Plains Indians—the Apaches and Comanches. The influence of the mission Indians on San Antonio differs greatly from that of the Plains Indians, who fiercely defended their hunting grounds against each other as well as against the invading forces of the Spaniards, the Mexicans, and the Anglo Americans.

Mission Indians in the area came from more than seventy groups. As an example, just the group whose names began with "p" were the Pacao, Pachalaque, Pajalat, Pamaque, Pampopa, Pana, Pasnacan, Pastia, Patalca, Patumaco, Payaya, Peana, Piquique, Pinto, Pitalac, and Pootajpo.

Apaches, Comanches, Tejas, Xarame, Zacuestacan, and others were represented at the missions. The largest number of groups were classed as belonging to the Coahuilteco linguistic affiliation, yet the language relationship of some was Karankawa, some Caddo, some in other categories, and some unknown.

The Indians at the missions were taught leadership and management as well as arts and crafts. They were organized into *pueblos* or special towns as part of the missions. At Mission Concepción, for instance, Indians served in the positions of superintendent, foreman (*caporal*), overseer, and *fiscal* (supply officer). Others had special assignments based on specialized skills, such as cowboy, fisherman, barber, musician, tailor, cook, sheep shearer, and weaver. "Official Judges"—a governor and a mayor—were elected each year by the vote of the men of the mission. Women learned skills associated with the household and garden.

Each of the missions, including Mission San Antonio de Valero, had nearby farmlands for raising vegetables, fruits, grains, and poultry and farm animals. Beyond, they had extensive ranchlands for cattle, so the first "Texas cowboys" on big Texas "spreads" were Indians—trained by the soldiers and missionaries.

Today, near Floresville in Wilson County there is still part of the historic working ranch for Mission Espada; called *Rancho de*

Indians of Texas (Fred Himes illustration)

las Cabras, it is the only existing Spanish colonial ranch in the United States. In 1762, it had a stone house and 1,262 head of cattle, some 4,000 sheep, 145 saddle horses, eleven droves of mares, and nine donkeys. In 1768 there were twenty-six residents in a 500-foot-long walled compound. The Texas Parks and Wildlife Department has transferred some 100 acres of the *rancho* to the National Park Service for management, development, and preservation.

The missionaries must be credited with giving valuable training to the Indians that benefited the civil community later when the Indians became citizens. Instructions "written from experience for a missionary who has never been in charge of a mission and is all alone and does not know whom to consult for advice" were aimed at Mission Concepción. The instructions cautioned:

> . . . The missionary must keep in mind that it is the custom to alternate between the nations; the Pajalaches and the Tacames. The former also include members of other tribes. Thus one year the governor is a Pajalache and the mayor is a Tacame. The next year the governor is a Tacame and the mayor is a Pajalache.

The first textbook written in Texas was prepared by a missionary at San Francisco de la Espada. Father Bartolome García translated the text from Spanish into Coahuiltecan. Printed in Mexico in 1760, it was used by missionaries in their religious training of Indians in Texas.

Anthropologists say that the total Indian population at each San Antonio mission never exceeded 400 and in fact was rarely more than 300. Many of the Indians became potentially useful citizens and many became Christians—more than 5,000 were baptized by the five missions from the time of their founding. Not all,

---

How Do We Honor Our First Families?

There are few reminders in San Antonio that its first inhabitants, the Native Americans, the Indians, lived here off and on for many centuries. Inside the San Antonio City Employees Credit Union at 123 North Medina is a colorful stained glass window, twenty-two feet high and ten feet wide, depicting two Indian braves kneeling among the trees and peering across the river to a distant domed and towered mission. And on a pink granite plaque across from the Arneson River Theater there is a group of prayerful Indians with a missionary saying Mass in a makeshift shelter. Seldom seen by most people is the mural in the Federal Building where Indians can be viewed taking part in San Antonio's history.

---

of course, shed their native beliefs completely, preferring to hold on to certain deeply felt religious customs and traditions.

When the numbers of Indians at the missions began to diminish in the 1790s and early 1800s, the missions were closed—secularized—and members who wished to affiliated themselves with the church of San Fernando in San Antonio. Lands and tools of the missions were turned over to the former mission Indians, who became *vecinos* (responsible proprietors), but not all the natives held on to their possessions. The more sophisticated Hispanic residents of San Antonio soon acquired the property of many of the mission Indians, who had much less experience as civic-minded proprietors.

Yet after more than a century in San Antonio, Indians became an integral part of the community, continuing the cycles of training and mission-living for generations. At times, there were some 1,300 Indians in the five San Antonio missions; in addition, a number of them lived in the nearby community. According to census records, in 1793 the number of Indians had risen to 126, or 9.5 percent of the 1,321 residents of San Fernando. By 1800, the larger community had drawn native groups into its social and economic life.

The Indian Wars

The Apache Indians had a powerful influence on the way Texas developed from its earliest frontier days. Even before the founding of San Antonio de Béxar in 1718, the Spaniards were having problems with the Apaches in Texas—only partly because they had made friends earlier with the Tejas Indians in the eastern part of the region, who were deadly foes of the Apaches. In remote New Mexico, the Spaniards had been staving off attacks from the Apaches since the 1600s, so when the Spanish viceroy gave instructions to Governor Alarcón on his expedition to found the villa of San Antonio de Béxar, he included special warnings about them. And as soon at the Apaches heard of the new settlement, they began to harass it. The Spaniards tried to make peace with them, but their efforts were fruitless.

Why Mission San Antonio de Valero was Closed

On September 7, 1792, the president of the Texas missions, Father José Francisco López, wrote to the superiors of the Franciscan College at Zacatecas that the mission should be discontinued, and religious care of the Indians transferred. He explained that the Indians had been well-schooled in their religious and civic responsibilities. He wrote that "they are not now, nor can they be called neophytes, or even Indians, since most of them, being children of marriages between Indians and white women, are mulattoes or half-breeds, as can be seen by the census list. . . . It can therefore be inferred that this mission cannot be called a mission of Indians, but a gathering of white people. The few pure Indians who remain are, in trading and communication, as intelligent as the others." The mission was secularized on April 11, 1793, and the church records were transferred to the parish of San Fernando across the river.

In 1720, Spanish authorities in Coahuila made peace overtures to the Apaches. The Indians spurned any concessions, and instead demonstrated their hostile intentions by hanging red cloth (*bandera*) from arrows stuck in the ground near San Antonio. (This brandishment could have been the origin of the name of Bandera Pass and the town of Bandera.) Before the Marqués de Aguayo had conducted his expedition into Texas in 1721-22, the Apaches had already become so bold as to attack the supply trains from Coahuila to San Antonio, stealing mules and killing the drivers.

On August 23, 1723, a band of Apaches made a raid on the stock of the presidio in Military Plaza. Although the corral was locked and guarded by ten soldiers, the Apaches broke in and stole eighty horses. Their attacks continued. When the fifty-five Canary Islanders came to San Antonio de Béxar in March 1731, they found themselves faced with the same dangers hampering the families of the settlers who had come in 1718 and later.

Historical recorder Father Juan Agustín Morfi told how on September 18, 1731, a band of Apaches attacked the presidio, driving away horses. When the soldiers pursued them, the Indians led the soldiers into an ambush of 500. For some reason the Indians fled, but "carried away sixty beasts." Two soldiers were killed and thirteen wounded.

On the night of June 30, 1745, while the Spanish presidio soldiers were asleep, an advance force of a main Apache band of 350 struck the armed garrison in what today is Military Plaza. The other hostile Indians stayed hidden in ambush, while some gathered before the presidio. Luckily, a boy saw them and roused the presidio soldiers. They were joined in the defense by townfolk living around nearby Main Plaza, but the Apaches split forces and attacked the presidio from another street. The soldiers and citizens fought desperately, and disaster was averted only by the arrival of help from Mission Valero, including one hundred mission Indians.

Stories of the numerous attacks by Indians—first the Apaches and later the Comanches—against the town and its environs were recorded year after year for more than a century after the founding of San Antonio de Béxar. One of the principal reasons for the legal establishment of the Texas Rangers in 1835 was to safeguard the frontier against Indian attacks. As early as 1823, Stephen F. Austin employed ten men to serve as "Rangers" for armed protection.

The U.S. Army finally got into the war against the Native Americans, setting up a chain of forts across the western part of Texas. It fought the Indians all over the West, and officially lists the Indian Campaigns among all its other "minor wars." The Army records what it calls "the Apache Campaigns" as extending from 1871 to 1886, when these first Americans were finally displaced and subdued by their conquerors.

Army casualties during the Texas Indian wars from 1848 to 1881 totaled 180 soldiers; Indian casualties during the same period have been estimated at 536 (424 killed, 112 wounded). But these figures do not account for casualties on both sides during the great many more years of Spanish, Mexican, and Anglo military and civilian conflict with the Indians. Thousands of Texian and Tejano settler families were harassed off and on for decades with sneak attacks by the Indians, resulting in property destruction and large numbers of deaths, injuries, and kidnappings. According to historian T. R. Fehrenbach, in the year 1849 alone, some 200 Texans—men, women, and children—were killed by Indians or carried off into captivity.

It was an Apache named Geronimo who most symbolized the Indian Wars. He surrendered in 1877, more than a century after his forefathers had begun their attacks and counterattacks against the Spanish in Texas and the territory to the west. With his band of fellow prisoners, Geronimo was displayed to the visiting public in September and October 1886 by the U.S. Army at Fort Sam Houston before he was moved to Florida and later to Oklahoma. In his biography, Geronimo, whose Indian name was Goyathlay, was quoted:

> We are vanishing from the Earth, yet I cannot think we are useless, or Usen [God] would not have created us. . . .
>
> For each tribe of men Usen created, He also made a home. In the land created for any particular tribe, He placed whatever would be best for the welfare of that tribe.
>
> When Usen created the Apaches He also created their homes in the West. He gave them such grain, fruits, and game as they needed to eat. To restore their health when disease attacked them He taught them where to find these herbs, and how to prepare them for medicine. He gave them a pleasant climate, and all they needed for clothing and shelter was at hand.
>
> Thus it was in the beginning: the Apaches and their homes each created for the other by Usen Himself. When they are taken from these homes they sicken and die. How long will it be until it is said there are no Apaches?

On the streets of San Antonio today, you can see descendants of the Indians of early San Antonio. As former rector of San Fernando Cathedral Father Virgil Elizondo has observed, "They are not extinct nor living on reservations."

All the Little Alamos of Texas

W. K. Baylor, born in 1846, lived until after World War I, which ended in 1918—but what he remembered most vividly when he was in his late 70s were the years of spasmodic attacks and counterattacks between the Texans and the Native Americans who were trying to resist the invasion of their lands.

Few people realize today how bitter was this warfare in Texas, which began when the Spaniards came in the late 1600s and continued through the Mexican regime and into the 1880s, twenty years after the Civil War. Thousands of Texans were attacked in their homes and in their travels, as the Indians fought and died for their ancient territory. The fighting was cruel on both sides, and, over the years, thousands of Indians died.

Baylor wrote in the September 1924 *Frontier Times*, published in Bandera, Texas:

> People now look at you in amazement and ask: "Why did you stay in such a country?" In looking back to those years, I wonder myself why people lived there and voluntarily endured the hardships incident to a frontier life, as our frontier then was. But our settlers stayed and fought to the bitter end, many of them made the supreme sacrifice, and much is due them, for what that part of the state now is.
>
> Little do they realize that while at San Antonio we have a single Alamo made sacred by the blood of martyrs, that all along our frontier of those days are little Alamos where no messenger was left to tell the story of unutterable murder and cruelty, and there is many a Thermopylae Pass as well.
>
> These little Alamos have crumbled to dust, nothing marks the spots where they stood. They are only a memory, but a sacred one, and their memory should ever be kept green in the hearts of the people of Texas. A monument ought to be erected to keep alive the memory of "The Old Settlers of Texas," and their gallant deeds and achievements properly commemorated.

On Commerce Street Bridge there is a monument in high relief of an Indian in full headdress. "First Inhabitant" was commissioned early in 1914 and placed on the bridge as part of the project that widened Commerce Street. The sculpture is an uncommon reminder that the first families of San Antonio were native Americans—American Indians.

The Living Missions

For a century and a half, San Antonio's four missions, besides the Alamo, have been considered "must-sees" on the itineraries of most visitors—whether they have come from other parts of North America or from another continent. Nowhere else in the United States are there so many ancient Spanish missions near a city.

The eastern approach to the river, along which the San Antonio missions were established south of town, formed for a visitor from Mexico in 1828 "a superb background that lost itself in the horizon, charming the eye and filling the heart of the spectator with an unknown joy." José María Sánchez, draftsman with an expedition of Gen. Manuel de Mier y Terán, wrote: "We crossed the Cíbolo, a small creek, and at a short distance saw the mission of La Espada. The view of this temple and the few small houses that surrounded it made an impression upon me that I cannot express."

The leader of the great influx of German emigrants to the Hill Country in Texas, Prince Carl of Solms-Braunfels, marveled at the missions in 1844. He wrote, "San Antonio de Béxar looks like a single great ruin from Spanish times—the Alamo, all the splendid monuments of Spanish architecture, the missions of San José, La Concepción, San Juan, and La Espada lie in ruins—I feel here like Scipio on the ruins of Carthage."

The first Texas mission churches and their surrounding buildings were nothing like the stone edifices we see today. Until the mid-1700s and later, they were temporary wooden structures built to house the missionaries and Indians and provide places for teaching and worship, as well as shelter for equipment needed in hunting and basic farming. A few soldiers helped protect them from hostile tribes.

"First Inhabitant" is the title given by Waldine Tauch to this Indian figure she sculptured for the new Commerce Street Bridge after receiving a commission of $1,000 from the publisher of the San Antonio Express. Miss Tauch was a longtime protégé of Pompeo Coppini, the sculptor of the Cenotaph in front of the Alamo. The figure of the Native American is seven feet tall, and holds in each hand a shallow bowl to be used as a drinking fountain, but these were soon vandalized and their pipes disconnected. The sculptor was honored in June 1915 at a street-widening celebration led by the Rotary Club with bands, banners, parades, and orations. Miss Tauch created many works in Texas, including the statue of Moses Austin near the Spanish Governor's Palace. (Photo by author)

Because temporary shelters and Indians to occupy them were about all that the teaching friars needed, these missions were at first nearly as mobile as the missionaries. All but one of the five missions at San Antonio in the 1700s—San José—had been transferred from elsewhere. Another, Mission San Francisco Xavier de Nájera, was begun in 1722 near the area later occupied by Mission Concepción but never completed. There is a plaque telling about that nearly forgotten mission a half mile south of Mission Concepción on the left side of Mission Road, near the boundary of the Riverside Municipal Golf Course. It says, in part: "Approximate location of Mission San Francisco Xavier de Najera. Established in 1722. Its Indian neophytes, few in number, passed into the care of the missionaries of San Antonio de Valero in 1726."

San Antonio's four missions today are San José y San Miguel de Aguayo (named in honor of the governor of Coahuila and Texas, the Marqués de San Miguel de Aguayo), Nuestra Señora de la Purísima Concepción, San Juan de Capistrano, and San Francisco de la Espada. All four missions—which were for many years in ruins—have been restored and again serve Roman Catholic members.

No longer an active religious center, Mission San Antonio de Valero—the Alamo—was established in San Antonio in 1718, but it had been founded as Mission San Francisco Solano near the Rio Grande in 1700. Three of the other missions were transferred to San Antonio from East Texas in 1731. San Antonio's Mission San Francisco de la Espada originated in 1690 in East Texas as San Francisco de las Tejas. It was the first institution to carry the Texas name.

Mission Nuestra Señora de la Purísima Concepción de los Hasani, which we refer to as Mission Concepción, was founded on July 7, 1716, in East Texas near present-day Nacogdoches, in the principal settlement of the Hasinai Indians (also called Hasani, Asenai, Assoni, Asenay) of the Caddo Indian confederacy. These Indians used a word sounding to the Spaniards like "Texas" when referring to themselves or their allied tribes. It meant "friends" or "our own people."

Concepción was among six missions founded in 1716 and 1717 by Franciscans from two apostolic colleges in the towns of Querétaro and Zacatecas south of the Rio Grande in New Spain. The "de los Hasani" designation was dropped from the mission's name when it was moved to San Antonio. It then became Nuestra Señora de la Purísima Concepción de Acuña—Acuña being the family name of the incumbent viceroy.

Mission San José had a different beginning. Although founded on the east bank of the San Antonio River on February 23, 1720, it was moved to a second site on the west bank sometime between 1724 and 1727; then, after an epidemic in 1740, to its third site so as to be on the higher ground it now occupies. Founded by Franciscan Father Margil (Antonio Margil de Jesús), of the College of Nuestra Señora de Guadalupe de Zacatecas, it is the only San Antonio mission not established by the Franciscans from the College of Querétaro.

Father Margil, generally considered the most noteworthy of all the missionaries in New Spain, spent thirty years organizing missions in Yucatán, Costa Rica, and Guatemala before coming to Texas in 1716 and founding five more. He also spent years as the president of the missionary college at Zacatecas that he had founded. His extraordinary achievements among the Indians, and stories of an unusual spirituality, of humbleness, of long journeys always on foot, and of purported miracles resulted in 1771 in his being placed under consideration by the Vatican for sainthood. His title in the church was elevated to "venerable" in 1836, and he remains under consideration for sainthood.

Seeing the almost fortress-like missions today, it is easy to forget that all of them began in temporary buildings made of sticks, branches, grass, and mud, and later of heavier wood or of adobe bricks. The stone churches were completed many years later: San José in 1782; Concepción in 1755; San Juan and San Francisco de la Espada in 1756. Mission San Antonio de Valero had the stones laid for its first substantial church on May 8, 1744; because it had collapsed, the second church, the present Alamo, was begun in 1756 but never was completed during mission days.

Mission Concepción is the only San Antonio mission that has not required extensive restoration. Not only is it the oldest unrestored stone church in the United States, and the oldest named for the Immaculate Conception, but it is the oldest building in Texas.

The four missions south of the former Mission San Antonio de Valero have been preserved and maintained in recent years by the combined efforts of the Archdiocese of San Antonio, the San Antonio Conservation Society, the Texas Department of Parks and Wildlife, the City of San Antonio, the County of Bexar, the State

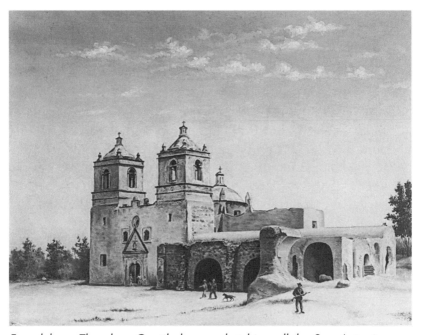

French-born Theodore Gentilz began sketching all the San Antonio Spanish Colonial missions in 1844 and for years made a variety of paintings of them. Mission Concepción is the best preserved of San Antonio's missions. First built of temporary materials—rough timber roofed with grass—in 1731, it was constructed in stone in 1755, taking advantage of a natural rock-solid foundation. (Daughters of the Republic of Texas Library photo)

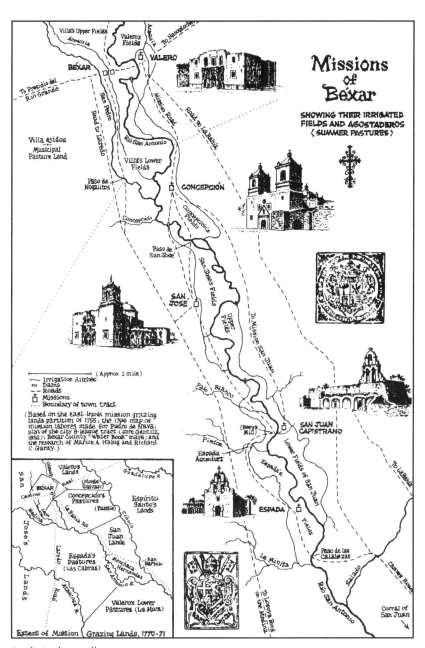

Jack Jackson illustration

The artistry demonstrated by the sculptor of the rose window outside the sacristy of Mission San José is almost matched by the mysteries of its origins. No one is entirely sure of the name of the sculptor or the exact date of the work's creation. We do know that it has drawn admirers from near and distant places for decades and is replicated in churches, the facades of buildings, and wherever else its beauty seems needed. Roses are associated with Our Lady of Guadalupe, and with the name of the Apostolic College of the missionary Franciscans in Zacatecas. The opening was used for a time as a two-way pulpit. The story of the sculptor from Spain and his broken heart over the drowning of his betrothed Rosa is only a legend. The author of San Antonio's Mission San José, Fr. Marion A. Habig, said he believed the sculptor could be Pedro Huízar, a carpenter and surveyor from Mexico, who completed the work around 1790. (Fred Himes illustration)

of Texas, and the National Park Service of the United States. Mission San Antonio de Valero, "the Alamo," is a State Historic Site in the care of the Daughters of the Republic of Texas.

In 1978, the San Antonio Missions National Historical Park was established by the United States Congress, making the U.S. Department of Interior's National Park Service responsible for stabilizing and preserving the historic mission structures and grounds. The four beautifully restored missions are spaced less than three miles apart along the river south of San Antonio encompassed in a 475-acre historical park. By cooperative agreement with the Archdiocese of San Antonio, three of the mission churches remain active Roman Catholic parishes while they also are open to the public as historic sites. Missions San José, Espada, and San Juan Capistrano are active Catholic parishes, while Concepción functions as a mission shrine of St. Cecilia Catholic Church.

In 1778, Father Juan Agustín Morfi (descended from Irish immigrants named Murphy who settled in Spain) described Mission San José. "It is, in truth," he said, "the first mission in America, not in point of time but in point of beauty, plan, and strength, so that there is not a presidio along the entire frontier line that can compare with it." Another Irishman serving Spain, Colonel Hugo Oconor (O'Connor), commandant inspector for the viceroy, had witnessed the laying of the cornerstone in Mission San José's church in 1768.

Mission San José has become an especially popular attraction for visitors who attend the noontime Sunday Mariachi Mass there. The church quickly becomes packed with parishioners and tourists who have lined up after 11 A.M. at an entrance on the Rose Window side.

Mission San Juan—still seemingly lost in an ancient woods—evokes, as it has for 200 years, a feeling of a time beyond memory, an era of enchantment. Its ancient acequia, now being refurbished, will be flowing again from the San Antonio River to serve a Spanish colonial demonstration farm.

In the shaded greenery not far from Mission Espada's west gate, an acequia carries water from an archaic dam in the San

Antonio River over a Spanish aqueduct of stone. Espada dam and aqueduct are the best surviving examples of Spanish Colonial irrigation systems in the United States.

A project called Mission Trails is under way to provide a distinctively landscaped, urban-to-rural series of intertwining roads and hike and bike trails from the Alamo to Mission Espada. The scenic route will be 10.4 miles long, the direct route 6.8 miles. The hike and bike trails will run 32.4 miles.

The facade of Mission San José as visualized in its original beauty by Ernest Schuchard. Engineer and historian as well as artist, Schuchard meticulously studied and recorded the colorful frescoes and fragments of exterior and interior decorations of Missions San José and Concepción in the 1920s and 1930s. In this perspective of the church, the high dome that is some distance behind the entrance is not seen, nor is the top of the church's single bell tower at the right. Today, you can see Schuchard's frescoes painted more than sixty years ago on one side of the church's bell tower and inside the mission's restored granary. (Daughters of the Republic of Texas Library photo)

Theodore Gentilz painted a wedding party approaching Mission San Juan Capistrano in the 1800s. After the mission was established in 1731, the padres had by 1762 baptized 847 Indians and given Christian burial to 645. Many Indians had learned farming and ranching skills as well as certain rules of community self-governance. In an adjoining building, Indians wove cotton and woolen fabrics on three separate looms. The granary was filled with 2,000 bushels of corn and beans, and the mission herds had multiplied to 1,000 cattle, 3,500 sheep and goats, and 500 horses. In 1794, the mission was secularized and land and property turned over to the few remaining Indians. As with the other missions, it has been restored so that today it looks much as it did in the mid-1700s. (Daughters of the Republic of Texas Library photo)

This is one of several paintings of Mission San Francisco de Espada done over the years after 1844 by Theodore Gentilz. It shows the mission before its restoration was begun by French-born Father Francis Bouchu, who was first assigned as an assistant at San Fernando Church in 1868. Bouchu died in 1907, remembered not only for his work as a religious but as a bricklayer, stonemason, carpenter, photographer, printer, historian, and lawyer. Mission Espada represents all the others in the Coat of Arms of Bexar County. (Daughters of the Republic of Texas Library photo)

5

The Hispanic Tradition

San Antonio is a rare gem of ancient Hispanicity in an Old West setting. Novelist Graham Greene observed in 1939 that San Antonio was "half Mexico and half Will Rogers."

Stanley Marcus, the Dallas merchant known for his insightful contributions to the famous Neiman-Marcus stores, has described San Antonio as "one of the most charming cities in the country." San Antonio, said Marcus, "has been flavored by its Hispanic culture, to which it has added a graciousness of the old South and an imaginative understanding of the importance of core city planning."

Larry McMurtry wrote in his book *In a Narrow Grave* that San Antonio "is of Texas, and yet it transcends Texas in some way, as San Francisco transcends California, as New Orleans transcends

Louisiana. Houston and Dallas express Texas—San Antonio speaks for itself, and much of its charm is in the way it embodies its past. Not a little of its charm, like that of El Paso, is attributable to the presence of Latins, who almost always improve an Anglo-Saxon town."

An understanding of San Antonio's mystique must include (1) the story of the Canary Islanders who came in 1731 to found the Villa de San Fernando, and who have kept their traditions before the public with insistent pride even to this day; (2) the first settlers of Villa de San Antonio de Béxar, who came from south of the Rio Grande more than a decade before the Canary Islanders; and (3) the role of the Hispanic Texans—the Tejanos—who helped shape the city for two and three-quarters centuries, giving all who spend time there today a memorable "sense of place."

Who Were the Canary Islanders?

The first city government in Texas was formed in the early 1700s by Canary Islanders sent to San Antonio by the king of Spain. To this day, they have exerted an influence on the city far out of proportion to their numbers.

In the 1730s, King Philip V ruled virtually all the South American continent as well as Central America. He also claimed what is now Mexico and the southwestern United States all the way to the Pacific Ocean, plus Florida and the islands of the Caribbean. British possessions in the Western Hemisphere were mostly on the Eastern Coast of North America, and the French claimed a vast V-shaped area stemming narrowly north from the banks of the Mississippi River in New Orleans and rising like a flared champagne glass into Canada.

As part of a plan begun years earlier to establish a Spanish presence in the region of Texas to forestall French encroachment from Louisiana, King Philip wanted to found a city at San Antonio as a halfway point between the Rio Grande and Nacogdoches far to the east. He decided to send Canary Islanders as settlers.

The Canary Islands are in approximately the same latitude as San Antonio, which is twenty-nine degrees, thirty-one minutes,

When the fifty-five Canary Islanders arrived at the future site of San Fernando de Béxar on March 9, 1731, they were greeted by some of the more than 200 residents who had come north from below the Rio Grande in 1718 and later. (Drawing by José Cisneros)

Why Are Hispanics Unique?

What makes the Spanish people—the original source of Hispanism—so distinctive? Why were the Canary Islanders and other Hispanics clearly different from the English, the French, the Germans, the Irish, and other "European" San Antonians of the 1800s? The answer, of course, lies in the distinctive history of Spain—as it differs from all other countries. It is the source of the people's language, institutions, art and architecture, their religion and attitude toward life. The culture of Spain was shaped uniquely by the interaction for centuries of the wisdom and learning of Christians, Moslems, and Jews.

Like virtually all nationalities, the Spanish are a mixture of peoples. The Iberian peninsula on which they live juts out from the southwestern edge of Europe, with coastlines on the Mediterranean Sea and the Atlantic Ocean. It is the closest link between Europe and Africa and has been a vital crossroads for many centuries. The first known inhabitants, the Iberians, were followed by Phoenicians, Celts, Greeks, and Carthaginians, all of whom established colonies.

After 218 B.C., when the Carthaginian leader Hannibal came from Africa to attack the Romans, the Roman general Scipio invaded the Iberian peninsula, and the people there gradually were unified in the Roman province of Hispania. The Romans brought to Hispania the Latin language, the Christian religion, irrigation systems, paved roads, and urban planning. But in the fifth century A.D., the Visigoths, a Germanic tribe, crossed the Pyrenees and ended the rule of Rome. The Visigoths were Arian Christians, while the Hispano-Romans were Catholics, and the latter religion eventually prevailed.

In 711, Moors from North Africa invaded Iberia and occupied nearly the entire peninsula except for Asturias in the mountainous northwest where the Christian warriors took refuge. The Moors were Arabs from the Middle East and Berbers and mixed Arab-Berbers from North Africa. The Moors (*Moros*, in Spanish) had spread their Islamic faith from east to west across North Africa, and now they were to establish their culture in Hispania. They called Spain *"al-Andalus,"* a name that survives as "Andalusía." During the next several centuries, they created one of the medieval world's leading cultural centers.

The Moors demonstrated a superior knowledge of medicine, science, geography, philosophy, and fine arts. They introduced a more advanced irrigation system and improved agricultural techniques, including horse breeding, which they had developed in North Africa. More than a quarter of all the words in the Spanish language come from the Arabic. Jewish intellectuals created significant compilations on legislation, astronomy, and world history. Carlos Fuentes has observed, "One can say that the Jews fixed and circulated the use of the Spanish language in Spain."

Eventually, the Christians in the north of the peninsula developed military strength, a crusading spirit, and a determination to move southward. By the thirteenth century, they had pushed the Moors back to the extreme south. Granada fell to the Christians in 1492, but it was not until 1609-1610, during the reign of Philip III, that the last of the Jews and Moors were expelled from Spain. Moors who were Christianised (*Moriscos*) remained.

---

fifty-three seconds north. The thirteen volcanic Canary Islands thrust up from the Atlantic Ocean with a total land area of 2,807 square miles—somewhat larger than the state of Delaware. The island nearest the mainland of Northwest Africa is about sixty-seven miles west of the coast of Morocco on the African continent.

Mountains and volcanos give the islands a variety of soil types and climates. The highest mountain, Pico de Teide on Tenerife, is 12,198 feet and snowcapped. The islanders can trace their roots to the Guanches, the ancient natives going back to the Stone Age, who have been described as robust, fair-skinned, and handsome.

The Canaries suffered invasions by a variety of exploiters—Romans, Moslems of the Arabian Peninsula, Phoenicians, and voyagers from Italy, Portugal, France, and Spain. Even English raiders appeared at times. In the 1500s and later, Spanish and other European immigrants settled in the islands, often mixing their families with the earlier inhabitants. By the time Spain came to the New World, the Canary Islanders were fundamentally Spanish in their institutions and culture. The islands got their name from the Latin word for "dog" (*canis*) because of the large numbers of ferocious canines that lived there many centuries ago; then canary birds were named for the islands. Christopher Columbus found them a convenient stopping place on his voyages. Some of the islanders shipped on with expeditions as sailors. They brought back stories of great opportunities to be found in the Western Hemisphere.

According to historian Francisco Morales Padrón, the average Canarian "from the moment he acquired the use of reason, longed for America as his true homeland." For most of the islanders, life was not easy. The Spanish government kept tight control of their trade. Their most successful products and crops, such as wine, cereals, fruits, and sugar, could be exported, when allowed. The islands suffered from many calamities besides invasions and raids. Besides limited arable land, there were volcanic eruptions, epidemics, bad harvests, and famines. But still, in 1729 when King Philip V issued his invitation for volunteers to go to Texas, it took eight months to enlist the prospective settlers and prepare them for their voyage.

Finally, on March 27, 1730, they embarked from Santa Cruz on Tenerife Island. In May, they stopped over in Havana and arrived in Vera Cruz, Mexico, in July—eighty-four days after sailing from Tenerife. Next came the long overland journey to San Antonio, which they reached on March 9, 1731.

The *Isleños* consisted of fifteen families plus four bachelors who were considered the equivalent of one family in the allotment of supplies and, later, land. Fortunately, when these fifty-five people arrived at Presidio de Béxar they were welcomed by the soldiers and their families and others who had been living and farming in the vicinity for more than twelve years. The Isleños

A variety of citizens can be seen here in José Cisneros' drawing of the interior of the cabildo—the offices of the municipal corporation made up of regidores or councilmen—in San Fernando de Béxar in the 1700s. The coat of arms on the wall symbolizes the Spanish kingdoms of León (Lion) and Castile (Castle). (Courtesy Institute of Texan Cultures)

Here, José Cisneros depicts a presidial soldier and a girl in Canary Island dress in front of his concept of how Mission San Antonio de Valero, later known as the Alamo, might have appeared in the 1700s. (Courtesy Institute of Texan Cultures)

Artist José Cisneros made this drawing to depict the different peoples living in the town in the 1700s. In the Plaza de las Islas in front of the San Fernando Church are a mulatto, an Indian, and Europeans. (Courtesy Institute of Texan Cultures)

were sheltered and fed by the original settlers until they could fend for themselves.

In August 1731, five months after the arrival of the Canary Islanders, the new settlers had formed a "city council"—appointed by the captain of the presidio—and, in the first election in Texas, had chosen two judges. The new municipality was called Villa de San Fernando.

For some years, the town was called either San Fernando or Béjar or Véjar or Béxar, or San Antonio de Béxar, or simply San Antonio. There were three separate communities: the missions, the presidio residents, and the town governed by the Canary Island immigrants. Sometimes their special interests clashed but eventually they learned to work together. Finally the city became San Antonio, the county became Bexar, and San Fernando was the name of the cathedral in the ancient church building whose construction was begun by the Isleños.

The presidio captain, Don Juan Antonio Pérez de Almazán, had appointed the recognized leader, Juan Leal Goraz, the number one alderman (alcalde)—a kind of mayor—for life. Although

An old postcard shows San Fernando Cathedral in the horse and buggy days before removal of the decorative cupolas atop the 1891 City Hall in the background. The main part of the cathedral and its facade were designed by François Giraud, a French-trained engineer. They were constructed in 1873. There have been a number of renovations over the years since the cornerstone was laid in 1738, but many of the earliest parts remain, including the original walls of the sanctuary built around 1750 beneath the dome. The dome is the official center of San Antonio from which measurements of distance are made. To the right of the cathedral were the businesses of the Texas Stockman & Farmer and Frost National Bank. In 1922, Frost National Bank built San Antonio's first twelve-story office building on this site.

Leal was untrained in reading and writing, as were all but two of the aldermen, the first Isleños apparently had little need of formal education to enable them to sink their roots into the new world. After the land had been surveyed and apportioned among the fifteen families for housing and farming, the new settlers went about the task of helping to make the first municipality in Texas a town that would endure, grow, and prosper.

To this day, the Canary Islanders, the Isleños, have not forgotten the honor bestowed upon them in 1731 by the king for their pioneer work on his behalf. Each male person of the first Canary

Islanders in Texas was given the title of "Hidalgo"—literally, *Hijo de Algo* or "Son of Something." It was a social rank of modest nobility, but the Isleños naturally saw it as putting them above all other residents.

Thousands of San Antonians—many with English, Irish, German, or other family names besides Spanish—trace their lineage to a Canary Islander. Many belong to the Canary Islands Descendants Association. Typical of the high standing of Canary Islanders among San Antonians is the fact that five of the nine women who established the Alamo Mission Chapter of the Daughters of the Republic of Texas in 1906—ousting the thirteen-year-old De Zavala Chapter—proudly claimed descent from the families who came to San Antonio in 1731. Ironically, none of them had Spanish surnames.

The Bexareños

Settlement of San Antonio was begun more than a decade before the Canary Islanders were sent by the Spanish Crown to establish a formal city. When the Islanders arrived in 1731, according to historian Jesús F. de la Teja, the first village, located around today's Military Plaza, had about twenty-five civilian households, including former soldiers, and a total population of about 300. These first settlers along with the Canary Islanders were eventually called *Bexareños*.

The Alarcón expedition of 1718 that established a presidio and mission brought seventy-two immigrants, including seven families. The composition of the colonists fell somewhat short of the staffing the governor had been instructed to follow: fifty selected married soldiers, preferably Spaniards, a carpenter, a mason, a blacksmith, and a weaver. The governor had been directed to help the missionaries found one or two missions and supply them with provisions, cattle, tools, and a guard of ten soldiers. Instructions called for the Indians to be pacified by "peaceful and affectionate means." They were to receive gifts, such as tobacco, flour, and trinkets, and dealt with through their chiefs. The expedition included cattle, sheep, goats, hogs, chickens, six droves of mules laden with clothing and provisions, and 548 horses.

The new settlers had come from what we now call Northern Mexico, especially the province of Coahuila. Most of them had frontier experience. It was possible for the soldiers, most of whom were of mixed-blood heritage, to gain officer status and even the title of *don*, an opportunity not often available in the New World. Intermarriage with civilian families, acquisition of land, and accumulation of monies were more important in acquiring social rank than the nationality of one's forebears. It is estimated that by 1820 about thirty percent of San Fernando de Béxar married couples were mixed Spanish and mestizo.

Today's Americans benefit from a vast array of contributions brought by Spanish civilization in the 1500s. Latin Americans have created their cultural heritage "with the greatest joy, the greatest gravity, the greatest risk," writes noted author Carlos Fuentes. Few cultures in the world possess a comparable richness and continuity, he believes. He traces those values to their origins. "There is not a single Latin American, from the Rio Grande to Cape Horn," he writes, "who is not heir to each and every aspect of our cultural heritage." If one could see the whole of Hispanic culture in one picture, as in the story by the Argentine author Jorge Luís Borges, "The Aleph," writes Fuentes, we would "*find ourselves* as Hispanics." He explains:

> What we would see in the Spanish-American aleph would be the Indian sense of sacredness, communality, and the will to survive; the Mediterranean legacy of law, philosophy, and the Christian, Jewish, and Arab strains making up a multiracial Spain; and the New World's challenge to Spain, the syncretic, baroque continuation of the multicultural and multiracial experience, now including Indian, European, and black African contributions. We would see a struggle for democracy and for revolution, coming all the way from the medieval townships and from the ideas of the European Enlightenment, but meeting our true personal and communal experience in Zapata's villages, on Bolivar's plains, in Tupac Amaru's highlands.

Jack Jackson illustration

A Cultural Mix Unique in the World

It is regrettable that most Hispanics in the United States—let alone non-Hispanics—do not appreciate the richness of the culture that they have inherited from the confluence of civilizations in the New World. The unusual character of the Tejano is the foundation of San Antonio's notably enchanting aura. Just as many non-Hispanic Texans have identifiable characteristics differentiating them from persons in other states, so do many Texan Hispanics—*Tejanos*.

Texan Hispanics generally have inherited their names, language, and much of their culture from Spain. Most trace their lineage to Mexico, but many have roots in the Canary Islands or to countries in Central or South America or the Caribbean area. These latter, of course, are not Mexican Americans.

Most Texas historians prefer the term "Tejano" to "Latino" when speaking of Hispanic Texans. They see Latinos as belonging to a broader group, embracing the Latin-based languages and cultures not only of Spain but of Italy, France, Portugal, and Romania. The majority of Mexican Americans prefer not to be called "*chicanos*," a name generally connected to groups seeking political redress of what they see as social injustices. Since 1980, the U.S. Census has designated *Hispanic* an ethnic category. The census literature explains that "Hispanics can be of any race," and a majority have identified themselves as white.

Hispanic Texans began to be called *Tejanos* in the 1830s, when Anglo-American Texans and their non-Hispanic supporters began identifying themselves as *Texians*. According to *The New Handbook of Texas*, the term "Texian" generally is used "to apply to a citizen of the Anglo-American section of the province of Coahuila and Texas or the Republic." It was used from about 1835 to 1868. As president of the Republic, Mirabeau B. Lamar used the term to foster nationalism, says the *Handbook*.

Mestizo

The Tejano heritage includes not only that of the multicultured Spaniards but also European, black, Indian, and "mixed" or *mestizo.* A portion of today's Tejano heritage was in the blood of the people who came across the Bering Strait from Asia between 10,000 and 40,000 years ago and trailed south across North America to the lands below the Rio Grande. In the blood of the Tejanos— the majority of today's San Antonians—could be genes of Olmecs, Toltecs, Mayans, or Aztecs, as well as of Indians who lived from coast to coast north of the Rio Grande. All these people flour- ished in great civilizations many centuries before the Europeans came to the New World some 500 years ago.

Indian

It is easier for most Americans to appreciate the contributions of Spanish culture to the New World than the contributions of the Indians. This probably is because we know more about the European and Judeo-Christian civilization at the roots of the Span- ish culture. As Jack Weatherford, author of *Indian Givers*, wrote: "Columbus arrived in the New World in 1492, but America has yet to be discovered." After reading his book on "how the Indi- ans of the Americas transformed the world," one is startled by its well-authenticated statements, such as:

The caucus in which politicians meet and voters select candidates is an Indian word and invention.

The American Federal system derives not from Europe but from Indian tribal organizations—Benjamin Franklin and George Washington, both highly knowledgeable about Indian society, could attest.

Some 60 percent of the food eaten in the world today is of American origin. Corn, potatoes, tomatoes, beans and squash, for example, revolutionized diets around the globe. So did chocolate, vanilla and peanuts. Our Thanksgiving turkey was originally all American. Tobacco, tequila, cocaine and chewing gum (chicle) from the Americas affected lifestyles everywhere. Chiles, mistakenly called peppers, enlivened the cuisines of China, Hungary and Italy, as well as Mexico.

Indian achievements in urban planning, architecture and agriculture were phenomenal. They had a road system that rivaled that of the Romans and "agricultural experiment stations" in the high Andes.

The Indians offered a sophisticated pharmacy that contributed much to modern medicine in the form of aspirin-related tree bark extracts, laxatives, painkillers, antibacterial medicines, petroleum jelly and many other pharmaceuticals and healing techniques. They had an attitude toward the natural world that anticipated modern ecology, and religious concepts and spiritual insights that were and are profoundly enriching for the rest of humanity, laws often more humane than their European equivalents, a collective *summa* of wisdom and experience almost totally ignored by newcomers to the Americas.

Both our language and our cuisine have been enriched by Indians of the Americas. Language historian Charles L. Cutler says that more than one thousand Native American (North American Indians north of Mexico plus Eskimo and Aleut) words, and more than fifteen hundred Latin American Indian loanwords have entered the English vocabulary. One of the most popular legacies that the early natives of South America gave to Mexico and to the entire world was the chile, the wild *capsicum*, long before any Asian or European had gone to the Americas. Archaeologists have found the cultivation of chiles as far back as 6,000-7,000 B.C. somewhere in the area of what is now Brazil, Bolivia, and Paraguay.

Aztec

There is a plaque in Mexico City on the Great Pyramid of Tlatelolco, in the Square of the Three Cultures, that gives sharp insight into the nature of the Mexican of today:

On August 13, 1521, Tlatelolco, heroically defended by Cuauhtemoc, fell into the power of Hernán Cortéz. It was neither a triumph nor a defeat, but the painful birth of the Mestizo people who are the Mexico of today.

Cultural anthropologists call the region of central and southern Mexico and parts of Central America "Mesoamerica"—Middle America. They call the "Indians" who lived there originally Mesoamericans. During the early colonial period in Mexico, the Spaniards brought a relatively small number of Negroes with them. Other ethnic groups, including Asians, also merged into the life of the country. By the 1700s, there were more than twenty designated social elements stemming from those basic human components and their later mixtures.

The sophistication and culture of Montezuma's empire astonished Cortez and his army when they arrived in 1521. Tenochtitlán, the Aztec capital, was almost rectangular and laid out in the middle of a lake in four symmetrical parts. An engineered aqueduct system brought fresh drinking water to the large populace from distant mountain springs. The Spaniards estimated the city to have more than 80,000 people. Historian William H. Prescott estimated the population of the great city at 300,000, but even 80,000 would be very large for the time. This was a population greater than most of the European cities of that time, since only four of them— Paris, Naples, Venice, and Milan—had more than 100,000 inhabitants. Spain's largest city, Seville, had only 45,000 in 1530.

Tenochtitlán had palatial homes with beautiful gardens along canals. The Great Temple stood on what is now Zócalo, the main plaza in Mexico City. Beside it were schools teaching music and dance for the Aztec warriors and priests. The ruling classes wore rich garments and artistic jewelry of gold and precious stones.

Bernal Díaz, who recorded the Spanish conqueror's impressions of the Aztec city, wrote:

Some of the soldiers among us, who had been in many parts of the world, in Constantinople and all over Italy, in

Rome, said that so large a marketplace and so full of people, and so well regulated and arranged, they had never beheld before.

Díaz added that on seeing the spectacular city, with its great palaces and homes of the lords, "we were amazed and said that it was like the enchantments they tell in the legend of Amadis, on account of the great towers and temples and buildings rising from the water, and all built of masonry. And some of our soldiers even asked whether the things that we saw were not a dream."

The Aztecs were anything but primitive, even though their view of life was greatly different from that of the Christian Europeans. They had acquired a knowledge of mathematics that had come from the Olmecs and Mayans—a sophisticated system used even earlier than Europeans, who did not have the zero until the Arabs introduced it in the Middle Ages. They had a knowledge of

---

"Like Quebec—City of the Oldentime"

San Antonio was described in *Frank Leslie's Illustrated Newspaper*, New York, in 1859:

San Antonio is like Quebec, a city of the oldentime, jostled and crowded by modern enterprise. . . . Walking about the city and its environs, you may well fancy yourself in some strange land. The houses, many of them built of adobe, one-story high, and thatched, swarm with their mixed denizens, white, black and copper-colored. The narrow streets, the stout old walls which seem determined not to crumble away, the aqueducts along which run the waters of the San Pedro, the Spanish language, which is spoken by almost everybody, the dark, banditti-like figures that gaze at you from the low doorways—everything in the Mexican quarter of the city especially, bespeaks a condition widely different from what you are accustomed to behold in any American town.

---

astronomy. From the Maya, the Aztecs had also inherited the Mesoamerican calendar that meshed the 365-day solar year with the 260-day lunar year.

The Aztecs had an expressive oral language and a system of writing. They had poets and artists. They exercised concepts of law and justice, and adhered to special social rules for respectful living. They had programs for education and training, a thriving merchant class, and a variety of skilled craftsmen. They engaged in public sports, such as *tlachtli*, which used a small, solid rubber ball and was played in well-constructed courts in the temples. As in ancient Greece, they used many slaves and, as with the ancient Romans who reveled in blood sports, their empire was militaristic and predatory. Their religion demanded a great deal of blood from human sacrifices. Yet, theirs was one of the great civilizations of history—and their architecture and art plus their remarkable agricultural and culinary developments attest even today to their lasting contributions to the world.

Every Tejano or Tejana bears within himself or herself a continuity of great civilizations from more than one continent, combined with the special heritage of the early Texans who lived for ten years in an independent world republic.

San Antonians Embraced the Tejano Legacy

Visitors see evidence of the exotic Tejano heritage when they come to San Antonio. It is this distinctive cultural manifestation that has evoked enthusiastic exclamations over the years. It is blended with the Old West in a curiously symbiotic Anglo-Hispanic ambiance. It is found in the old buildings, the friendly people with their graceful language, the green plazas, the pleasant river, the piquant food, the startling art, the Stetson hats and Lucchese boots, the rollicking music and swirling dancers with their staccato-stamping feet. The Tejano heritage is found in the never-ending series of celebrations—big ones virtually every week of the year. Here it is easy to share a heartfelt appreciation of life's joys.

Non-Hispanic San Antonians have embraced the culture that the Tejanos represent. Their architects have paid tribute to the

Hispanic New World heritage, as well as to the Mesoamerican, in public buildings and theaters. Museums and galleries specialize in the ancient arts of the Americas. The city's leading force for cultural preservation, the San Antonio Conservation Society, has for more than forty years replicated seasonally a number of primarily Tejano social and even religious traditions.

Dress

Among these Tejano customs is the practice by San Antonio women of wearing Mexican ethnic dresses or fashionable gowns notably affected by the Mexican culture. Especially during Fiesta time in April, but frequently throughout the year and often when they are entertaining, San Antonio women wear the cool, comfortable, and colorfully embroidered Oaxacan dresses. The dress often is called the *San Antonino* for the city in Oaxaca from which it comes. Another popular fashion is the *puebla* dress (named for a state in Mexico), which is usually calf-length or shorter. There is a legend of a Chinese princess who introduced the *china poblana* costume after a pirate brought her to Puebla, Mexico, from a ship en route to Acapulco; it is the national folk costume worn by girls and women of all social classes. It is the dress of those who dance the *jarabe tapatio* and of the *charras* who accompany the *charros*.

Men often wear the comfortable Hispanic-style *guayabera* shirt.

Aztec Theater

Maya, Toltec, Aztec, or Spanish art and architecture are especially evident in two major downtown theaters. Before the Aztec Theater was constructed on the corner of St. Mary's and Commerce, a team of designers was sent to Mexico by the developers to study the ancient sculptures, art, and buildings found in the ruins of the Mesoamerican civilizations. They spent several months photographing, sketching, and modeling Aztec, Maya, Zapotec, Mixtec, and Toltec sculptures, symbols, and architectural elements on view at archaeological sites and at the National Museum in Mexico City. Many of these works were lavishly replicated or slightly abstracted in the extensive decorations of San Antonio's Aztec Theater.

The theater opened on June 4, 1926, and for years it has glo-
ried in the startling artistry of these amazing peoples. The theater
itself has long been considered a colorful work of art, and we see
it today because it was preserved from destruction by the San
Antonio Conservation Society, which purchased it in 1988. The
Society sold it in 1993 to Aztec Theater Ltd. for a planned conversion into a dinner theater featuring laser and electronic shows
and live performances, but the unusual building's future use is
still in the planning stage.

Majestic Theater

The Majestic Theater, across from the Camberley Gunter Hotel on Houston Street, was designed by nationally known theater
designer John Eberson. It opened on June 14, 1929. Some sixty
years later, on September 19, 1989, San Antonians celebrated the
theater's restoration to its original beauty. Eberson had turned to
San Antonio's Spanish roots for his designs, and also to the Moorish
art nurtured in the Spanish people during their centuries under
the Moslems. Its walls convey the ambiance of a Spanish village.
Typical of some theaters of the 1920s is the high, vaulted ceiling
with an azure sky, "stars" that seem to twinkle, and "clouds"
that float across the sky, propelled gently by unseen power.

In 1993, the Majestic was designated a National Historic Landmark by the U.S. Department of the Interior, joining seven other
such landmarks in San Antonio: the Alamo, Fort Sam Houston,
Espada Acequia, Hangar 9 at Brooks Air Force Base, the Spanish
Governor's Palace, and Missions Concepción and San José.

Alameda Theater

In January 1995, the City of San Antonio purchased the historic Alameda Theater and adjacent International Office Building
on West Houston Street as a step toward a plan to establish a hub
for Tejano arts and for promoting a better appreciation of the
Mexican-American heritage. The 2,000-seat theater was the
nation's largest and most lavish Spanish language movie palace
when it opened in 1949. "It may be the most significant building

in the nation relating to Mexican-American culture and history," according to Tomás Ybarra-Frausto, an associate director of arts and humanities for the Rockefeller Foundation in New York. Architecturally, the building is art deco. In 1982, the San Antonio Conservation Society led a successful campaign to prevent its demolition.

This "cultural zone," as visualized by Henry Muñoz III, chairman of Alameda, Inc., would include Milam Park, Market Square/El Mercado, Spanish Governor's Palace, Navarro House, Main Plaza, Santa Rosa Medical Center, San Fernando Cathedral, UTSA Downtown campus, Centro de Artes, International Center, and Military Plaza.

Other Buildings With Local Flavor

Another prominent San Antonio building of exotic architecture inherited from Hispanic history is just west of the Commerce Street bridge, near Navarro. The building, designed by George W. Brackenridge, housed the first chartered bank in Texas. It has many Moorish details, from the windows to the granite-columned entrance.

The Casino Club Building on the river at West Crockett Street, built in 1925-1926, features brick and cast-stone trim detailed in Mayan reliefs, but most of San Antonio's New World-rooted architecture is Spanish Colonial. An example is the Municipal Auditorium, built in 1926, which architects describe as Spanish Colonial Revival. The Southern Pacific Passenger Depot, built in 1903, is Mission Revival. Across the street is the Heimann Building, built in 1906, which also reflects the Mission Revival style. Closer to downtown is La Mansión del Río Hotel, with its Spanish Colonial style. Originally built in 1857 as St. Mary's School from designs by François P. Giraud, La Mansión del Río was remodeled and opened as a 200-room hotel in 1968, altered in 1979, and extensively remodeled in 1985.

Two of the most spectacular examples of San Antonio's Hispanic-influenced architectural style are Thomas Jefferson High School—which, because of its beauty, has been featured in *Life*

and *National Geographic* magazines, among others, plus Hollywood motion pictures—and the Randolph Air Force Base administration building nicknamed the "Taj Mahal." The high school,
with its four-story domed tower, reflects the Spanish Colonial
Revival style. It was built in 1932 and added to the National Register of Historic Places in 1983. The style of Randolph's Taj Mahal
dome was derived from a number of mid-nineteenth-century
Mexican churches, especially the Pociti Chapel in Mexico City.
The tracery on the shaft of the tower was inspired by Moorish
Spain. At both Fort Sam Houston and Randolph AFB, the Hispanic architectural influence is seen on every side.

A *Guide to San Antonio Architecture,* published in 1986 by the
San Antonio Chapter of the American Institute of Architects, presents photographs and descriptions of many of San Antonio's most
interesting buildings. It says this of the synagogue built in 1927
at 211 Belknap: "The design of Temple Beth-El deftly combines
square and spherical forms, unified by the consistent use of terra-
cotta ornament and clay tiles. In this most Spanish of Texas cities,
even a synagogue is designed with decidedly Iberian-Renaissance-
style ornament, most notably the marvelous cornice composed of
scallop shells."

Robert H. H. Hugman's grand plan for the River Walk centered on his vision of "old cities in Spain," graced by narrow
winding streets, lined with shops, barred to vehicular traffic. And
the Arneson River Theater, on both banks of the river near La
Villita, includes a Spanish Colonial backdrop with bell tower and
stage where a half-dozen major Tejano entertainments are presented throughout the year.

The tradition of Hispanic or Mesoamerican architecture continues in San Antonio. One of the most notable re-creations of the
latter style is the nine-story Pyramid Building at San Pedro Avenue and Interstate 410 not far from the airport. It was built in
1980 by the San Antonio Savings Association, then headed by
former mayor and head of a notably civic-minded family, Walter
W. McAllister. The huge concrete and limestone structure is highly
reminiscent of a Mayan temple pyramid.

The influence of the Tejano culture has spread across the country in a thousand forms—in architecture, food, music, dress, and countless other areas affecting the American way of life. At the World's Columbian Exposition in Chicago in 1893—dedicated to celebrating the 400th anniversary of the arrival in the New World of "the Admiral of the Indies"—one of the most admired structures was the Texas State Building. It was described in a Rand McNally book with this comment beside an engraving of the building:

> In the treatment of the design the architecture has not deflected from the traditions of the "Lone Star State," which from the first has been marked by a Spanish tinge, whose architectural feeling and beautiful botanical effects lay down a chain of thought far too beautiful to forsake for that of this modern day. Therefore the architect has designed the building, colonnades, grounds, fountains, foliage, etc., to present a Spanish vista, a bower of beautiful Texas foliage, comprising the banana, palm, magnolia, pomegranate, Spanish dagger, orange, and many rare tropical plants common to Texas.

The award-winning Texas State Building was financed entirely by the women of Texas. Its architect was James Riely Gordon, whose family had come to San Antonio from Winchester, Virginia, when he was ten.

Tejano Art

A visit to the San Antonio Museum of Art or to the Guadalupe Cultural Arts Center can provide a better understanding of the flavor of the Tejano culture. Examine some of the displays and obtain a copy of the illustrated booklet *Art Among Us—Arte Entre Nosotros*. It portrays the folk art that expresses the community-based social and cultural life of San Antonio's Tejanos.

The Guadalupe Cultural Arts Center nourishes Hispanic creativity and production of literature, dance, music, and drama.

Among its programs are the Tejano Conjunto Festival, the San Antonio Inter-American Bookfair and Literary Festival, and the San Antonio Cine-Festival, described as the country's oldest and largest Chicano-Latino film festival.

San Antonio has many art galleries displaying the work of professional Tejano artists. On May 7, 1994, the voters approved $1 million for a Latin American Art Center to be added to the San Antonio Museum of Art. Designed to house the museum's more than 8,000 pieces of Hispanic art, the two-story center will eventually cost more than $9 million and will open in 1998. Most of the cost will be borne by foundations and individual subscriptions. The center will display pre-Columbian art, Mexican folk art, Spanish colonial art, and contemporary Latin American art.

Folk art abounds in the front yards of many homes on the West Side and in the murals on the walls of public housing there. In some yards are religious grottoes, which complement the small but elaborate altars inside many homes. Rooted in centuries-old artistic expressions, the folk art reflects themes of religion, myth, magic, machismo, politics, and death.

Tejano and Conjunto Music

San Antonio has been the heartland of *conjunto* music for decades, and since 1980 has become recognized as the "Tejano Music Capital of the World." And here again, as with other Texas-Mexican art, the music reveals the unique soul of the Tejano. It is as Texan as the German Hill Country and as Hispanic as San Antonio's West Side. *Conjunto*, meaning "group" music, is the result of the blending of the accordion-based German polka and the richly traditional Mexican music of the *rancheras* and *mariachis*. Tejanos dance to *conjunto* music.

Tejanos have always loved to dance, and the story of their public dances in the 1800s—which they called *bailes* for the more formal balls, and *fandangos* for the lesser affairs—makes for interesting reading. Often the sole source of music for fandangos was a violin. The dances were held several times a week and were often frequented by visitors from "the States" or from foreign coun-

Nowhere else but in San Antonio could you enjoy this scene of festively costumed Tejana dancers—with the Alamo, Old Glory, and the Tower of the Americas in the background. (San Antonio Express-News photo)

tries when they were in San Antonio. Generally, the outsiders found them fascinating. But they didn't hear *conjunto* music then; it came much later.

Conjunto, according to Jim Beal, Jr., *Express-News* music columnist, was invented in South Texas. He says, "Born when European dances such as polkas, waltzes and schottishes met South Texas and northern Mexican musical forms, *conjunto* is ruled by the button accordion and aided by the bajo sexto—a large twelve-string bass guitar—drums, bass, and lately almost every other musical instrument." Tejano music is the sound of *conjunto* that has been modernized with a blend of country, blues, and rock.

There are many places in Bexar County for listening to Tejano and *conjunto* music. Lerma's Nightclub, near the corner of Zarzamora and Culebra, is a historic place for this kind of music. It has been host to leading *conjunto* players three nights a week since 1947—and to dancers on its eighteen-by-thirty-foot dance floor. But there are newer and larger clubs, too—for example, Tejano Rodeo, which has an 18,000-square-foot room with an elevated stage.

Conjunto and Tejano music is often heard at El Mercado in Market Square, as well as mariachi music by roving players. And *conjunto* or Tejano music is on the jukebox in San Antonio's ice houses.

The Ice House

To experience more intimately one aspect of the Tejano culture, visit an ice house. This is like a neighborhood tavern—something like a British or Irish pub. A *New York Times* reporter compared the San Antonio ice houses to the street cafes of Paris and coffee houses of Vienna.

The ideal ice house—now becoming rare—is a place where families can go and where (in a few) you'll sometimes see children playing—but it is mostly a place where men go to drink beer, talk, listen to music on the jukebox, shoot pool perhaps, or watch

---

The Mexican-German-French Social Connection

Mexicans, Germans, and other folk contributed to a distinctive cultural blend from which ice houses could borrow traditions of public socializing. Mexican traditions of outdoor eating, music and dance in the fiestas and fandangos had imprinted the city's night life. The French contributed the merchants and engineers who established the manufactured ice business. Germans contributed tradesmen and industrialists, in particular the brewers. Menger and Degen's "City Brewery," perhaps the city's first manufacturing enterprise, opened next to the Alamo in 1855. The brewery drew so much traffic from surrounding towns to its aged, bottom-fermented lager (the "light" beer of its day) that in 1859 Menger built an accommodating hotel next door.

—Tom Denyer, *The Social Science Journal*, Vol. 28, No. 4, 1991

---

television, especially sporting events. Sometimes live music is played by individuals or bands.

Beer drinking was introduced to San Antonio by the Germans, according to political scientist Tom Denyer. In 1876, there were five breweries in town. Because in the early days beer was not pasteurized, its wide use depended on ice. At first, ice was transported in sawdust from New England by ship and hauled in wagons from the Gulf of Mexico. Breweries and ice plants were developed simultaneously. San Antonio got its own ice-making plant in 1862. In 1886, the city had 169 establishments that sold beer and forty-four that sold both whiskey and beer—a state record. Germans especially enjoyed their concert gardens, where beer was sold; there were eleven in 1892.

As the city began to spread out in the early 1900s—especially after World War I—ice stations were established in various neighborhoods where ice could be stocked for sale to individuals and where residents could buy fresh produce such as watermelons, as well as milk, soft drinks, and beer cooled by ice. Many ice houses sold groceries and sundries. Some sold baked goods, candy, and snacks. Ice houses became places where people wanted to tarry and talk.

A San Antonio ice house today often has an adjoining open area with picnic tables and benches for sitting in the shade of live oak trees. This is essential most of the year because ice houses are not usually air-conditioned. Some have pool tables and dart boards. Some have an attached restaurant or kitchen.

These neighborhoods can be roughly described as predominantly Mexican-American, African-American, and Anglo working class. In contrast, most of the city's urban growth since 1970 has sprawled in an affluent arc from Loop 410 (seven miles from the center) north to the Hill Country foothills. With few exceptions, ice houses have not been part of this pattern.

From 1924 to 1929, there were some thirty ice houses in San Antonio. In 1975, there were about 281; in 1987, about 119. Their numbers continue to diminish—while nostalgia, for some folk, increases.

Market Square

Market Square, about two blocks east of where City Hall now sits, inherited the folklife of Military Plaza. The Plaza (originally *Plaza de Armas*) was the old town's place of barter, trade, and commerce. After the Civil War, life in Military Plaza reflected the mingling of American, German, French, Mexican, and other vendors and patrons. One heard at least four languages, but many non-Hispanic San Antonians spoke Spanish when conducting business, just as did nearby ranchers of every national origin.

A resident observer concluded that "the political border was on the Rio Grande, but Military Plaza was the commercial and social border between the countries." Military Plaza was vital to the life of the town. It was a chief source of fresh produce, staples, supplies, hardware, and feed. Before the railroad came in 1877, the fuel supply for cooking depended almost entirely on the Tejano wood peddlers who congregated with their laden burros in Military Plaza.

"And this place is in the United States!" exclaimed an *Express* reporter in 1879. He observed Military Plaza filled with "mustangs, mules, donkeys, ox teams, wagons, lumber, hides, cotton, whites, blacks, half-breeds and Mexicans." The scene at night was, he said, filled with "foreign tongues, strange costumes, and a band of fantastically dressed Mexicans discoursing in loud strains a kind of wild music." The whole spectacle, he said, "surpasses the best Theater; if variety is the spice of existence, here it is on San Antonio's Military Plaza."

More than 100 years ago—after the cornerstone of City Hall was laid on September 16, 1889—the vendors in Military Plaza where the new building was rising began moving a couple of blocks west to the site of today's Market Square, while others moved to Washington Square, just to its south.

From the 1890s on, El Mercado drew visitors who had come to San Antonio to savor the Hispanic culture at first hand—to eat chili con carne and tamales spiced with local chiles and listen to the exotic music. At that time, the west end of Market Square was called *Plaza de Zacate* or Haymarket Square. Of course, every city

There is Mexican-style singing, including mariachis, any day of the year at the largest Mexican market in the United States, El Mercado. Latin-American entertainers are a fixture there, where almost every week a celebration draws big crowds. It is an exotic and entertaining place of relaxation, with food and handicrafts for sale. A popular twenty-four-hour restaurant there, Mi Tierra, has become a Texas tradition. (San Antonio Express-News photo)

in the United States in the 1800s had a haymarket, because it was hay that fueled their transportation.

El Mercado

On almost any weekend of the year, El Mercado offers many elements of the traditional fiesta—Tejano-style music, roving mariachi groups, dancing, Tejano foods, street artists, entertainers and vendors, colorful banners, *piñatas*, and joyful folk.

This is the largest "Mexican market" in the United States, primarily because circumstances of history and an unstated bureaucratic tradition have ensured that virtually every tenant of the city-owned part of the market has a Hispanic name or is married to a Tejano or Tejana, or subleases from one. Shops are kept in the family. In contrast, other large markets throughout the country have a noticeable variety of ethnic representation.

The Chili Queens

The Tejano West Side—west of San Pedro Creek—has always fascinated curious visitors to San Antonio. One of the principal attractions was food—most notably, chili con carne, which was first discovered by out-of-town visitors in San Antonio in 1828. The vivacious young *señoritas* who sold the spicy dish—always chaperoned by an older family member—became known as "chili queens."

In 1987, Concepción Chavez, age seventy-five, recalled for the *San Antonio Light* her days as a chili vendor, working alongside her mother-in-law. One of the last of the chili queens, Mrs. Chavez described how they used to prepare the food at home and take it to the plaza in the afternoon. After the vegetable and fruit sellers had departed and the place had been hosed down, they would begin setting up their tables—boards on sawhorses. The women

"A Mexican Dinner," says the caption that accompanied this illustration in a San Antonio visitors' guide published in 1894. Military Plaza was the probable setting. There, the "chili queens" served chili con carne, tamales, and other Mexican food along with light banter loved by visitors "from the states." Chilli is a Nahuatl (Aztec) word for the peppery fruit of the capsicum, which Spaniards spelled chile and others spelled chili. San Antonio is recognized as the place where chili con carne first came to the attention of Anglo Americans—as far back as 1828.

would start their charcoal-fired grills to keep the food warm—chili con carne, tamales, tacos, and *albóndigas de sesos*, or brain patties smothered with cheese and chili. Setting lanterns on the tables, they served far into the night. Their usual customers were ranchers, produce vendors, and neighbors.

What was a chili queen's recipe for chili con carne? Concepción's mother-in-law would slice the meat and fry it in fat, making use of a little flour. Next, she added spices, including ground chile, then water, and left it to "simmer to perfection." No beans.

The chili queens were banished from the plazas in 1936, as they had been more than once in the past. Encouraged by Mayor Maury Maverick, they returned in 1939, encumbered by the requirement of sanitation laws to enclose their tables in flimsy screened structures. Their numbers diminished. Finally, in 1943 they ceased operations entirely after city health authorities objected to their dishwashing facilities.

Farmers Market Plaza

Other changes took place at Market Square over the years. In 1955, the great Terminal Produce Market was moved to South Zarzamora Street. Later, a Farmers Market was built in Market Square to sell fresh produce, but in 1993 it was converted to a diversified shopping area. Now somewhat modernized, it is called Farmers Market Plaza and maintains its Hispanic flavor, although open to more than seventy-five vendors of diverse backgrounds.

A bust of the revolutionary leader who became president of Mexico, Francisco I. Madero, stands across the street in Milam Square, where he is honored in a city-led ceremony each November. It was in San Antonio in 1910 that Madero signed a call for revolution that was printed and then distributed in Mexico as the *Plan de San Luís Potosí*. Madero urged that at 6 P.M. on November 20, 1910, Mexicans should take up arms to overthrow the government of Porfirio Díaz. His revolution succeeded. Díaz was ousted and Madero was elected president in 1911, but he stood at the pinnacle only briefly before he was assassinated on February 15, 1913.

Exotic Food and Drink

A hundred years ago, the foods of this area were astonishing to the uninitiated. Now, in the 1990s, this kind of fare has been embraced not only by San Antonians but by the whole country. Chili con carne, the state's official dish, has been canned since 1911 when the German William Gebhardt, the first to can chili powder, began canning chili as well as tamales in San Antonio.

There are more than 450 Mexican food restaurants in Bexar County. Not surprisingly, they have a larger share of the market than any other kind, including hamburger, pizza, and barbeque restaurants. Tortillas are made in more than sixty San Antonio establishments including restaurants. Mission Foods produces 500,000 corn and flour tortillas a day. The Mexican food restaurants of San Antonio use, altogether, more than one million tortillas daily. Many more are eaten in San Antonio homes. Per capita tortilla consumption in San Antonio is estimated at 620 per year, or about a dozen a week. One large grocery chain sells 10,000 bags of tortillas daily. Nationally, tortillas are the fastest growing part of the baking industry. Americans spent more than $2 billion on sixty billion tortillas in 1995, and we now eat more tortillas than bagels, muffins, croissants, and pita breads combined.

San Antonio is the home of Fritos. Fried tortillas were first marketed as Fritos here in 1932. *Fajitas* have been a favorite way of eating beef for decades in San Antonio—at least as far back as the early 1970s, when they were used in South Texas because the meat was very inexpensive. The skirt steak (*"faja"* means "belt" in Spanish) was often cast off as too tough in early days when meat was more plentiful. Traditionally, slices were tossed directly on the hot coals and then folded into tortillas to be eaten.

La Margarita Restaurant in Market Square introduced *fajitas* to the general public many years ago. Pace Picante Sauce, a national favorite, began in San Antonio in the late 1940s. The recipes for both Fritos and picante sauce came from Tejanos.

Spanish words such as *tortilla* and *picante* have become part of the English language, but *tamales* have not yet captured the national appetite as have other Mexican foods. In fact, they are virtually unknown in most parts of the country. President Gerald Ford delighted San Antonians during a visit in 1976 when he innocently bit into a *tamal* without first removing the corn shuck surrounding the delicacy within. The *tamal* is made with a dried shuck that has been soaked and filled with a mixture of cooked meat and *masa* dough. The dough is made from a special corn flour (*masa harina*) mixed with lard or a substitute, salt, and broth or water. A variety of meats can be boiled, shredded, seasoned, and enveloped with the *masa* dough, then wrapped in the shuck and steamed.

Traditionally, tamales—usually homemade—are favorite snacks during Christmas season in virtually every Tejano family in South Texas, but they no longer are sold on the streets of San Antonio by vendors on rickety carts behind the reins of their burros as they plaintively cry "*¡Tamales calientes!*"

Usually available only on weekends, *barbacoa*, the pit-cooked head of a cow or pig, is very popular—especially on the West Side—but it is now sold in many larger meat markets everywhere. *Menudo*, a hot and spicy soup of tripe, pig's foot, and hominy, can be found at any of the larger full-menued Mexican-style restaurants in San Antonio. *Cabrito,* which is kid or baby goat, is another specialty.

San Antonio lays claim to the margarita—not only because of the great quantity consumed in the city to accompany Mexican food, but because a local society hostess, Margarita Sames, says she invented the drink at her Acapulco hacienda in 1948. Sames points to documentation in *Town & Country Magazine* and the fact that Cointreau has made her an official spokeswoman for the liqueur.

Another favorite food for years, originally used widely by the Aztecs, is the *aguacate*, the source of *guacamole.* According to the California Avocado Commission, San Antonians consume more avocados per capita than residents of any other city in the world.

The West Side

During the first four decades of the 1900s, great numbers of immigrants came to San Antonio from Mexico, and the city

The West Side

In certain neighborhoods
the air is paved with names.
Domingo, Monico, Francisco,
shining rivulets of sound.
Names opening wet circles
inside the mouth,
sprinkling bright vowels
across the deserts of
Bill, Bob, John.
The names are worn
on silver linked chains,
Maria lives in Pablo Alley,
Esperanza rides the Santiago bus!
They click together like charms.
O save us from the boarded-up windows,
the pistol crack in a dark backyard
save us from the leaky roof,
the rattled textbook that never smiles.
Let the names be verses
in a city that sings!

Naomi Shihab Nye, from "West Side,"
in *Hugging the Juke Box*

became the center of Mexican influence in the country; the Mexican population increased from 13,722 in 1900 to 82,373 in 1930. By 1940, 50 percent of the Mexican population in San Antonio was foreign-born. The ethnic Mexican population in 1940 was 103,000 (46.3 percent of total), almost equal to the Anglo population of 131,221 (46.7 percent of total). The African-American population was 18,235 (7.0 percent of total). San Antonio's total population was 254,053.

The majority of the newcomers settled on the West side of town—"across the San Pedro." At the turn of the century, some San Antonians called the west side of San Pedro Creek "Chihuahua" or "Laredito." Freighters who drove the ox carts or mule wagons that traveled to Laredo or Chihuahua in Mexico lived or often laid over here. (It is more likely, though, that "Chihuahua," an Aztec word for dry, sandy, or dusty, was a reference to the condition of the land west of Alazán Creek rather than to the far-away town.) Laredito also had a cultural connection to the Laredo Road, which ran south of the neighborhood. A visitor in mid-nineteenth century described the houses as mostly *jacales* with hard clay floors.

Drive west of Market Square on Commerce Street for a dozen blocks, returning on Buena Vista—or head south from Buena Vista to Guadalupe Street. Read the signs written in Spanish and English and get the feel of a Texan Mexico: Contreras Ice House; Casos de Amnistias (where they handle immigrant amnesty cases); La Iglesia (church) Católica del Sacrado Corazón de Jesús; El Brasero Mexican Restaurant, "The Best Food Across the Alazán Creek"; Marmolejo (marble pieces); First Sacraments—Baptism and First Communion Apparel; El Charro TV Rental, Appliances and Furniture.

In these mostly one-story buildings are restaurants, lounges, nightclubs, auto parts stores, butcher supplies, beauty salons, a barber shop/liquor store, an old (1917) pecan shelling factory, insurance office ("auto liability, no down payment"), funeral homes, civic center, library, grocery, chiropractor, tailor shop, auto body shops, loan offices—many of the necessities of life and death.

A Long-Forgotten Tourist Attraction

One priceless curiosity from the past that most San Antonians are not even aware of was featured prominently in guidebooks for visitors in the early 1900s. It was the shrine of *El Señor de los Milagros* (Our Lord of Miracles), known also as "the Chapel of Miracles," a place held dear by many Tejanos but not sanctioned by the Catholic Church.

A colorful San Antonio guide published in the early 1900s by the Chamber of Commerce featured the chapel as within walking distance of "San Antonio's Bowery—a place of considerable interest and amusement lying on West Commerce Street a block from Military Plaza."

The 1909 visitors' guide said that at "No. 115 Ruíz street, you will find the *Capilla de los Milagros*, or the Wonder Chapel, a shrine of miracles where hundreds of people, they tell you, have been cured of 'incurable' diseases. In proof of which you will see the crutches they left behind and their grateful offerings to the shrine. It is a quaint and curious place in a class with the Shrine of the Lourdes in France or that of St. Anne de Beau Pre near Quebec." This booster's puffery is, of course, a great exaggeration.

Another visitors' guide, published in 1924, told how to drive to the chapel in an automobile from the Post Office on Alamo Plaza—or how to find a trolley that could take you to the site. Drivers were expected to reset their automobile mileage meters to zero before they began their trip. Instructions started the odometer with zero at the Post Office:

> *Motor*: 0.0, Post Office, west on Houston Street.
> 1.1, Turn right at I. & G. N. Depot—continue.
> 1.6, With car line 7 blocks to Ruiz St.

> *Trolley*: Post Office, walk one block west on Houston St.
> Take West End car; get off [at] Ruiz and Medina.
> No. of house is 109.

Today, the Chapel of Miracles may seem little more than a tiny, cream-colored, stuccoed, steepled church beside a small house, sitting in an island of greenery surrounded by a maze of concrete streets and flanked by a multilevel super highway. The little chapel, which was once on the west bank of San Pedro Creek, is located at the probable site of San Antonio's first mission, San Antonio de Valero, before its first move. This could be the site where San Antonio was founded on May 1, 1718. The historic creek at this point flows forever imprisoned beneath the concrete highways. That the chapel has been saved from obliteration by "progress" and urban renewal is, some might say, a "miracle."

Because extensive urban renewal has left only a massive city-owned warehouse and sprawling public housing virtually surrounding the chapel, the streets have changed and the shrine can be found now in the shadow of Interstates 10 and 35, near the corner of North Frio and North Salado. The chapel has been owned from its beginning in the early 1870s by the Ximénes-Rodríguez family. The building provides a sanctuary for an ancient Spanish crucifix, said to have been entrusted to the family when services at the church of San Fernando were suspended for a time after a devastating flood. This is *El Señor de los Milagros*. Until the crucifix was placed in the chapel, it had been in the home of the family, where it attracted visitors. A somewhat less than life-sized image, the body of the Christ figure, carved in wood, bearded and dark-skinned and colorfully painted, hangs on a cross against the east wall of the tiny chapel. Pinned to the red cloth around the figure's loins are dozens of silvery tin medals, about an inch in height—*milagros*, shaped like arms, legs, heads, bodies, hearts, eyes, or other images. These have been placed there on behalf of prayerful believers in supplication or in thanksgiving for favors sought or granted, and the medals represent the focus of their problems.

Devout supplicants still find relief from their troubles at the foot of the cross or close to a variety of statues in this folk chapel; there are traditional images of the Sacred Heart, the Blessed Virgin, or Our Lady of Guadalupe, St. John the Baptist, St. Anthony of Padua, and a score of other saints. Votive candles flicker beyond the seats and kneelers in the tiny semi-dark room. Supplicants quietly enter the chapel, buy a candle, have it lighted, go to one of the kneelers to pray for a while, then perhaps pin a *milagro* to a cushion provided near the more popular framed reproductions on the wall—or lay the *milagro* beside a statue.

Certainly this is a refuge dear to many San Antonians—a place that has profoundly touched the hearts of countless numbers for more than a century, and today continues the tradition of its past. Near the chapel entrance, a metal plaque states: "Entered in the National Register of Historic Places 1980."

Unmistakably, San Antonio is, at first glance, a Tejano city, with its Spanish and Mesoamerican architecture and art, the lilting language and russet skins of the Aztec, the Mayan, or the Payayan on all sides. Yet many of the city's Spanish and Indian roots are all but invisible—even though, over the centuries, their influence on the non-Tejano culture of the city can be easily detected.

6

The German Catalyst for Progress

In the mid-1800s, large numbers of German immigrants carried a great European culture to San Antonio, complementing the city's already exotic mix of Texians, Tejanos, and a sprinkling of Old World ethnic groups—and infusing a markedly new character into the community.

Most visitors to San Antonio are surprised to learn that in 1876 there were more German-speaking people in that town of 17,214 than any other nationality—including Hispanics or Anglo Americans. They are surprised too when they are told of the other "German" towns, such as New Braunfels, Comfort, and Fredericksburg, or the Alsatian town of Castroville that grew in the vicinity of San Antonio.

When and why did many thousands of Germans come from several provinces in the kingdom of Prussia to live in Texas? Why were they willing to uproot themselves, sail on eight- to twelve-week ocean voyages, and trust their futures to untried life in a frontier country? And why did so many of them settle in and around San Antonio?

The first Germans to arrive in Texas settled for the most part in the area around the Brazos and Colorado rivers, founding small communities in what became Austin, Fayette, and Colorado counties. That was in the 1830s and early 1840s in the vicinity of the town of Industry, founded by Friedrich Ernst from Germany. Ernst had acquired a grant of land in 1831 from the Mexican government and soon began farming. His enthusiastic letters back to Germany were published in newspapers there and in a book describing travels in Texas. He sparked the dreams of the folk back home with visions of a land of milk and honey and political freedom. During the decades that followed, many Germans came to Central Texas, some to settle near Friedrich Ernst, some to farm in the verdant Hill Country. They were escaping a life with little promise of an improved economy or political freedom. By 1890, the census showed 48,843 German-born Texans.

The largest number of immigrants had been persuaded by an association of promoters—wealthy, titled Germans who were interested in overseas colonization for both philanthropic and money-making reasons. The nobles called their organization the *Mainzer Adelsverein* or the *Verein zum Schutze Deutscher Einwanderer in Texas*. It later was known simply as the *Verein* or the German Emigration Company.

The Adelsverein bought about three million acres between the Llano and Colorado rivers, which comprised the Fisher-Miller Land Grant. As events turned out, however, title to the land was questionable, and the area was isolated, inhabited by hostile Comanches, and not highly fertile. Only a handful of German settlers ever moved there.

A few came to the Llano River in 1847, including a group of intellectuals not associated with the Adelsverein. They tried living in a utopian communal settlement but it proved impractical and they disbanded. Dr. Ferdinand Herff, later a leading Texas surgeon, lived there for a time before moving to New Braunfels and then to San Antonio.

The German immigrants had sailed in ships to Galveston and then to Indianola, the Adelsverein port on Matagorda Bay in the Gulf of Mexico (later destroyed by hurricanes). Some had come overland from Galveston. The task of colonizing in Texas was supervised first by Prince Carl von Solms-Braunfels and later by the more businesslike Baron Ottfried von Meusebach, a resourceful man who in 1847 made a historic treaty with the Comanches that helped ensure preferential treatment for German settlers.

From 1844 to 1846, the Adelsverein brought 7,380 Germans to America, but in 1847 the organization became bankrupt, stranding thousands along the road from Indianola to the Llano River, many in deplorable conditions. However, immigration continued from Germany in large numbers for some years, with the newcomers choosing to settle in the same general areas as their predecessors—from the coast at Indianola to San Antonio, New Braunfels, and the Hill Country.

Castroville, twenty-five miles west of San Antonio in Medina County, is often included in accounts of German immigration because most of its people—many from the Alsace region on the French border with Germany—spoke German or Alsatian. From 1842 to 1865, Henri Castro, a French empresario, brought 2,134 settlers, not only from French Alsace but from Germany, Switzerland, Belgium, and Holland. His primary communities were Castroville, D'Hanis, Quihi, and Vandenberg.

The immigrants who settled in Texas either because of Henri Castro or the Adelsverein or Friedrich Ernst were special in the sense that they had the money, energy, and pioneer spirit to invest in a long and dangerous enterprise. These attributes made them a select group.

Settlers with the Adelsverein were able to pay not only for their food but for transportation by sailboat and wagon to their final destination, where they had been promised they would get

A traveler wrote in 1878: *After one has been whirled through the dust, cinders and smoke, at the rate of twenty-five miles an hour for a thousand miles or more, it is a relief to change the rail-car for that dear old relic of the past—the stage coach—with its four prancing horses, its ever-merry driver with tin horn ever ready to signal a station or a start.*

From the stage coach one can see the country, enjoy the scenery along the route, and be sociable without splitting one's throat in the endeavor to be heard above the din and rattle, as is the case in railroad traveling.

While the stage coach, like many other institutions that were held in high esteem in the earlier history of this country, has been forced to fall back before the onward march of the inventive genius of the age, still there is a luxury in that medium of traveling that neither time nor improvements can efface. The above thoughts were suggested while making a trip from San Antonio, Texas, to Fredericksburgh [sic] on the popular and well managed Four Horse Mail Coach Line of K. C. Bain and Companies.

—From Southern and Western Guide, *1878*

a log cabin, 320 acres per family, fencing and seeds, and access to church, school, hospital, grain mills, and saw mills.

Settling in San Antonio

Many of the settlers who had come with Castro and with the Adelsverein moved later to San Antonio, where they saw more opportunities. According to District Court records, by far the largest number of foreign immigrants to settle in San Antonio from 1846 to 1860 were from the European states that later were unified to become Germany. As late as 1880, the population of San Antonio was one-third German.

History remembers only a few of the many outstanding San Antonio Germans who were well known in their day as doctors, teachers, musical and theatrical directors, artists, writers, architects and builders, prosperous businessmen, bankers, scientists, and social, civic, and religious leaders. History forgets, as individuals, the great majority of men and women whose lives and talents were spent in a wide variety of pursuits. To read the list of these specialties is to come just a little closer to those "unknown" people who spent their years giving to San Antonio something of themselves and their exemplary approach to living—and, incidentally, adding to the peculiar mixture of cultures that so many visitors found so enchanting in the 1800s and early 1900s.

By the late 1800s, these Germans were involved in work described as follows in the rolls of Saint Joseph's Catholic Church: "saddle and harness manufacturing, hardware retailing, lumber, drugs, groceries, clothing, shoes, leather and findings, commission merchants, dry goods, blacksmithing, wines and liquors, brewing, book selling, hide and wool merchandising, carpentering, farm and ranch implements, jewelry repairing, tea and coffee, tailoring, windmills, tinsmith, cabinet maker, pumps and pipes, camp yards, physician and surgeon, cigar making, cooperage, bookkeeping, flour mill operator, building contractors, insurance, stone mason, photography, livery stables, engineering, dentistry, music teacher, buggy, carriage and wagon makers, banking and Western Union operator."

Clubs for All Tastes

Important in their day were the associations—the cultural and social clubs—and the celebrations and enjoyment of life that the Germans brought to San Antonio. The Casino Association began as a group of intellectuals meeting in the home of Carl Hummel. In January 1858, it moved into its new club and opera house at 210 Market Street. Built by John H. Kampmann, it stood between what is today's Hertzberg Circus Collection in the old Main Library and the site of today's Hilton Paseo del Rio Hotel. The club and opera house building has now been replaced by the San Antonio Water System's Market Street Pump Station above the river near South Alamo Street.

In 1925, the San Antonio Club and the Casino Club were consolidated as the San Antonio Casino Club and moved to their new six-story building. Its art deco facade with Mayan reliefs is still evident on West Crockett Street, around the corner from the Hyatt Regency, beside the river.

Hard Work—"The German's Favorite Pastime"

When former San Antonian Alex E. Sweet wrote in 1905 a wryly humorous book with his friend J. Armoy Knox, titled *On A Mexican Mustang Through Texas*, he gave high praise to the German emigrants. The authors observed: "They are a most industrious and desirable class of citizens. They have brought over all their German pastimes and amusements, and working about fourteen hours a day is one of them. While the Texas-American has gradually succeeded in overcoming his aversion to lager-beer, his prejudice against working very hard in the field between meals still exists. The German from the old country could not stop working, even if he were to make every effort to do so. His ancestors for a thousand years have worked harder than people in this country have any idea of, and he has inherited the industrious disposition of his forefathers in his bones."

Beginning in the 1850s, Casino Club members formed their own theatrical group and made the building's stage and 400-person seating capacity available to traveling companies of actors. Members were among the first to sponsor dramas and concerts in San Antonio, and they also presented a variety of dances for the German community. Families were invited every month to attend a concert or a play, which was followed by a "hop." A children's ball (*Kinderball*) was held on Christmas Day and a masked ball (*Maskenball*) on Shrove Tuesday (before the Lenten period). On New Year's Eve, fathers formally introduced their daughters to society.

Each day, Casino Club members gathered to talk, drink wine or beer, play skat, or bowl in the alleys in the basement. The stone building had a barroom, a ballroom, rooms for reading, billiards, and poker, and a ladies lounge. Except for officers of the U.S. Army and of local military-social associations such as the Alamo Rifles and the Alamo Guards, membership was restricted to persons who spoke German.

The San Antonio *Herald* reported on October 30, 1860:

The Ball of the Alamo Rifles, which transpired at the Casino Hall on Saturday night, proved to be a very pleasant *recherché* affair. The hall was tastefully decorated with the paraphernalia of military life. . . .

Among the military notables present we noticed Col. [Robert E.] Lee, Capt. King, Capt. Blair, Capt. Potter, Lt. Williams, and Lt. Jones of the U.S.A., in addition to the members of the "Rifle" corps, who turned out in full uniform under their commander, Capt. Wm. Prescott.

Singing, dancing, and athletics were important traditional ways for the hardworking Germans to relax. They met in their favorite public houses, restaurants, and social clubs. La Villita had become a largely German neighborhood that San Antonians began to call "Little Rhein." The newcomers had converted a number of the flat-topped Tejano homes to meet their tastes, including the addition of peaked roofs. A popular place there was Vauxhall Garden, with its summerhouse surrounded by greenery.

Beer gardens flourished in the neighborhood, with signs such as: "Schlagen & Vertragen's Bier Halle," "Beowulf Dreizehn," "Kap der Guten Hoffnung," and "Der Blaue Donner, Schooner, Pretzel and Wiener Wurst, five cents." One could go for drink and music in the afternoon, dancing in the evening, and occasionally watch entertainers.

East on Alameda, now East Commerce, was a garden-surrounded hall near the old powder house. In 1854, Alameda Hall had, according to the San Antonio *Ledger*, a "well-conducted bar," and a band of musicians who played on Sundays. Also on Sundays, one might go to San Pedro Park where William Mueller had a restaurant offering food, beer, and band music

San Antonio's first street railway, using a mule-drawn car, began going regularly to San Pedro Park from Alamo Plaza in June 1878. Before that, visiting the park meant riding by omnibus,

---

San Pedro Springs—A Merry Place for German Families

The San Pedro is commonly known as a creek, but has many a beautiful nook along its banks, and in one of them the Germans have established their beer garden, at what is called "San Pedro Springs." There, in the long Sunday afternoons, hundreds of families are gathered, drinking beer, listening to music and singing, playing with the fawns, or gazing into the bear garden and the den of the Mexican panther.

There too, the *Turnverein* takes its exercise, and in a long hall dozens of German children waltz, under the direction of a gray-haired old professor, while two spectacled masters of the violin make music. This is the Sunday of great numbers of citizens of San Antonio, Germans and Americans, and is as merry, as free of vulgarity or quarreling, as any beer garden in the Dresden Fair.

—Edward King, *Scribner's Monthly Magazine*, 1874

German-American gymnasts of the San Antonio Turnverein perform at Bowen's Island, which today is beneath the tall, green-topped Tower Life Building at 310 South St. Mary's Street. (Daughters of Republic of Texas Library photo)

wagon, carriage, or horse. Many walked from downtown—an exercise people took in stride in those days and evidently enjoyed.

The Germans contributed to the city's experience in athletics and sports with a Turnverein gymnastic society they started in 1853 and opened to all interested San Antonians. On May 2, 1870, after an all-day celebration at San Pedro Springs, the Turnverein staged a wrestling match in which the contestants stood on boats floating on the river. Probably the athletic prowess, comradeship, and public spiritedness of the young men of the Turnverein were the reasons they formed the nucleus of the first volunteer firemen in San Antonio.

Turner-Halle (Turner Hall) just north of the Menger Hotel was the site of the Germans' first athletic club. A larger one was built when the hotel was expanded in 1875. Standing on the southeast corner of Houston and St. Mary's, it became the principal theater of the city, and internationally famous performers such as Lillie Langtry entertained there. Turner Hall activities finally were moved to a strikingly interesting building at 411 Bonham, whose architect was James Wahrenberger. It is now a popular nightclub.

Politics for Music Lovers

Music was even more characteristic of the German enjoyment of life than sports. It seems that almost every time groups—notably the men—assembled, they were moved to sing. Germans who remember the history of Texas *Sängerfests* like to recall the story of the day in 1845 when the cable that New Braunfels settlers had strung across the swollen Guadalupe to ferry provisions on a wagon bed broke and a barrel of wine cracked open on the riverbank. According to legend, using hats and whatever utensils they could find, "the men drank the wine until their jubilation rose above the rush of the waters, singing the song put to verse by Prince Solms himself and set to music by Capt. Alexis Bauer, 'Durch des Weltmeers Wogen.' "

A Texas Musical Center in the 1880s

San Antonio has developed her taste for music, her reputation as a musical center having long been established. This taste is exhibited on every occasion when musical entertainments are presented to our people, be they amateur or professional performances. Nothing draws like music in the Old Alamo City. Only let a concert be announced, and the Grand Opera House, or Turner Hall, or the Casino, as the case may be, is filled to overflowing, and the enthusiastic applause which greets every meritorious performance attests to the strong hold, the abiding place which musical entertainments have in the affections of the people.

—*The San Antonio Light*, December 28, 1888

Besides impromptu vocalizing, the Germans loved singing in clubs, recitals, and competitions. The first Texas Sängerfest was held in New Braunfels in October 1853. The second took place in San Antonio on May 14, 15, and 16, 1854, attended by singing societies from Austin, La Grange, New Braunfels, and San Antonio. New Braunfels alone was represented by eighty singers. Unexpectedly, the festival had political repercussions that affected both Germans and other Texans for decades—but especially during the period of the Civil War, which began seven years later. On the last day of the state Sängerfest, a special German convention was held in Vauxhall Garden on Alamo Street. The convention program had been suggested by some of the well-educated freethinkers of Sisterdale, a Hill Country settlement thirty-five miles northwest of San Antonio that was called "the Latin Colony"—one of several such clusters of literary people and other intellectuals in the area.

At the convention, a position paper was presented asking for abolishing capital punishment and prohibiting speculation in land. Moreover, the policy presentation declared that slavery should be abolished in conformity with the Constitution of the United States, which stated that "all men are free." The declaration included this pronouncement:

> Slavery is an evil, the removal of which is absolutely necessary according to the principles of democracy. Since slavery concerns only the states, we demand that the federal government refrain from all interference in matters pertaining to slavery. However, if a state determines on removal of this evil, it may call on the federal government for aid in the execution of its decision.

The proclamation was seized upon by the Know-Nothing political party in San Antonio, a national semi-secret organization (also called the American Party) that was both anti-foreigner and anti-Catholic. Because of the generally unfavorable reaction to the disturbing declaration—especially among the many who sympathized with slaveholders—the Know-Nothing party unexpectedly won the municipal elections in San Antonio in 1854.

The local German newspaper, *San Antonio Deutsche Zeitung*, which had been founded by Adolf Douai in 1853 and expanded in 1856 by Gustav Schleicher, helped make the German point of view well known and politically influential in San Antonio, because the German third of the population made a practice of voting.

San Antonio's Germans have always been associated with good music. A second music hall, built in 1895, was called Beethoven Hall because it was designed to house the Beethoven Männerchor, a men's choir organized in 1867 by Wilhelm C. A. Thielepape as the Beethoven *Gesangverein*. It played an influential role in development of the city's musical life. Opera was presented there as well as the concerts of the first two temporary symphony orchestras in 1904 and 1916.

In 1921, the San Antonio Symphony Orchestra was the only such orchestra south of St. Louis, but it fell into decline until the arrival in 1939 of a young German conductor and refugee from European anti-Semitism, Max Reiter, under whose talented leadership the Symphony Society of San Antonio was founded. Today, the orchestra offers a well-rounded program of classical music, lightened by pop concerts, and features performances by notable guests.

Beethoven Hall stands today on South Alamo Street, across from La Villita; it was destroyed by fire in 1913, rebuilt the next year, and then somewhat effaced during the widening of South Alamo Street in preparation for HemisFair '68. It is scheduled to be renovated and its face restored to resemble architect James Wahrenberger's original design. The restoration will be part of the development of a German-Texan cultural center in the new German Heritage Park dedicated on May 2, 1992, by the President of Germany, Dr. Richard von Weizsäcker. When completed, say the planners, the park is expected to be "a showcase of German history, arts, culture and commerce which can be studied and enjoyed in a family environment, filled with the sights, smells, sounds and tastes of early German Texas."

The new park was brought from idea to dedication by the San Antonio Liederkranz, a male choral group formed on July 11, 1892, at St. Joseph's Church. More than 100 years ago, John C. Dielmann became the first president of the Liederkranz. In May 1992, his great-grandson, William V. Dielmann II, president of the San Antonio Liederkranz, led the dedication of the German Heritage Park. Dielmann's father and grandfather, as well as his great-grand-father, have headed the organization.

Starting a School and a Fraternal Society

Germans were interested, of course, in more than concerts, singing, gymnastics, shooting contests, theaters, dancing, and celebrating to relieve their hard work and long hours. They believed not only in politics to protect and further their interests but also in education to maintain and improve the quality of their lives.

To educate their children, they established the German-English School in 1858. It was moved in 1859 to South Alamo Street, across from Beethoven Hall. The German-born, self-made builder and architect John H. Kampmann, one of the trustees, was given the contract to construct three buildings.

The curriculum of the privately financed school was patterned after the *gymnasium* system used in Germany. All subjects were taught in both English and German. Religion was not a subject, although the Bible was used for exercises in spelling and copying. The school term lasted eleven months, six days a week, from eight o'clock to twelve and from two to four. The advanced class studied English and German grammar, history, and mathematics. The juniors studied reading and writing in both English and German, arithmetic, geography, natural history, and physics, with electives to be chosen from singing, drawing, physical education, and swimming.

In 1897, the school was sold for debt and the City of San Antonio bought it in 1903 and refashioned it as the George H. Brackenridge grammar school. In 1926, the University Junior College moved in, remaining for a quarter of a century. Its name was changed to San Antonio College in 1948, and in the early 1950s the institution took shape with buildings going up on the thirty-seven-acre San Pedro Avenue campus. It is now the largest single-campus community college in Texas.

On October 7, 1992, the restored buildings of the German-English School served as a backdrop in the outdoor ceremony for the initialing of the historic North American Free Trade Agreement by the chief executives of Mexico, Canada, and the United States. A plaque commemorates the event. The old school is currently used as the Plaza San Antonio Conference Center.

The first fraternal benefit society in San Antonio, the Grand Lodge of the Sons of Hermann, still is going strong after more than a century. With their penchant for organizing to achieve their objectives, San Antonio Germans formed the Grand Lodge on July 6, 1861, coordinating eight member lodges across the state. Texas was part of the Order of the Sons of Hermann headquartered in New York. The national society was named for a German folk hero who lived in the days of conflict with the early Romans. It provides insurance as well as *volksfests*, concerts, dances, parades, and other recreation and fellowship activities.

Now an autonomous Texas organization, the Sons of Hermann has 160 lodges in the state. Some 50 percent of its 80,000 members are German Americans. On October 7, 1990, about 7,000 people celebrated the organization's centennial with food and dancing at Joe and Harry Freeman Coliseum.

German La Villita and King William

Germans played a leading role in designing and constructing many of San Antonio's distinctive buildings. Architect James Wahrenberger—who designed Turner Hall, the old Alamo National Bank, and Our Lady of the Lake and St. Mary's universities—was born in Austin to parents of German descent and studied architecture in Germany. San Antonio architect Albert F. Beckman also was trained in Germany. The two had a hand in designing and constructing what we see now as the San Antonio Museum of Art, then a large brewery. Many downtown buildings reflect the interests of the German architectural school.

For a time, the Germans who came to San Antonio in the mid-1800s were isolated both of their own volition and by the attitude of others. This was a result of their ignorance, at first, of the prevailing English and Spanish languages and of their own self-sufficiency and natural clannishness; but their isolation was short-lived, and they soon fitted themselves actively into the community. They built homes on both sides of South Alamo Street in the vicinity of La Villita and east and south of the Alamo along Alameda (now East Commerce), and in the area later demolished to make room for HemisFair.

Today, La Villita reflects both its Hispanic and German history. Some of its buildings can be traced to the houses of the Alamo soldiers from south of the Rio Grande and their families in the early 1800s. In one, Mexican Gen. Martín Perfecto de Cós signed surrender documents in December 1835 after his failure to defend San Antonio, including the Alamo, from the attacking Texians. The two-story stone building at 231 South Alamo, built in 1855 and used today by the Little Rhein Steak House, displays the work of German builders. (It is owned by the San Antonio Conservation Society and leased out.)

The Little Church of La Villita, restored and renamed in 1957, was originally the German Methodist Church, built in 1879 with stones carted from what is now the Sunken Gardens in Brackenridge Park. For a time after 1895 it was used by the Episcopal Diocese of West Texas as a school for African-American girls. In 1956, Rev. Paul Soupiset began using it as a personal mission where he raised funds to feed the poor. Since 1945, it has been owned by the city, and now the "Little Town" with its quaint buildings is registered as a National Historic District and attracts visitors who enjoy its artists, craftsmen, shops, and restaurants.

Farther south of La Villita, a number of more affluent Germans had their homes built in the vicinity of King William Street. The street had been named for King Wilhelm I of Prussia by the first German resident on the street, Ernst Altgelt, a surveyor, lawyer, and real estate investor who previously had founded the town of Comfort in the Hill Country. In 1867, he built his first San

Antonio house at 236 King William and bought nearby lots for a garden and space for the family's horses and cows.

Down the street at the river, Carl Hilmar Guenther established a flour mill in 1860, and there he also built a stone house where he raised his family. The King William area reflected San Antonio's new prosperity in 1867, two years after the Civil War ended, and Carl Guenther could write to his mother in Germany:

> San Antonio has changed since the war. Every ball demands new gowns for the ladies. Just imagine it! They study the fashion magazines and then try out every new style. Even I had to buy a white satin vest and it is most uncomfortable in this heat.
>
> Before the war we all drank our San Antonio Menger beer. Now that is not good enough; it has to be Bremer beer, English port and ale, Chicago beer and every kind of imported wine. That the ladies need not feel slighted, there is an elegant ice cream parlor where they can get all kinds of ices.
>
> There they meet their friends for a social hour, discuss the new fashions and step over to the stores and millinery shops, which are all well stocked, and buy what they wish.

Many Texans Were Loyal to the Union

Texas entered the Civil War after delegates to a state Secession Convention voted on February 1, 1861, to secede from the United States, and Texas voters approved the decision on the twenty-third. However, at least 40 percent of Bexar County citizens were against secession. Most Germans opposed the idea of separation. Texas Confederates killed thirty-five Unionists from the Hill Country and wounded several others when they intercepted them near the Nueces River as they tried to flee Texas. A monument in Comfort, Texas, bearing the inscription "Treue der Union" (Loyal to the Union), memorializes them.

Guenther himself had two ice machines in his ice plant to cool beer for "thirsty males" and to supply the elegant ice cream parlor for the "special enjoyment of the ladies." His plant grew into the Southern Ice Company and eventually became the Southern-Henke Ice Company, an important industrial institution taken over years later by Southland Corporation. The Guenther family home is now the Guenther House Restaurant, which includes a museum and the San Antonio River Mill Store. The home has been restored to its turn-of-the-century decor, while an art nouveau style of the 1920s was used in decorating. Next door is the much enlarged and still-prospering Pioneer Flour Mills that Guenther founded.

San Antonians used to call the area along the river on the west side of South Alamo "Sauerkraut Bend," because of the Germans' fondness for the dish. Interestingly, except for several homes there by architects Albert Beckman and James Wahrenberger, most were designed by San Antonio architects of other schools, such as those by the prolific Alfred Giles from England and by James Riely Gordon from Virginia.

The King William area, with its late nineteenth-century homes loosely called "Victorian," became a prestigious residential section of San Antonio, inhabited not only by Germans but by other prosperous San Antonians as well. In 1972, the approximately twenty-two-block area, with seventy-nine historic structures, was entered in the National Register of Historic Places. The King William Historic District, and the La Villita Historic District with its twenty-seven buildings restored in 1939 and registered in 1972, became the first two such districts in Texas.

The mansion at 509 King William Street—designed by Alfred Giles and known as the Steves Homestead—is owned by the San Antonio Conservation Society, and the house, with its priceless antiques and furnishings and the surrounding grounds, is open every day to conducted tours.

In 1991, a new name was applied to an old San Antonio neighborhood. Now "Southtown" is a favorite place for artists to make their homes. It encompasses the King William District and much of South Main Street as well as surrounding streets south of Durango Boulevard. Approximately, it is bounded on the east by Presa Street and on the west by the river. The Southtown Association, guided by a director, is concerned with historic preservation and neighborhood revitalization. It sees the area as a primary "historic and cultural corridor" for the city.

In the 1800s, prosperity came to many of San Antonio's Germans because they had brought with them marketable knowledge, crafts, and skills. The 1860 census showed them leading all the other "foreign" San Antonians in numbers of merchants, clerks, and professionals. They nearly matched the Tejanos in numbers of craftsmen.

The *Southern and Western Texas Guide for 1878,* published by the Galveston, Harrisburg & San Antonio Railway, said that San Antonio's "German, Polish and Alsatian elements are the largest property holders, the American next in magnitude." These figures were based on the total valuation of taxable property of all kinds, including real estate, personal property, merchandise stocks, and banking capital.

Architect in the Guinness Book

Hundreds, probably thousands, of Germans—from the first settlers to their descendants—have made lasting, though not obvious, marks on San Antonio's unique ambiance. A second-generation German, architect Leo M. J. Dielmann, whose father had studied architecture in Germany, has left his mark most indelibly in international record books.

He designed the Gift Chapel, the central chapel at Fort Sam Houston, which was donated to the post by the people of San Antonio; the Spanish Colonial church-style chapel near the Taj Mahal tower at Randolph Air Force Base; the lofty-spired Conventual Chapel at Our Lady of the Lake University; the Second Baptist Church in San Antonio; and the Protestant and Catholic churches in a number of nearby communities including the impressive Gothic structure for St. Mary's Church in Fredericksburg, built of native stone in 1908.

A Record-Breaking Anaqua Tree

On the grounds of Plaza San Antonio Hotel at 555 South Alamo Street is one of only three national championship trees in Texas. (The other two are a huisache in Big Bend National Park and a Texas madrone in the same area.) Near the hotel swimming pool is a forty-two-foot-tall anaqua, spreading its crown over forty-six feet. It has clusters of fragrant white blooms in March and April and sometimes after a fall shower. The flowers become globe-shaped yellow or orange fruits that birds, animals, and humans find sweet and juicy. It surpasses the historic anaqua in Refugio, still standing, that shaded Gen. Sam Houston when he made a noted speech there in January 1836.

But Fairmount Hotel's anchor building on the corner of South Alamo and East Nueva streets—across from La Villita and HemisFair Park—brought Leo M. J. Dielmann's name to world attention in 1985. That is when the 1,600-ton, three-story structure designed by Dielmann was moved on thirty-eight gigantic dollies one-half mile through downtown San Antonio to its present location, suffering only minor surface cracks. It set the record for the largest building move ever, according to the 1986 *Guinness Book of World Records*.

When the foundation for the transplanted hotel was dug in 1985 on the city-owned property that the Fairmount Partners group leases, artifacts uncovered confirmed that the site had held one of Santa Anna's artillery batteries during the siege of the Alamo in 1836.

Dielmann had designed the Italian Victorian-style structure as a hotel for drummers (traveling salesmen) on the second and third floors, with commercial establishments on the first. It was built in 1906 of brick, limestone, and wood by contractor J. P. Haynes. The hotel's rumbling, six-block move from 857 East Commerce, where Foley's department store now stands at Rivercenter, took from March 30 to April 4, 1985. National television followed the suspenseful six-day trek of the 3.2-million-pound building,

In 1985, the Fairmount Hotel was moved six blocks, from Bowie and Commerce streets to 401 South Alamo, during a six-day period. The historic structure of hard red brick was designed by noted architect Leo M. J. Dielmann and opened in 1906. The transfer was recorded in the Guinness Book of World Records as the largest building ever moved through city streets. (San Antonio Express-News photo)

which involved turning two corners, crossing the San Antonio River Walk, and rotating the structure 90 degrees before it was backed onto its foundation.

German Churchgoers

Most German churchgoers were either Lutheran or Roman Catholic. It was not until 1852 that a Lutheran pastor came to San Antonio. In one of his first letters home to Switzerland, Rev. P. F. Zizelmann wrote:

> Because of the many nationalities represented among the immigrants that flocked into the city after Texas became

part of the United States, San Antonio is a Babel on a small scale. The Catholics assemble for worship in the old partly ruined Mexican Church, whereas the various Protestant denominations have only a primitive adobe house at their disposal, and this is used mainly by the Episcopalians and Methodists.

Mr. Zizelmann organized St. John's Lutheran Church in 1857. Its cornerstone was laid on March 5, 1860, at a site on Nueva and South Presa streets, and services were conducted in the unfinished church until it was completed after the Civil War. Its steeple was added in 1875 and was long remembered for the weathervane atop it, shaped like a rooster; St. John's became known as the "Rooster Church" until a new edifice was built in 1886.

The Alamo might instead be a Catholic Church today had circumstances been just a little different. It came close to being adapted permanently in 1856 for use as a parish church for San Antonio's German Catholics. The Alamo property was owned by the Catholic Church at the time but leased by the bishop to the U.S. Government as an Army quartermaster depot. Bishop Claude Marie Dubuis of Galveston asked the Army to release the Alamo church for use by the Germans but was told the space was vitally needed by the quartermasters for storage, so the bishop made land available near the Alamo, beside the acequia—the Alamo Madre Ditch that flowed south from near the river's head, past the Alamo, through the Menger Hotel, and onward across today's East Commerce Street.

Coincidentally, this site of St. Joseph's Church is about where the Alamo church (Mission San Antonio de Valero) was located when it was moved from its earlier location on San Pedro Creek. The mission was moved to its third and final site after a hurricane destroyed its huts and small stone tower in 1724.

The St. Joseph's Church we see today at 623 East Commerce was begun in 1868 and completed in 1876. Sometimes called "the German Catholic Church," its Gothic Revival design is that of Theodore E. Giraud, a South Carolina architect of French descent and brother of the esteemed former mayor of San Antonio

(1872-1875), François Giraud. The limestone walls were complemented in 1898 by the Gothic spire designed by James Wahrenberger.

Its famous stained-glass windows, imported from the Emil Frei Art Glass factory of Munich, were installed in 1902. It is noted also for the two paintings by the third pastor of the church, Father Henry Pefferkorn, which appear above the side altars. The pastor painted the striking depictions of the "Assumption of the Blessed Virgin" and the "Ascension of Jesus" not long after he began serving St. Joseph's in 1878. Some say that Father Pefferkorn also painted the Stations of the Cross that grace the interior walls, while others dispute this. After eighteen years as pastor of St. Joseph's, he became chaplain of Our Lady of the Lake College in San Antonio.

Today, oldtimers refer to St. Joseph's Church as "St. Joske's," because Joske's Department Store, which once called itself "The Largest Store in the Largest State," was built on three sides of St. Joseph's after its owners failed in their attempt to buy the entire property. The church's most prominent neighbors now are Dillard's department store and the spectacular Rivercenter shopping mall that embraces an arm of the river along the River Walk.

"The Triple Nationality"

The distinctive German legacy is still alive in San Antonio, the Hill Country, and much of Texas. There are still German names on some buildings on the north side of West Commerce Street, but gone are the signs printed in German that once distinguished those stores.

Yet history especially remembers the sign at the Commerce Street Bridge on which was printed a warning in three languages. Sidney Lanier wrote in 1873 that the sign was an unconscious satire of the Anglos, the Tejanos, and the Germans because the translations differed. The sign read:

Walk your horse over this bridge, or you will be fined.
Schnelles Reiten über diese Brücke ist verboten.
Anda despacio con su caballo, o teme la ley.

Lanier noted that the "American's warning" appealed "solely to the pocket." The German, he said, was told: "So, thou quiet, law-abiding Teuton, enough for thee to know that it is forbidden simply." Lanier interpreted the message for the "Mexicano" to be: "Slow there your horse or fear the law."

On the streets of San Antonio, said Frederick Law Olmsted in 1854, "the triple nationalities break out into the most amusing display"—the "sauntering Mexicans," the "sallow Yankees," and the "bearded Germans." Marveling at this enchanting mixture of cultures, he said:

> We have no city, except, perhaps, New Orleans, that can vie, in point of the picturesque interest that attaches to odd and antiquated foreignness, with San Antonio. Its jumble of races, costumes, languages and buildings; its religious ruins, holding to an antiquity, for us, indistinct enough to breed an unaccustomed solemnity; its remote, isolated, outposted situation, and the vague conviction that it is the first of a new class of conquered cities into whose decaying streets our rattling life is to be infused, combine with the heroic touches in its history to enliven and satisfy your traveler's curiosity.

7

San Antonio's Ethnic Richness

Historians have yet to ferret out individuals among the Indians who made a major impact on the development of San Antonio in the 1700s and 1800s, but they can name many of the people whose rare but surprisingly compatible Anglo-Hispanic-German mixture of cultures in the 1800s made San Antonio unique among North American cities.

A dictionary defines "Anglo" as "a white resident of the United States who is not Hispanic." Historian T. R. Fehrenbach says that the term Anglo-Texan "indicates a full participation in the English-speaking American culture as contrasted with adherence to the still Spanish-speaking Mexican way of life."

San Antonio's story was woven by some truly heroic as well as totally bizarre people who still seem "bigger than life," even

140

John Coffee Hays, a Ranger who begon service as a sergeant for the Texas Republic in 1836, became in a few years the Deputy Surveyor of Béxar District in San Antonio, while keeping his Ranger status. "Captain Jack" trained a party of about ten men to survey land and to fight the Indians who resisted any movement into territory they claimed. As a fighter of Indians and outlaws and leader of volunteers in the War with Mexico, Hays became a colonel and a Texas legend. His San Antonio home can be seen today at the corner of Nueva and Presa streets. (San Antonio Express-News file photo)

when their lives are examined closely. Consider, for example, the fearless Indian fighter Ranger Colonel Jack Hays, who later became the sheriff of San Francisco and a founder of Oakland, California. It was Hays who staged the first rodeo in the United States on the west side of San Pedro Creek.

Other amazing pioneers were Deaf Smith, the resourceful and heroic scout in the war for the Republic; Bigfoot Wallace, the rawboned frontiersman, fighter, and storyteller—the subject of fanciful dime novels even in his lifetime; Samuel Maverick, who established a dynasty of civic-minded leaders; and Roy Bean, for whom San Antonio named a neighborhood "Beanville" before the "judge" became "the Law West of the Pecos."

But people never stop making history. There are fascinating stories about those who have made San Antonio the truly different and charming city it is today—men and women of each century since the 1700s. The French, for example, are remembered for their schools, which enriched many minds among the populace, and for their work with the sick and with orphans and others who needed compassionate help and education. Their spiritual uplifting and healing continues.

The Irish are remembered for their leadership in civic work, commerce, and banking. The Bryan Callaghan family provided mayors, off and on, for eighteen years between 1885 and 1949. The Jews came early and were productive merchants and widely respected as public benefactors. The British were among leaders in the sheep and wool industry, and the work of architect Alfred Giles can still be seen. The beloved Scottish humanitarian Dr. George Cupples was the first president of the Texas State Medical Association—one of many Scottish achievers.

Many of the Poles came originally to the first Polish settlement in America—Panna Maria, Texas—and contributed much to San Antonio's intellectual climate. The Italians came with their appreciation of good food and as merchants of fresh fruits, vegetables, spices, and herbs, the imaginative use of which they demonstrated in their restaurants. The Belgians specialized in truck farming, producing much of the community's vegetables, fruits, nuts, and flowers and establishing central markets. The African Americans contributed notably to the city's political stability and education programs while they broadened the community's appreciation of life with their exceptionally fine music and food— reminding us that much of what we call "American Southern cooking" is rooted in Africa.

Colonel T. C. Frost

The largest space in an extensive history of San Antonio would be devoted to the Anglo Americans, who were the most numerous ethnic group during much of the town's history and among whom were some of its most fascinating knaves and greatest leaders and heroes. One of those Anglos was Col. Thomas Claiborne Frost—a lawyer, freighter, retailer, wool warehouse owner, and banker—the first of a bankers' dynasty that flourishes today in San Antonio under Tom C. Frost as Frost National Bank in more than a dozen locations. Frost, fourth-generation descendant of the founder and a nationally respected financial leader, is senior chairman of San Antonio-based Cullen/Frost Bankers, Inc.

Robert B. and Rena Maverick Green

Some San Antonians of note were benefactors or philanthropists such as George W. Brackenridge, whose name is seen in the great city park and who contributed much to Texas education. Others such as Robert B. Green are remembered especially for their extra-ordinary decency, sense of justice, vision, and civic leadership. Green was the first commander of the Belknap Rifles in 1884, a volunteer civilian drill team that became known nationally for its precision. Before he died at age forty-two, he had been a district judge, county judge, and State senator. He introduced fiscal responsibility and long-range planning to Bexar County government, provided the first gravel road surfaces in the city, and was widely acclaimed as an exemplary judge.

Green was a strong advocate of a county charity hospital, and in 1915, eight years after his death, the Robert B. Green Memorial Hospital was named for him, with his young son George turning the first spadeful of dirt to start construction. In 1981, the hospital was enlarged and became the Brady-Green Community Health Center. In 1994, it was renamed University Health Center Downtown, part of the Bexar County Hospital District.

Green's wife also made her mark on San Antonio. Rena Maverick Green, granddaughter of Samuel and Mary Maverick and one of the founders of the San Antonio Conservation Society, was a persistent historic preservationist. Her books *Samuel Maverick, Texan: 1803-1870* and the *Memoirs of Mary A. Maverick* are valuable contributions to San Antonio and Texas history.

"Fatal Corner"

San Antonio was a frontier town, besieged off and on by hostile Apaches or Comanches for more than a century and a half, a jumping-off point for the law-enforcing Texas Rangers, trade and transport center, major crossroads for cattle drives and military routes. San Antonians could see saloons, music theaters, female entertainers, fandango dance halls, gunfighters, gamblers, and desperados—and the often wild, rollicking life where cowboys, freighters, stagecoach drivers, cattlemen, soldiers, land speculators, European

*San Antonians and collectors of Western outlaw lore have been
fascinated since the 1800s by "the Fatal Corner." Eight or more deadly
shootings occurred at various times at the corner across Main Plaza
from today's Court House. The most famous was on March 11, 1884,
when Ben Thompson, notorious gambler, gunman, and former city
marshal of Austin, and his friend King Fisher, a deputy sheriff of
Uvalde, were killed in the Vaudeville Theater at 401 West Commerce
Street. Jack Harris, owner of the theater, had been killed by Thompson
two years earlier in the same building and there was bad blood
between Thompson and Joe Foster, who had been a close friend and
employee of Harris and was now partner with Billy Simms in running
the theater.*

*Illustrator Fred Himes based his interpretation of the event on court
testimony and jury findings at the inquest and other accounts, as well
as studio photos of the key participants. He shows Ben Thompson with
his back against the wall while King Fisher, in dark suit, clutches his
chest. Foster, in shirt sleeves, lies on his side in the foreground, shot
allegedly by Ben Thompson. On the floor beside Foster is Simms.
Jacobo Coy, a special policeman, lunges at Thompson to grab his
pistol. The three men on the balcony were purported to be the real
killers, according to the rumor from "sporting men in the know"
reported by Frank Bushick, editor of the San Antonio Express from
1892 to1906. When police came, both Thompson and Fisher were
dead, and Foster died in a few days. An inquest jury—which named
only Foster and Coy as firing the fatal shots—found the killings
justifiable self-defense. Austin citizens called it a massacre.*

"remittance men" who lived on money mailed from home, and other adventurers of all kinds prowled the narrow streets and ample squares seeking diversion.

The intersection of Main Plaza and Soledad became known as "The Fatal Corner" because of the many shootings that took place in the vicinity before the turn of the century. On the northwest corner was Hart's Cigar Store, and above it the gambling rooms of Jack Harris that connected to his Vaudeville Theater next door. The most popular saloon in town, the theater had the first electric lights in San Antonio, and people came from miles around to see the "refined entertainment" and stare at the lights.

On July 11, 1882, a few months after the lights went on, Harris, who had become a political power in the city, was shot and killed in his theater lobby by Ben Thompson, noted gunman and then Austin city marshal. Two years later, Thompson and King Fisher were shot in the same theater by friends of Harris, a story that made the front page of the *New York Times*.

Judge Roy Bean

Although not identified widely as a San Antonian, Judge Roy Bean—"the Law West of the Pecos"—was a long-time resident. He was the subject of a television series and three motion pictures that made much of his passion for Lillie Langtry. He wrote the English actress that he had named a town for her in West Texas, and at his invitation she stopped by to visit her namesake town on January 4, 1904, but her adoring fan had died ten months before.

Judge Bean resided in San Antonio for twenty years, putting an unforgettable stamp on the city and developing a reputation that made him a legend even while he lived. When he died, he had spent just about as many years of his life in San Antonio as in West Texas.

During his many years in San Antonio, Bean's neighborhood became known as Beanville. On November 14, 1909, the *San Antonio Light* carried a feature story headlined: "Suburb of City Is Named for Famous Pioneer Judge." The article said that "the City of Beanville as it generally is styled" had been there "since the

After longtime San Antonian Roy Bean moved to the railroad town of Langtry near the Rio Grande and Pecos rivers in the 1880s, he became widely famous for his saloon, the Jersey Lilly, where he offered ice cold beer and served as a judge advertising himself as providing "law West of the Pecos." He was the kind of confidence man who amused as many people as he flimflammed. He revealed little about his background. He was born around 1825 or 1830 in Kentucky, died in 1903, and is buried in Del Rio. Roy Bean lived in San Antonio about twenty years and his neighborhood became known officially as Beanville. One house he lived in with his family is on East Glenn Street not far from Mission Concepción. (Fred Himes illustration)

days of '64" and was "but four blocks in length and two in width." Roy Bean lived in several homes during many years in Beanville, which in 1880 had a population of twenty-five to thirty families. Today, one of his places of residence still stands. A one-story stone building with five rooms and four fireplaces, it was originally used in the 1700s as the home for a livestock supervisor of Mission Concepción. Each year, an Indian would be elected by his peers at the mission to move his family to the house and perform his *ranchería* duties from that location. It was a cherished responsibility. Bean's former home is well cared for today by an ardent private preservationist.

A Flying Family

The Stinson family for whom San Antonio's Stinson Airport is named made their marks in San Antonio history. Three women— two of them among the world's earliest female pilots, and the third, their mother—opened a flying school in San Antonio only five years after the first military flight in Texas and established San Antonio's first municipal airport. Katherine, who passed the final test to earn her pilot's license on July 12, 1912, helped teach not only Marjorie but brothers Jack and Eddie as well. The two women pilots became known internationally. Marjorie trained more than eighty Canadian male students who came to Texas to learn to fly for Great Britain in World War I. Her older sister, Katherine, the fourth woman in America to be issued a pilot's license, barnstormed in Canada, England, Japan, and China as well as around the United States—her flying acrobatics and world records drawing newspaper headlines, vast crowds, and fan clubs. These two women helped the early aviation industry gain popular acceptance worldwide.

The Inventive Genius of Tom Slick, Jr.

Another history-maker whose mark can be seen on the city today was Tom Slick, Jr., who founded the Southwest Foundation for Biomedical Research, one of the three largest independent institutions of applied research in the world, providing an extraordinarily valuable service both to private industry and to governments worldwide. Its major focuses are heart disease, genetic studies, AIDS research, and neonatal medicine. It has the world's largest colony of breeding baboons—more than 2,500— and produces baboons for the entire U.S. biomedical research community. It also has a menagerie of other research animals. The foundation's overriding mission is to improve human health through biomedical research.

In 1947, Slick founded Southwest Research Institute. By the 1990s, the Institute had 2,500 employees and twelve operating divisions. Each year, it takes on more than 1,000 major nationally and internationally sponsored research and development projects. It is the nation's third largest non-profit, independent, applied research and technology organization.

In 1958, Slick created the Mind Science Foundation to research the potential of the human mind and brain—exploring parapsychology, creativity, imagination, learning, and the mind's role in healing. Today it sponsors an annual series of lectures on facets of these subjects.

Also in the 1950s, working with New York architect Philip Youtz, Slick developed the Youtz-Slick method of construction, using precast, reinforced concrete slabs lifted into place by hydraulic jacks. The system was used by San Antonio's colorful architect O'Neil Ford in most of the structures of Trinity University from the early 1950s until the mid-'60s. The lift-slab process influenced the design of many of the buildings on campus at 715 Stadium Drive.

The six-story-high building near the top of the 750-foot tall Tower of the Americas—which houses a revolving restaurant and, at 605 feet, an observation deck—was constructed first as a steel frame near the tower's base and raised by oversized cranes and the Youtz-Slick hydraulic jacks. Publicists like to include the tower atop the restaurant and observation platform in figuring the height of the Tower of the Americas, making it 750 feet tall.

Although he died in 1962 (in the crash of a private plane), Tom Slick's ideas and accomplishments continue as a catalyst for bringing similar scientific and research organizations to San Antonio, including biotechnology, giving the city potential as a major new center in the United States.

USAA and General McDermott

Another reminder of Anglo-American contributions is the largest privately owned, single-occupant office building in the United States on San Antonio's Fredericksburg Road. Measured at more than five million square feet, the structure, christened "the McDermott Building" in 1994, rests in a campus-like setting on 286 acres. The enormous headquarters houses a major part of the staff of the United Services Automobile Association (USAA), the fifth largest insurer of private automobiles in the nation and highly rated nationally for its enlightened personnel policies and high morale. In 1993, USAA—which employs 14,600 people worldwide and 9,400 in San Antonio—was named among the top five companies in the United States as "best to work for."

USAA was started in San Antonio on June 20, 1922, by Major William H. Garrison of Kelly Field and about twenty-five other Army officers meeting at the Gunter Hotel. As outstanding, in a way, as the USAA building, is Brig. Gen. Robert F. McDermott, USAF retired, who was a combat pilot in Europe in World War II. He was the first faculty dean at the U.S. Air Force Academy, established in the 1950s. When he retired from the Air Force, McDermott was selected for the chairmanship of USAA and was its chief executive officer and chairman from 1968 until 1993, when he assumed the position of chairman emeritus. The extraordinary achievements of USAA attest to the quality of his leadership.

For San Antonio, the USAA chairman's achievements outside his work have been even more fundamental than heading one of the top insurance and financial institutions in the nation. He organized the Economic Foundation in 1975, served as its chairman until 1980, and continues to work with it in bringing new business to San Antonio. Focusing on developing biotechnology in the city, McDermott founded and serves as the chairman of the

Texas Research and Technology Foundation, which is developing the Texas Research Park. Together with the University of Texas Health Science Center and other institutions, the Texas Research Park forms the core of biotechnology for San Antonio.

Extraordinary Men and Women

There are scores of other Anglo Americans whose life stories would reveal the many ways they are now contributing or have contributed to making San Antonio the enchanted city it is—and not all of them lived in the 1700s and 1800s.

For instance, there are the dynamic women who have headed the San Antonio Conservation Society from 1924 until today and who are among the primary reasons that San Antonio has never lost its distinctive ambiance. The Society owns and manages eight historic sites. Not only do its members concentrate continually on preserving historic treasures and maintaining them, but they sponsor educational programs.

There was the unforgettable Hondo Crouch, the white-haired, white-bearded man in the beat-up cowboy hat, wrinkled cowboy boots, and worn Levis who made the ghost town of Luckenbach famous as the place "where everybody's somebody." Hondo spent part of his time in San Antonio, where he and his pickup added to the local color. No stranger could guess that the old cowboy with the down-home ways was John Russell Crouch, a former All-American swimmer at the University of Texas. When he died in 1976, newspaper headlines called him "the Clown Prince of Luckenbach." The little settlement with its old general store, ancient dance hall, and other weathered buildings attracts many tourists today.

Currently, Jim Cullum brightens the name of San Antonio with his jazz band on the River Walk, which is heard by more than a million listeners weekly on more than 200 radio stations, including the nation's largest cities. The Public Radio International program, "Riverwalk, Live From the Landing," has a twenty-six-week season. Thousands of visitors to San Antonio throughout the year are entranced by the Jim Cullum Jazz Band playing at its own club, The Landing, in the Hyatt Regency Hotel.

In 1975, Lila Cockrell was the first woman mayor of a large metropolitan city. After her terms were over, she gave strong support to a promising young city councilman named Henry Cisneros, who also became mayor and then a member of President Bill Clinton's cabinet, and later president and chief operating officer of Univision, the largest Spanish-language television network.

8

Why the Alamo?

The heroic stand at the Alamo of the Texians and Tejanos against the overwhelming forces of the Mexican general, Santa Anna, has become an internationally known paradigm of sacrifice for a cause. It became in 1836 not only a new symbol in world history—an American event in the mold of self-sacrificing patriotism as at the Battle of Thermopylae in Greece in 480—but led to the Battle of San Jacinto, which reshaped the United States and Mexico geographically, politically, and culturally.

The story has been told many times in great detail, but after all these years historical researchers find that still not everything about the conflict is known or understood. As Walter Lord wrote in *A Time to Stand*, "It is a rash man indeed who claims he has the final answer to everything that happened in the Alamo. The best that can be done is to offer some careful conclusions—always

On July 19, 1821, the Spanish governor of Texas, Antonio Martínez, along with the town officials, clergy, soldiers, and citizens of Béxar, took an oath of allegiance to the new Mexican government, which had overthrown the government of New Spain. (Drawing courtesy José Cisneros.)

subject to correction—that might throw new light on a few of the many intriguing riddles."

Lord lists the pros and cons of several such riddles: How did David Crockett die? Was he captured and then executed, as a number of respected historians have concluded? Where in the Alamo was James Bowie when he was killed? Is the story true that William Travis drew a line in the dirt with his sword, asking those who would volunteer to remain in the fort to show their willingness by stepping across the mark?

As a turning point in the history of three nations, the conflict should be understood in terms of the many events that led to it. A war fought to the bloody and decisive end probably was inevitable when one considers the inexorable advance of large numbers of Anglo Americans into the Mexican territory of Texas, and the deep concern of the Mexican government about this rapidly growing population overwhelming the native Texans.

Historians estimate that between 1821, when Mexico became independent, and 1835, when the armed struggle between Mexico and the Texans began, some 35,000 Anglo Americans flocked across the border into Mexican Texas, outnumbering the Mexican Texans, or Tejanos, by a ratio of ten to one. Mexican Texans had become a relatively small minority and Anglo Americans showed a critical awareness of the distinct cultural differences between them as exemplified by language, appearance, and customs.

Mexican government leaders were concerned about what they believed were expansionist desires of the American government, and they had good reason to be. Many influential Americans had visions of territorial expansion. Thomas Jefferson, for example, had said in an 1820 letter to President James Monroe that "the province of *Techas* will be the richest state of our union, without exception." Jefferson believed that when the United States had purchased Louisiana from France in 1803 while he was president, the territory extended to the Rio Grande, embracing Texas. Later, in the 1820s, President John Quincy Adams wanted to purchase Texas. And even later, the Mexican government was distressed by the widely publicized expansionist views of Andrew Jackson, who was president from 1829 to 1837.

The Mexican government had opened Texas to immigration in the 1820s, after Moses Austin and his son, Stephen F., had made acceptable overtures. At the time, Mexico's leaders believed that if it were more heavily populated—even by Americans—their land would prosper for the benefit of all. But from the late 1700s, various Americans had been making armed incursions into Texas, some stating openly that they had come to "liberate" the land and make it an independent nation.

By 1828, it had become clear to the Mexican government that the Anglo Americans were notably more industrious than the first settlers and were taking over. The Mexicans appointed Gen. Mier y Terán to lead a scientific expedition, study the Texas territory to establish its boundaries, and propose steps to keep it secure from further encroachment.

In his report to the Minister of War and Navy, completed on November 14, 1829, Gen. Mier y Terán wrote:

> The department of Texas is contiguous to the most avid nation in the world. The North Americans have conquered whatever territory adjoins them. In less than half a century, they have become masters of extensive colonies which formerly belonged to Spain and France, and of even more spacious territories from which have disappeared the former owners, the Indian tribes. . . .

He added:

> If war should break out, it would be expedient to suppress it in a single campaign—a less expensive method than to be always on the defensive. But even this would be useless until a colony of one thousand native Mexican families is planted there, an economical measure when it is remembered that the funds spent once in establishing a colony would be spent many times in maintaining garrisons.

Six years later, the war Gen. Mier y Terán spoke of did indeed erupt. But what were the Anglo Americans fighting for in a country where the majority of them had lived less than ten years?

They had come to a land of promise. They had been invited by entrepreneurs, mostly Anglo Americans who represented the Mexican government. These *empresarios* had offered them rich land at little cost and an opportunity to build new lives as farmers, tradesmen, merchants, and professionals.

The moneymaking opportunities presented by the vast lands that could be acquired cheaply and sold for much more were irresistible to almost everyone at every level who could position himself to profit. Accumulating land in a new frontier had begun with colonial America in the days of George Washington and the signers of the Declaration of Independence—and Stephen Fuller Austin, Sam Houston, and Ben Milam were only the best known of the Texans who sought to prosper from the land, although this was not their overriding objective.

Land in Texas could be bought for five to ten cents an acre, when an acre in the United States was selling for $1.25. Commercial real estate groups were formed in the United States to use political influence to obtain vast tracts of land for resale. They used public orators and newspaper stories to promote interest in Texas. The Anglo Americans had little concern, if any, for the native inhabitants' moral or legal rights to the land they possessed and fought bravely to defend. There was widespread feeling among the Anglo Americans that it was the "destiny" of the people of the United States to expand their territory all the way to the Pacific Ocean.

Some of the more than 1,000 people per month streaming into Texas by 1835 were not prospective farmers or ordinary settlers. As happens with the opening of any frontier, some of the newcomers from the United States were fleeing their past, or were adventurers, outlaws, confidence men, or other unsavory fortune hunters. But the great majority of the new Texans were in the vanguard of the inexorable movement of Americans, not long from Europe, who spread out toward the West from America's East Coast and from Gulf Coast ports—always seeking new land to work and new opportunities for themselves and their families.

At first, the new settlers from the North believed they could enjoy this land of opportunity under a Mexican government with its enlightened rule—the Constitution of 1824—which provided many of the freedoms they valued. There was one major drawback: Since 1824, Texas had been combined with the state of Coahuila and its capital was in Saltillo, Mexico, so the Texans suffered from their inability to make their needs known in the distant capital. Then in 1830, a central administration of the Mexican government passed sweeping laws that halted further U.S. colonization and reimposed customs duties that Texans would have to pay to trade with New Orleans and other centers. The government sent an army to enforce the laws.

Stephen F. Austin went to Mexico City in 1833, when Gen. Antonio López de Santa Anna was president, to petition for statehood for Texas as a Mexican state independent of Coahuila—a status that had been promised in the Constitution of 1824. He also asked for repeal of the oppressive decrees of 1830, but he was rebuffed on both counts.

In 1835, the war began with the settlers' defiant and triumphant clashes with the Mexican army at Gonzales on October 2 and San Antonio on December 5-9. During this period, representatives from a number of Texas towns met at San Felipe in what they called a "Consultation." On November 7, 1835, they issued a "Declaration of the People of Texas in General Convention Assembled," which they quickly had published in both English and Spanish. Although it avowed the loyalty of Texas to the former Mexican republic, the declaration stated:

> *Whereas.* General Antonio López de Santa Anna and other Military Chieftains have, by force of arms, overthrown the Federal Institutions of Mexico, and dissolved the Social Compact which existed between Texas and the other Members of the Mexican Confederacy—Now, the good people of Texas, availing themselves of their natural rights,

SOLEMNLY DECLARE . . . that they have taken up arms
in defense of their rights and liberties, which were threatened by the encroachments of military despots, and in
defense of the Republican Principles of the Federal Constitution of Mexico of eighteen hundred and twenty-
four. . . .

The battles of the Texans with the Mexican forces that had
begun in late 1835 were followed by the historic stand at the Alamo
from February 23 to March 6, 1836, the massacre of 342 Texans
by the Mexican forces at Goliad on March 27, and the defeat of
Santa Anna's army by the Texans at San Jacinto on April 21.

Why Mexican Texans Fought for Independence

A significant number of Tejanos fought alongside the Anglo Americans in the battles of 1835 and 1836. They advocated restoration
of the Constitution of 1824 and wanted more freedom and independence for Texas.

In fact, four years before the Texas Declaration of Independence was framed and issued, the city council of San Antonio de
Béxar had prepared a "petition" to the legislature of the state of
Coahuila and Texas in the Mexican Republic, outlining a list of
fourteen grievances. It said, "by these events the Constitution
was violated and the people of Texas were insulted and given yet
another just cause to separate from a state which has given so
many proofs of its lack of respect for fundamental laws, the sover-
eignty and rights of an aggrieved people, and for the principles
of the republican federal system that governs us."

The petition had been discussed and agreed upon by forty-
nine Bexareños and signed by seven members of the *ayuntamiento*
(town council). The title the council gave this historic declaration, signed on December 19, 1832, was: "Petition Addressed by
the Illustrious *Ayuntamiento* of the City of Béxar to the Honorable
Legislature of the State: To Make Known the Ills Which Afflict
the Towns of Texas and the Grievances They Have Suffered Since
Their Union With Coahuila."

The council sent copies of the petition to *ayuntamientos* of Goliad, Gonzales, Nacogdoches, and Stephen Austin's colony, San Felipe. At San Felipe it was translated into English, and Austin had copies of it printed. It also reached officials in Mexico City.

Called the *Representación*, it was the second Texas declaration of independence originated in San Antonio. The first, in 1813, had been the work of leaders of invaders who called themselves the Republican Army of the North, many of whom were from the United States. Yet, years later, a Mexican historian and a general for Santa Anna, Vicente Filisola, blamed the authors of the 1832 *Bexareños Representación* of San Antonio for Mexico's losing Texas. Too few Americans today are aware that many Tejanos wanted Texas to be independent as a nation.

Speaking of the *Representación*, Stephen Austin said in 1833— three years before the Battle of the Alamo—that the Bexareños "have taken a bold stand for Texas . . . in very energetic terms. This document will be of great use to Texas for it recapitulates all our grievances and the violations of the Constitution etc. This from the ancient capital of Texas and from native born Mexicans will burn bright all over the nation."

Is This Cause Worth Dying For?

The men defending the Alamo were unaware that on March 2, 1836, a Declaration of Independence for a new Republic had been approved by a convention at Washington-on-the-Brazos, but some, if not all of them, knew that a declaration was being worked on. The commander of the Alamo garrison, Colonel William Barret Travis, wrote from the Alamo on March 3: "Let the Convention go on and make a declaration of independence, and we will then understand, and the world will understand, what we are fighting for. If independence is not declared, I shall lay down my arms and so will the men under my command. But under the flag of independence, we are ready to peril our lives a hundred times a day."

The Declaration presented a list of grievances against the Mexican government and, patterned after the U.S. Declaration of

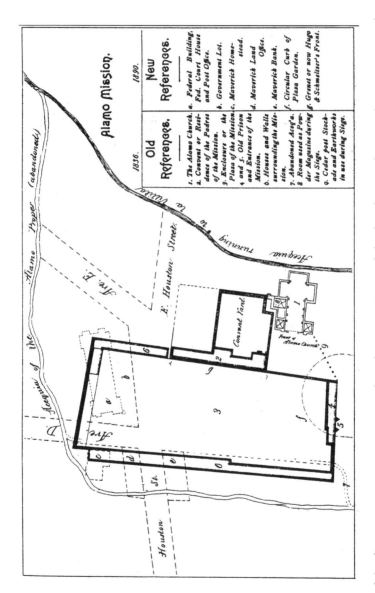

Map of the former Mission San Antonio de Valero in 1836, with broken lines indicating the property and street boundaries of 1890. Published in San Antonio de Bexar by William Corner. (Courtesy Mary Ann Noonan Guerra.)

Independence, stated that "when a government has ceased to protect the lives, liberty and property of the people from whom its
legitimate powers are derived," the people have the right "to abol-
ish such government and create another in its stead. . . ."

Although a messenger had not yet reached the Alamo defenders with the news that the Texas Declaration of Independence
had already been signed, the men and women there knew that
they had a cause for which to fight, and, if need be, for which to
die. Political grievances had been widely discussed in Texas for
years; newcomers soon shared the dissatisfaction with the Mexican government, which by 1834 had become a centralized regime
under the dictatorship of Santa Anna, who had begun calling
himself "the Napoleon of the West."

In December 1835, Stephen F. Austin had concluded, as he
wrote to a friend:

> The character of the struggle in which Texas is engaged, is
> now clearly developed; it evidently is one of life or death,
> "to be, or not to be." It is no longer a mere question about
> the forms of political institutions; it is one of self-preser-
> vation. The people now understand their situation.

Many of the Alamo defenders had heard how, in May 1835,
Santa Anna had defeated the forces of the rebellious Mexican city
of Zacatecas and ordered his army to burn and loot the city and
massacre some 2,500 nonparticipants, male and female. And they
knew also of the bloody battle in Béxar in 1835, when Santa Anna
had sent his brother-in-law, Gen. Martín Perfecto de Cós, to San
Antonio to lead the Mexican forces in Texas. The battle that followed, when the Texans had opposed the Mexican army, had forced
Cós to retreat to Mexico. The armed conflict was a training ground
for the fight that would come later when Santa Anna and General
Cós would return for revenge.

The Texan victory in 1835 had been a turning point in the
revolution, and later a grateful Texas government gave land grants
to 504 veterans of the "battle for San Antonio." Daniel William

Cloud, a twenty-four-year-old lawyer from Kentucky, had come to the Alamo as a mounted volunteer, having enlisted as a private and a rifleman at Nacogdoches in the Volunteer Auxiliary Corps of Texas. He wrote in a letter to his brother on December 26, 1835:

> Ever since Texas has unfurled the banner of freedom, and commenced warfare for liberty or death, our hearts have been enlisted in her behalf. The progress of her cause has increased the ardor of our feelings until we have resolved to embark in the vessel which contains the flag of Liberty and sink or swim in its defense. . . .
>
> If we succeed, the country is ours, it is immense in extent and fertile in its soil, and will amply reward all our toil. If we fail, death in the cause of liberty and humanity is not cause for shuddering. . . .
>
> I hope I shall recover entirely the hardships I am destined to undergo. . . .

Alamo commander Travis spoke for those who had chosen to remain in the fort when he sent this letter by messenger to the town of Gonzales on February 24:

> To the People of Texas and all Americans in the World— Fellow Citizens and Compatriots—I am besieged, by a thousand or more of the Mexicans under Santa Anna—I have sustained a continual bombardment & cannonade for twenty-four hours & have not lost a man—The enemy has demanded a surrender at discretion, otherwise, the garrison are to be put to the sword, if the fort is taken—I have answered the demand with a cannon shot, and our flag still waves proudly from the walls—*I shall never surrender or retreat.* Then, I call on you in the name of Liberty, of patriotism & everything dear to the American character, to come to our aid with all dispatch—The enemy is receiving reinforcements daily & will no doubt increase to three or four thousand in four or five days. If this call is

Juan N. Seguín is probably the least known of the major heroes of the Alamo as well as the Battle of San Jacinto. He acted as a messenger on dangerous missions and led his own force of mounted volunteers. Later, his life also was tied to San Antonio during the 1850s as justice of the peace, election precinct chairman, and co-founder of the Democratic Party in Bexar County. He became a controversial figure in Texas-Mexico relations, especially after he fled to Mexico in 1842 and served for a time in the military there. A town near San Antonio is named for him. (San Antonio Express-News *file art*)

James Bowie, a Kentuckian who lived for a time in Louisiana dealing in land sales with his brother, came to San Antonio in 1828. He married Ursula María Veramendi, daughter of the vice governor of Texas, in San Fernando church in 1831, fought against Mexican forces in the Battle of Béxar in 1835, and on March 6, 1836, was killed in the Alamo church where he lay ill on a cot. (San Antonio Express-News *file art*)

William Barret Travis, an attorney and adventurer from South Carolina, was commander of the Texian and Tejano volunteers at the Battle of the Alamo. He is honored as a hero along with David Crockett, James Bowie, and James Bonham in the fight for Texas independence from Mexico. Travis, Crockett, and Bowie are portrayed in this book, but no true-to-life likeness of South Carolinian James Butler Bonham is known to exist. (San Antonio Express-News file art)

David Crockett, former militia colonel, Tennessee state legislator, and U. S. Congressman, is remembered as a hero in the defense of the Alamo, where he died in 1836. (San Antonio Express-News file art)

Antonio López de Santa Anna was president of Mexico five times, although he spent much of his life as a professional soldier. In 1833, he was elected president of Mexico as an advocate of democracy, but in the following year he became an autocratic Centralist. As a general, he used an overwhelming force of trained Mexican soldiers to defeat the relatively small number of Texian and Tejano volunteers defending the Alamo on March 6, 1836. Fighting heroically to the last man, the Texans lost 189, while Santa Anna lost as many as 600 killed or wounded, one-third of his assault force. In the following month, on April 21, his forces were defeated at the Battle of San Jacinto by volunteers under Gen. Sam Houston. Santa Anna was captured, but soon released—and in later years he again served Mexico. (San Antonio Express-News file art)

neglected, I am determined to sustain myself as long as possible & die like a soldier who never forgets what is due to his own honor & that of his country—VICTORY OR DEATH.

William Barret Travis

Lt. Col. Comdt.

P.S. The Lord is on our side—When the enemy appeared in sight we had not three bushels of corn—We have since found in deserted houses eighty or ninety bushels & got into the walls twenty or thirty head of beeves— Travis

After twelve days of siege, including heavy cannon fire, Santa Anna's soldiers moved on the Alamo at dawn on the sixth of March. Mounting ladders, they scaled the walls surrounding the mission. Wave after wave of attackers engaged the defenders with firearms and hand-to-hand fighting, using bayonets. The numbers of Mexicans were overwhelming. By about eight o'clock in the morning, some 189 Texians and Tejanos lay dead inside and outside the Alamo. The lives of the few women and children in the fort were spared.

Much of the fighting took place in the old two-story *convento* of the mission, which had been turned into a long barracks for housing the soldiers. Some 600 Mexican soldiers of Santa Anna's attacking army of 1,800 were dead or wounded.

The heroes of the Alamo were many—not only Travis, Bowie, and Crockett, whose stories are so often told and who are memorialized in so many places, but men such as James Bonham, who was sent as a messenger to get reinforcements and who returned to the Alamo—and to almost certain death—on March 3 with the disheartening news that no aid was coming to the outnumbered defenders.

There were other heroic messengers, such as Juan Seguín, who rode through enemy lines to Goliad, about 100 miles away, in a vain effort to get help. John W. Smith, who later was thrice mayor of Béxar, was sent out three times as a messenger. He served as scout and guide for the Gonzales Ranging Company's reinforcement of the Alamo on March 1, after which he was sent out for the last time.

Perhaps the most remarkably courageous of all the Texans were the thirty-two volunteers from Gonzales, who rode their horses seventy miles to the Alamo to cast their lot with the desperate defenders of this classic sacrifice in the name of Liberty.

The young Kentucky lawyer Daniel William Cloud, who had written to his brother: "I hope I shall recover entirely [from] the hardships I am destined to undergo," had hoped in vain. He was one of the 189 who died at the Alamo. The dead were from Tennessee (33), Virginia (13), Kentucky (12), Pennsylvania (10), New York (7), North Carolina (7), South Carolina (7), Missouri (5), Massachusetts (5), Georgia (5), Mississippi (4), Louisiana (4), Alabama (4), Ohio (3), Arkansas (3), Connecticut (1), Illinois (1), Maryland (1), New Jersey (1), Rhode Island (1), and Vermont (1). Nine had

"The Fall of the Alamo" was painted in 1885 by Theodore Gentilz after years of study of the ruins of the walled former Mission San Antonio de Valero. It had become a fortress used in 1835 by Mexican soldiers against the Texas volunteers and in 1836 by the Texians and Tejanos. In 1844, only eight years after the battle, Gentilz began interviewing San Antonians and taking measurements and making sketches at the battle site. (Daughters of the Republic of Texas Library photo)

been born in Texas. From Ireland and England came twelve each. Four came from Scotland, two from Germany, and one each from Wales and Denmark. The birthplaces of twenty are unknown. All had died for their dreams of a better future. Recent research, endorsed by the Daughters of the Republic of Texas, recognizes no less than eight Tejanos who died beside their Texian comrades in the Alamo.

When we walk today in some areas near the Alamo—including the large plaza in front of the church that was once behind high walls—we tread on places where Texian and Tejano defenders and soldiers of the Mexican army died for the causes they represented.

When we walk southeast of Alamo Plaza, on East Commerce Street—an area once called the *Alameda*, Spanish for "tree-lined boulevard"—we may be stepping over the final resting places of

Sam Houston was a giant among Americans—he was six feet, four inches tall, weighed around 240 pounds, and before coming to Texas at age thirty-nine in 1832 he had served as U.S. Congressman and later governor of Tennessee, and in 1830 was ambassador of the Cherokee nation to the government in Washington, D.C. In Texas he showed his superb intellect, charisma, and eloquence—but he was not perfect. Historian Ralph Wooster said "he was egotistical, self-centered, vain, at times vulgar, but he had great vision—a rare ability to see the grand picture of the future of Texas." He was the commanding general at the defeat of Gen. Antonio López de Santa Anna's Mexican forces at San Jacinto on April 21, 1836. He had been a delegate to the Constitutional Convention. He was twice president of the Republic of Texas, member of the Texas Congress, U.S. Senator, and governor of the state of Texas. Houston died in 1863 and is buried in Oakwood Cemetery in Huntsville. (San Antonio Express-News file photo)

some of the Alamo defenders. The exact location of their remains is lost in history. They might lie under the concrete we walk on or drive over, in front of St. Joseph's Church on Commerce Street, near Rivercenter.

Several San Antonians recalled how, after the battle, General Santa Anna had the corpses of the Alamo defenders placed in two piles (some say three piles) near a peach orchard beside the street of the Alameda—stacked on alternating layers of wood, and covered with grease and tallow, then ignited. The pyres, some 250 yards apart, eight to ten feet long and ten feet high, burned for two days and two nights. Eyewitnesses quoted by journalist Charles M. Barnes in the *Express* in 1911 recalled that some of the charred remains were later moved to the Odd Fellows Rest at the cemetery on Powder Hill on East Commerce Street.

On April 12, 1997, the Daughters of the Republic of Texas dedicated the Alamo Wall of History on the Alamo grounds to provide visitors a colorfully illustrated story of a former Franciscan mission that became an inspiring symbol of heroism.

In Rivercenter, around the corner from the Alamo between Crockett and Commerce streets, the Alamo battle can be seen re-created in a spectacular motion picture, *Alamo . . . the Price of Freedom*. It is shown at the IMAX theater on a six-story-tall screen with six-track stereo sound that "puts you in the middle of the action." In the IMAX lobby is an interesting and informative diorama showing the scene of the battle in the walled mission compound as it might have been viewed from a balloon hovering directly above it.

At the Texas Adventure on Alamo Plaza, there is another dramatic portrayal of the Battle of the Alamo with the exciting sights and sounds of a multimedia show using state-of-the-art special effects in the *Encountarium F/X Theatre*. Moreover, an extraordinary, forty-two-square-foot diorama showing the last minutes of the Battle of the Alamo was added to the theater in 1995. It displays 800 colorful, hand-carved pewter figures of the Mexican, Texian, and Tejano fighters in mortal combat around and inside the walled former mission. Newcomers to the city often are advised to view one of these commercial presentations before visiting the Alamo grounds, as an aid to understanding the profound meaning of the confrontation and the nature of the historic battle.

News Traveled Slowly

It took almost six weeks for people on the East Coast of the United States to hear the shocking news about the Battle of the Alamo on March 6, 1836. The April 13, 1836 issue of *The Times*, a semi-weekly published in Hartford, Connecticut, headlined a story with "**Important from Texas** — FALL OF SAN ANTONIO AND MASSACRE OF TEXIAN TROOPS!!!" It then published three dispatches—from Gen. Sam Houston, from President Ellis, President of the Senate in Texas, and from "the passengers of the schooner Comanche eight days from Texas."

Houston's message was headed: "Headquarters, Gonzales, March 11, 1836. J. W. Fanning, Jr. Commanding at Goliad," and said: "Sir—Upon my arrival here, the following intelligence was received through a Mexican supposed to be friendly, which however, was contradicted in some parts by another which arrived with him; it is therefore given to you as rumor, though I fear a melancholy portion of it will be found true. Ansilma Burgura states that he left the Alamo on Sunday the 6th inst. and now is three days from Arochas Rancha; that the Alamo was attacked on Sunday morning, at dawn of day, by about 2300 Mexicans, and was carried a short time before sun rise with a loss of 520 Mexicans killed and as many wounded. Col. Travis had only 150 effective men out of his whole force of 187. After the fort was carried, seven men surrendered and called for Gen. Santa Anna and for quarter--they were MUR-DERED by his order. Col. Bowie was sick in bed and also murdered.

"The enemy expected a reinforcement of 1500 men under Gen. Condilla, and 1500 reserve to follow them. He also informs that Urgartrehear had arrived with two millions of dollars for the payment of the troops. The bodies of the Americans were burned after the massacre—an alternate layer of bodies and wood underlaid and set on fire. Lt. Dickinson who had a wife and child in the fort, after having fought with desperate courage, tied his child to his back and leaped from the top of a two-story building—both were killed by the fall. I have little doubt but that the Alamo has fallen. Whether the above particulars are all true may be questionable; you are therefore referred to the enclosed orders.

—I am, Sir, your Obedient Serv't. Signed.
SAM'L HOUSTON."

9

Twelve Battles
Remembered

A group of San Antonio students of history once listed twelve encounters among military forces in and around San Antonio—aside from the scores of deadly skirmishes that went on for more than a century. In 1970, the San Antonio Retired Officers Association published a brochure, now out of print, with maps showing the location of "Battlefields of San Antonio."

The list consists of the Battle at the Rosillo, March 29, 1813; the Battle at the Alazán, June 20, 1813; the Battle at the Medina, August 18, 1813; the Battle at Concepción, October 28, 1835; the Grass Fight, November 26, 1835; the Storming of Béxar, December 5-9, 1835; the Battle of the Alamo, February 23-March 6, 1836; the Council House Fight, March 19, 1840; Woll's Capture of San Antonio, September 11, 1842; the Battle at the Salado, September

18, 1842; the Dawson Massacre, September 18, 1842; and the Battle at Adams Hill, May 9, 1861.

Rosillo Creek

The battles at the Rosillo, at the Alazán, and at the Medina all occurred in 1813, when Texas was a province of Spain. It was a time when forces seeking independence from Spain were at work all over the Americas—south, central, and north. Between 1810 and 1826, independent Latin American governments drove out Spanish and Portuguese rule. In 1813, Mexico was seeking independence from Spain, and forces sympathetic to both Mexican independence and a new Texas began moving toward San Antonio to take control of the government.

On March 29, 1813, near the confluence of Rosillo and Salado creeks southeast of San Antonio on the San Antonio-La Bahía Road, the Royal Spanish Army was defeated by the Republican Army of the North made up of native-born Spanish Americans from the border, Indian allies, Tejanos, and volunteers from the United States.

Some Texas histories refer to the Army of the North's attack on the Spanish government in Texas as "the Gutiérrez-Magee Expedition." José Bernardo Maximiliano Gutiérrez de Lara, from Nuevo Santander, had made connections with high officials in the United States government advising them of his intentions. They did not discourage him from moving to "liberate" Mexico and Texas.

In New Orleans, he was introduced to William Shaler, a U.S. consular officer and special agent of the government, who would advise him. Another leader was Augustus William Magee, former lieutenant in the United States Army, a graduate of West Point. Magee's military capability was matched by that of José Álvarez de Toledo in the expedition of the Republican Army of the North against the Spaniards.

The Royal Spanish Army that was defeated at the Battle of Rosillo was commanded by Texas Governor Manuel María Salcedo, assisted by Col. Simón de Herrera, Governor of Nuevo León. Both governors and twelve of their officers were executed on April 3 in an unauthorized action by a vengeful group in the Republican Army of the North. They were interred in San Fernando Church (now a cathedral), where their remains lie today. Three days later, the rebels issued a Declaration of Independence and flew their green flag over San Antonio de Béxar.

Alazán Creek

On June 20, west of town and directly west of Alazán Creek, along the Camino del Río Grande, forces of the Republican Army of the North made a surprise attack against the Spanish Royal Army Forces and again were successful in defeating them.

Medina River

The following August, the Spanish Royalist Army led by Brig. Gen. Joaquín de Arredondo (accompanied by a young lieutenant named Antonio López de Santa Anna) defeated the Republican Army of the North. The actual battle site is no longer detectable and history does not record its exact location, but experts who prepared a study of the Caminos Reales for the State Department of Highways in 1991 believe the fighting occurred not far from the Old San Antonio-Laredo Road, about five or six miles south of the Medina River near the Bexar-Atascosa county line.

It seems strange that the battlefield of the bloodiest conflict in Texas history—which took more lives of Texans and their allies than the battles of the Alamo, Goliad, and San Jacinto combined—cannot be precisely located. The exact site of the Battle of the Medina has not been found because it is in a region covered with sand eight to twenty feet deep in a belt, once covered by "blackjack" oak trees, five miles wide and thirty miles long. It is in Atascosa County, named for the Spanish word meaning "boggy" because of the deep sand. So far, metal detectors have not been able to locate the usual evidences of battle (many of which were removed by the victors)—ammunition, harnesses, buckles, etc.— which have sunk far down since August 18, 1813.

Some 800 to 1,000 men of the Republican Army of the North were slaughtered in the four-hour battle or in the executions that followed. These men were in a force of about 1,400 volunteers made up of about 400 Americans, 800 or 900 Mexicans and Tejanos, and about 100 Indians, mostly Lipan Apaches. Commanded by Toledo, they were out-maneuvered and defeated by the forces of 1,830 Spanish Royalists under the command of General Arredondo. Only about 100 of these supporters of the Spanish king were killed, and then the general took his troops to San Antonio to punish its citizens.

This defeat brought a cruel end to what might have become a new Texas republic, but it lasted only from April 6 to August 18, 1813, during which time every Spanish official was removed from Texas and the new republic was ruled by a junta in San Antonio de Béxar under the green flag of the Republican Army of the North. There is a historical marker at Highway 281 and FM 2537, approximately ten miles from the presumed battle site.

Concepción

Four of "the twelve battles of San Antonio" were fought in 1835 and 1836, when the Texians, assisted by Tejanos, were attempting to drive the Mexican government forces from the area. One of these was the Battle of Concepción that followed the arrival of Stephen F. Austin and his volunteer forces, which had come from Gonzales by way of Goliad in October 1835. Austin sent detachments to various points near San Antonio de Béxar. He assigned James Bowie and James W. Fannin to secure the missions. They camped beside Mission Concepción.

On the night of October 27, they were startled by cannonballs falling nearby in the darkness. Some half dozen were fired by Mexican government forces from two miles away, using observers in the tower of San Fernando church at Main Plaza. No one was injured. The next day, when the Mexican infantry attacked they were defeated by the Texians and forced to retreat to the town.

During the rest of October and most of November, the peoples' volunteer army of Texas stayed in two camps. One, to the north, was near the Old Mill along the western bank of the San Antonio

River. (Today, the site of the Old Mill is the front lawn of Providence High School at 1215 North St. Mary's Street.) The southern camp was near Mission Concepción.

The Grass Fight

The skirmish dubbed the Grass Fight occurred on November 26, when a Mexican pack mule train was seen approaching the town near the confluence of Apache and San Pedro creeks. The Texans attacked it, believing it was carrying valuable cargo. The fighting continued with attacks and counterattacks as both sides were reinforced by troops, including cavalry. Finally, the Texans prevailed. They found to their chagrin that they had captured forty horses and mules loaded with fodder gathered to feed the animals of the Mexican army. The Texas Historical Commission marker at Sidney Lanier High School at the corner of Brazos and Durango commemorates this fight.

The Storming of Béxar

Not long after the Grass Fight, in early December 1835, the Texans consolidated their forces north of town and prepared to take it from Mexican forces commanded by Gen. Martín Perfecto de Cós. In house-to-house fighting around Main Plaza from the fifth of December to the tenth, the Texans finally defeated the Mexican forces.

General Cós surrendered. There had been some thirty to thirty-five Texan casualties, with five or six killed among the 780 who had participated. Mexican casualties were estimated at more than 100 killed, wounded, or missing.

The Council House Fight

The Casas Reales—called the Council House or Court House by the Anglo Americans—was the scene of one of the most consequential encounters that ever took place between the Texians and the Comanches. History records it as the "Council House Fight" or the "Council House Massacre."

Young Matilda Lockhart, captured and returned to San Antonians by the Comanche Indians, is featured in one panel of the mural by Howard Cook in the Federal Building near the Alamo. A misunderstanding at this meeting in 1840 at the Council House in Main Plaza resulted in a confrontation that ended with more than forty deaths. (Photo by Susan Riley Photography)

The misunderstanding occurred in March 1840, when the Indians failed to bring to the Council House all the Texan captives they had been expected to surrender at a meeting intended for peacemaking. The Comanches brought only one, young Matilda Lockhart. The treaty makers of both sides were armed. The Texans told the Comanche chiefs they would be held hostage until every one of their captives had been returned. In the fight that followed, both inside and outside the Council House, seven Texans were killed and eight wounded. Thirty-five Comanches were killed, eight wounded, and twenty-seven women and children plus two old men were captured.

This bitter and bloody fight left the Comanches feeling betrayed and swearing to wreak revenge—which, within five months, they determinedly carried out in massive attacks of burning and plundering on Linnville and Victoria. This was followed on August 1, 1840, by the "Plum Creek Fight" in which a large Comanche plundering party was returning north and was waylaid by a hurriedly organized army of volunteers near the present town of Lockhart. Their decisive defeat of the Comanches drove the war party to the northwest; never again would they make a stable peace with Texas settlers.

Woll's Capture of San Antonio

Two years later, Main Plaza was again the center of armed action. It was during a period when Mexican military forces were making occasional, brief incursions into Texas territory—even though their forces under General Santa Anna had been defeated at San Jacinto. The Mexican government ordered General Rafael Vásquez to lead his armed forces to San Antonio to demand its surrender. He arrived on March 5, 1842, with 500 men, took over the city unopposed, and hoisted the Mexican flag, but after only two days he returned to Mexico having done little more than declare new laws.

Six months later, the Belgian-born Gen. Adrián Woll rode into San Antonio with his army of 1,200 soldiers—pursuing Mexico's continuing effort to regain the province it had lost in 1836. On September 11, Woll took over the town including the Council House where the Fourth District Court of Texas was in session. When he started back to Mexico on September 18, he had among his captives fifty-three prisoners from the courthouse, including the presiding judge, lawyers, and jury. He also had removed irreplaceable city records. Several city leaders were held in the prison at Perote Castle halfway between Mexico City and Vera Cruz. Some of the more prominent captives, such as Judge Anderson Hutchinson and businessman Sam Maverick, received pardons the following year. Others died there or escaped or were released in the general amnesty of September 16, 1844, after two years of captivity.

The Alamo

This famous story is told in Chapter 8.

TEXICAN JUDGES AND JURY, AND MEXICAN SOLDIERY.

TEXAS AGAIN INVADED.—CAPTURE OF SAN ANTONIO.

(From the *New Orleans Bulletin*, Sept. 27.)

By the politeness of Captain Boylan, of the steam-packet Merchant, we have full files of Galveston, Houston, Matagorda, and Austin papers to the latest dates. The news from Texas is of a startling and important character, if we may place full credence in the following extract from the *Galveston* (extra) *Times* of the 20th. That paper says:—" We stop the extra to give the following information, but this moment received from a gentleman who has just arrived, and met the express the other side of Oyster Creek. San Antonio was completely surprised on the 11th instant, by 1300 Mexicans under General Wall. Fifty-three of the principal citizens taken."

When San Antonio was taken, the circuit court was in session, and the judge and the officers of the court were made prisoners—lawyers, clients, and all. It seems strange that the vigilant Texans should have allowed themselves to be " come over " so handsomely. A few months ago they took the alarm, and prepared for defence. But the immediate danger having soon passed away, the militia were discharged, and affairs were suffered to go on as if in the midst of a profound peace. Never since the declaration of independence was Texas more unprepared for a vigorous contest than at this moment. Her army is disbanded ; her ships of war lie idle at New Orleans for want of funds, when their presence is urgently needed on the coast of Texas and Yucatan ; her credit is utterly prostrate, and money she has none. Still, she has brave hearts and strong hands, and, when the crisis comes, we trust she will be found equal to it.

The news story above appeared in the Illustrated London News *on November 5, 1842.*

Salado

After the capture of San Antonio on September 10, 1842, by General Woll, Texian volunteers assembled on the Salado and provoked the Mexican force of some 1,100 to battle. General Woll attacked on Sunday, September 18. The most famous of the Texas Rangers, Jack Hays, led his fighting men along the Salado in support of Mathew Caldwell and his eighty-five followers. Among the 250 in the Texas army was the larger-than-life William Alexander Anderson Wallace—known as Bigfoot—legendary Ranger, hunter, Indian fighter, soldier, and storyteller. The Mexican forces retreated toward Mexico after losing about sixty men.

The Dawson Massacre

On September 18, 1842, the same day as the Salado Creek battle, a company of volunteers led by Capt. Nicholas Dawson was cut off while attempting to join the main body of Texan forces at Salado Creek. Discovered by Mexican cavalry about a mile and a half from the fighting, they took cover in a mesquite grove and prepared to resist attack. The Mexicans brought up two pieces of artillery and fired from beyond rifle range, killing thirty-five Texans including Dawson. Fifteen were captured and taken to Mexico, five were wounded, and three escaped.

Adams Hill

This was actually not a battle but a potentially bloody fight that did not materialize. It was a confrontation between two significant armed forces, with one backing down before the fighting could begin.

After Maj. Gen. David E. Twiggs surrendered the property of all the Union forces in Texas to Confederate representatives in San Antonio on February 18, 1861 (about two months before the Civil War began on the East Coast), some of his forces remained in the state for a time. His troops had been given permission to return to the Union but it was difficult to move large numbers of men and their supplies to the coast and transport them to the United States. Lt. Col. Isaac V. D. Reeve began moving his three infantry companies from Fort Bliss at El Paso to San Antonio at the end of March. By May 8, he and his men had reached Castroville, and then marched about nine miles closer to San Antonio and camped around a ranch house at Adams Hill near Lucas Springs.

The next morning, his headquarters was approached by two Confederate officers carrying a white flag. They demanded his unconditional surrender. After getting permission of the Confederate commander, Col. Earl Van Dorn, to send two U.S. Army officers to scout out the strength of the opposing forces and to return with the information, Reeve realized that he was greatly outnumbered and surrendered. About thirteen miles west of San Antonio on U.S. 90 West, on the east bank of the Medina River, is an official Texas Historical Marker, titled "Battle of Adams Hill."

THE ALAMO, SAN ANTONIO, GENERAL TWIGGS'S HEAD-QUARTERS.

The surrender in 1861 by Maj. Gen. David E. Twiggs of all United States military property in Texas to forces of the Confederates was noted in newspapers in the East. Fanciful sketches by artists far from the scene resulted in distortions such as this altered facade of the Alamo and inclusion of a nonexistent building beside it. Actually, the surrender took place in Main Plaza. (Daughters of the Republic of Texas Library photo)

This 1861 photograph from the files of the Library of the Daughters of the Republic of Texas is labeled: "Texas troops at San Antonio at the time of the surrender of U. S. arms." It shows the north side of Main Plaza, which the Bexar County Courthouse faces today. This was only one of the events occurring throughout the city of about 9,000 on February 18, when U. S. Maj. Gen. David E. Twiggs surrendered all U. S. military property in Texas to a force of some 800 Confederate supporters under Maj. Ben McCulloch. It was the U. S. government's first major loss in the Civil War. On the balcony of the Plaza House hotel in 1860, Governor Sam Houston heard a crowd cheer his proposal to keep Texas in the Union. Gen. Robert E. Lee lived for a time as a U. S. Army lieutenant colonel across the plaza at Read House. (Daughters of the Republic of Texas Library photo)

[Official.]

HEADQUARTERS DISTRICT OF TEXAS,)
GALVESTON TEXAS, June 19, 1865.)

General Orders, No. 3.

The people are informed that, in accordance with a proclamation from the Executive of the United States, all slaves are free. This involves an absolute equality of personal rights and rights of property, between former masters and slaves, and the connection heretofore existing between them, becomes that between employer and hired labor.— The Freedmen are advised to remain at their present homes, and work for wages. They are informed that they will not be allowed to collect at military posts; and that they will not be supported in idleness either there or elsewhere.　By order of

Major-General GRANGER.

(Signed,)　　　　　F. W. EMERY, Maj. & A. A. G.

*General Order announcing the emancipation of slaves in Texas.
Galveston Tri-weekly News, June 20, 1865. (Courtesy the Texas History Center, Austin)*

10

City of Exotic Spires, Domes, and Plazas

And that sweet City with her dreaming spires,
She needs not June for beauty's heightening.
    —Matthew Arnold, *Thyrsis*

Many of San Antonio's historic landmarks are associated with its first plazas—Main Plaza (*Plaza de las Islas*), Military Plaza (*Plaza de Armas*), Alamo Plaza, and Travis Park. Of all the ancient landmarks, it was the lone steeple and gray dome of the church of San Fernando standing between Main and Military plazas that early visitors remembered most. Surrounding it they saw sunbleached, one-story adobe buildings.

What is now called the clock tower at Fort Sam Houston was built in
1876 as a watch tower, used for sighting hostile Indians. The
design of the structure was the inspiration of Gen. Montgomery C.
Meigs, who had seen and admired such towers in Italy. The structure
stored 30,000 gallons of water in a tank at the top. A signal lantern
could be raised by pulleys to light part of the compound for sentries. A
clock was installed in 1882. The bell in the tower that chimes every
hour was once used at the Alamo when the U. S. Army occupied the
compound before moving to Government Hill. Fort Sam Houston is the
site of 900 buildings rated "historic"—nine times the number in historic
Williamsburg, Virginia. (Fort Sam Houston Museum drawing)

In the years since San Antonio's first church tower pointed to the heavens in 1749, San Antonio's spires have caught the eye of many visitors. In the 1750s and later, the spires of the Franciscan missions were added to the enchanting scene as their towers breached the skyline above the newly completed stone churches. Visitors saw an exotic city that seemed to belong to another world, another time. The English scientist William Bollaert noted how the city first appeared to him in 1843. "As we approached [the town from the east] we caught glimpses of the ruins of the Alamo, the towering steeple of the church and houses on the other side of the river through the dense foliage in the valley beneath us."

United States Commissioner John Russell Bartlett wrote in his report on the United States and Mexican Boundary Survey in 1850: "The view of San Antonio from a distance, as it is approached by the Victoria road, is exceedingly beautiful. The place seems to be embowered in trees, above which the dome swells with an air quite Oriental."

San Antonio is indeed a city of lofty towers and spires—from the four, 300-foot, minaret-like towers from which the nearly flat roof of its pavilion-like Alamodome is suspended, to the spires of many of its more than 500 churches. With the 750-foot Tower of the Americas for HemisFair '68, San Antonio punctuated its skyline, exclaiming exuberantly that at last it was making its mark on the twentieth century.

From the bell towers of San Antonio's four ancient mission churches to the twin towers of the Marriott Rivercenter, towers are in the city's heritage. The tower at Fort Sam Houston was inspired by an Army general who had admired the soaring towers of Siena and San Gimignano in Italy. Architect O'Neil Ford's tower at Trinity University also is reminiscent of the towers in the medieval Tuscan towns. The Taj Mahal tower at Randolph Air Force Base is a nostalgic beacon in the memory of millions.

But visitors were captivated also by the sight of the domed churches of San Fernando, Mission San José, and Mission Concepción. Visitors who gazed upon San Antonio from afar saw their romanticized vision of Granada in Spain or the exotic mosques of the Arabian Nights or the domes of Moorish Africa.

In itself, the very shape of a dome has an enchantment rooted deeply in the human psyche. Subliminally, the dome says "home," "shelter," "domicile," while, at the same time, when used in a great building its curved vault seems to form sanctuary under the arched firmament of the heavens.

As a city of domes and spires rarely seen in much of early America, San Antonio again and again seemed to imaginative world travelers an exotic work of art. The reasons are evident in the artifacts that make San Antonio so different: the incomparable Texas symbol of mortal sacrifice, the Alamo; the river that rises from the limestone caverns beneath us and flows with our dreams to the sea; and the gathering places of the townspeople and visitors; their icons; their businesses; their homes; their squares for merrymaking; their places of worship or contemplation or creation; their domes and "dreaming spires." These works of art are tokens, many of them touched by age, of what collectively has given San Antonio its enchanting aura over the centuries.

Main Plaza and San Fernando Cathedral

Walk past or step inside the San Fernando Cathedral today and imagine the history it has seen. Here, for centuries, amazing things have happened!

The building whose single spire and domed sanctuary first caught the attention of the earliest visitors to San Antonio—after 1749 and before 1890—was the village church of San Fernando, which in 1874 was made the cathedral of the new Diocese of San Antonio. Over the years, it has been greatly remodeled.

Interred inside this church lies a Paris-born military officer and former lieutenant governor of Louisiana who was appointed by the King of Spain in 1779 to be the governor of Texas. Despite his nationality this Frenchman, Athanase de Mézières, had been selected as the governor of a Spanish province because of his extraordinary rapport with many Indian tribes in Louisiana and Texas at a time when the Indians were the most frustrating problem faced by the Spanish crown in northern New Spain.

De Mézières was one of the French officers retained by Spain when French Louisiana became a province under the Spanish Crown between 1762 and 1769. His record for ten years as a brave and brilliant commander of the post at Natchitoches, Louisiana, and his unusual knowledge of tribal languages, as well as his fluency in both Spanish and French, would have made him an ideal governor of eighteenth-century Texas. But he died before he could take office, and was buried the next day, November 3, 1779, "in the parochial church of the villa of San Fernando and the royal presidio of San Antonio de Véxar." And there he rests today.

In 1749, while the cathedral was still under restoration, there was a treaty ceremony in *Plaza de las Islas (*Main Plaza) between a large gathering of settlers and Apaches in which the weapons of war—a hatchet, a lance, six arrows, and a live horse—were placed in a wide, deep hole in the plaza's center. The presidio captain and four chiefs joined hands and danced three times around the hole; the priests, the settlers, and all the Indians then did the same. When all had returned to their places, at a given signal they rushed to the hole and rapidly filled it—burying all that had been placed in it—to signify the end of a spasmodic war that had lasted thirty years. But as history has shown us, their pledge of peace was only a hopeful, yet unavailing gesture, broken too soon by actions on both sides.

In the battle for San Antonio in December 1835, Col. Francis W. Johnson raised the flag of victory in the steeple of the church after the Texans defeated the forces of Gen. Martín Perfecto de Cós from Mexico, some of whose troops were fortified in the Alamo. Several months later, the vengeful forces of General Santa Anna were sighted from the church tower as they marched toward San Antonio on February 23, 1836. Santa Anna and his personal staff dismounted in front of the church and proceeded to a house on the northwest corner of the plaza. Next day, he ordered a large, red banner of "no quarter, no mercy" to be flown from the church tower, where it was displayed until after March 6, when all the Texian and Tejano defenders of the Alamo had been killed.

Ben Milam led the victorious Texians in the Battle of Béxar in 1835. The Mexican forces were fortified in the Alamo. They also were in various parts of the town, some using artillery. Mexican sharpshooters were firing from the bell tower of San Fernando Church. Most of the fighting was house-to-house in the town of fewer than 3,000 people. Although it was largely through his initial leadership that the Texans prevailed, Milam was killed by a sniper's bullet to his head fired by a Mexican in a tree. (San Antonio Express-News *file art*)

Where Are the Bones of the Alamo Defenders?

There are those who say the remains of some of the Alamo defenders were interred in San Fernando Cathedral. Workmen making repairs outside the sanctuary railing near the steps in 1936 found a box of burned bones, but there are some who question whether they really were the bones of Alamo heroes that Col. Juan N. Seguín had said he buried in that part of the church a year after the battle. Seguín's 1899 story was contradicted by some of his contemporaries.

However, the remains are still kept in a place of honor in the cathedral. They were reburied in a special ceremony in May 1938. Archbishop Arthur J. Drossaerts led a procession from the sanctuary to the entrance of the cathedral, where a commemorative plaque was unveiled. The procession included a line of Catholic priests, descendants of the Canary Islanders, and city, county, and state dignitaries. The casket was borne through the rear of the church and around to the front, where it was lowered to its place on the right side of the sanctuary. The Archbishop paid homage to all the fallen heroes of the Alamo in his sermon following the Pontifical High Mass. The marble casket is now in an alcove to the left of the church's entrance.

There are no such questions about the remains of other historic personages buried at the cathedral. Parish records of baptisms, marriages, and burials go back to 1731 and include documents from Mission San Antonio de Valero.

Originally, the settlers were buried in crypts inside the church. Later, the burial ground (the *camposanto*, or "holy ground") was extended to the churchyard, which was surrounded by a wall. In 1808, the cemetery of San Fernando was again extended—this time to an area including today's Santa Rosa Hospital; south of it was Milam City Cemetery. Milam Park today is north of El Mercado/Market Square, and Santa Rosa Hospital stands north of the park.

Milam Park

The area is no longer a church cemetery, but markers in Milam Park memorialize those still buried in the vicinity. Most noteworthy, and near his statue, is the resting place of Ben Milam, hero of the Battle of Béxar on December 5-9, 1835, and of the Siege of Béxar, which began in October. His grave was first memorialized in 1897 by Adina De Zavala and her followers with a monument of gray marble. It was Milam who rallied the Texian forces against the Mexicans holding the Alamo fort and the town. The Mexicans under General Cós were defeated, but Milam was killed by a sniper as he stood outside the Veramendi House.

The Graves of Ruíz and Navarro

More distant from the church, San Fernando Cemeteries Number One, Two, and Three have extended the centuries-old burial grounds. The only two native Texans to sign the Texas Declaration of Independence from Mexico on March 1, 1836, lie in the San Fernando burial grounds. The first was José Francisco Ruíz, buried inside the cathedral. The second was his nephew, José Antonio Navarro. Both had been born in San Antonio.

José Antonio Navarro, along with his uncle José Francisco Ruíz, was one of the two native Texans to sign the Declaration of Independence from Mexico on March 2, 1836. Two others elected to represent San Antonio de Béxar, Jesse B. Badgett and Sam Maverick, also signed— Maverick on March 7. Navarro was born in the city in 1795, and spent most of his life in civic undertakings and political action. He held numerous appointive and elected offices under Mexico and later the Republic of Texas. He favored secession from the United States in 1861, and all four of his sons fought in the Confederate army. (San Antonio Express-News file art)

Navarro was buried beside his wife in San Fernando Cemetery Number One. In 1936, the Texas Centennial Commission erected a joint monument at their graves and also placed a statue of Navarro at Corsicana, Texas. Not far from the cathedral is the Navarro House, where he lived (at the corner of West Nueva and South Laredo streets). He had been an attorney, state legislator, and delegate to the federal congress in Mexico City, and he served on the committee of twenty-one that drafted the Constitution for the Republic of Texas at Washington-on-the-Brazos. He died in the house in 1871. Saved by the San Antonio Conservation Society, his home has been restored and is operated by Texas Parks and Wildlife Department. Today, in the gardens of the Texas Walk at Sea World, is a magnificent, life-size bronze statue of Navarro, along with fourteen other statues of notable sons and daughters of the Lone Star State. Closer to his original home is another statue of the great statesman on the southeast corner of Commerce and Santa Rosa streets.

José Francisco Ruíz was one of the four representatives of Béxar at the Convention of 1836, and, with José Antonio Navarro, one of only two native Texans to sign the Texas Declaration of Independence. He had represented Béxar in the Senate of the First Congress of the new republic. In 1813, he had taken part in the unsuccessful revolutionary action in San Antonio against Spain and had been forced to flee to East Texas and Natchitoches, Louisiana, where he lived for eight years among the Indians. When French scientist Jean Louis Berlandier published his landmark study of Indians in 1853 (The Indians of Texas in 1830), Col. Ruíz was described as his primary informant on the Comanches, their allies, and their enemies. In 1821, the government of Mexico offered him a full pardon if he would return to Texas and use his influence with the Comanches and Lipan Apaches as a commissioner to those tribes on behalf of Mexico. He later was commended for this and then became an officer for a time in the Mexican army. In 1842, when Samuel Maverick was released from a Mexican prison, his wife said she believed it was "through the influence of Don Francisco Ruíz," a longtime friend. (Daughters of the Republic of Texas file art)

San Fernando as Town Center

For centuries, the church of San Fernando has been the site of memorable San Antonio celebrations of many kinds—joyful, sad, and triumphant. James Bowie was married during a nuptial mass there on April 25, 1831, to Ursula María de Veramendi, daughter of San Antonian Don Juan Martín de Veramendi, vice governor of the Mexican state of Coahuila and Texas.

The church was the geographical center of San Antonio from its beginning—even before the building was erected. The site designated for its front door was the original point from which the city was measured off in all directions in 1731 by the new

*A bell, it is said, has a "universal tongue that any heart can under-
stand." If it is true that large bells have distinctive "voices," today you
can actually hear a voice from the 1700s, one that has called out to
San Antonians for centuries. It rings at about noon daily from the tower
of the Immaculate Heart of Mary Church on the Urban Loop that runs
behind 617 Santa Rosa Avenue. This was the lone bell in San
Fernando Church from the early 1700s until 1902; then it remained
silent until the church on the Urban Loop was dedicated on August 15,
1911. Today it has the same mellow voice that called out over the
centuries to announce good news and bad—births, weddings, deaths,
coronations, and alarms—virtually all the major religious and civic
events of San Antonians under Spain, Mexico, the Republic, the
Confederacy, and the United States of America. (Photo by author)*

settlers from the Spanish Canary Islands. In later years, the dome was designated the anchor measuring point. The Spanish Viceroy had named the villa after Don Fernando, Prince of Asturias. He was the second son of King Philip V, who had sent the settlers to Texas. Don Fernando became King Ferdinand VI in 1746 and ruled the Spanish Empire until 1759.

The name of the church, however, came from a different source. It was founded in the name of Saint Ferdinand, also known as Ferdinand III, a king of Castile who lived from 1199 to 1252. Called *"el Santo"* for centuries, he was canonized in 1671. The ancient, brightly painted statue of San Fernando stands inside the cathedral today.

San Fernando is the oldest continuous parish in the United States. Its cornerstone was laid in 1738, intended to be a stone structure similar to the church of Mission San Antonio de Valero, but a lack of funds and workers delayed its building for ten years, during which time the settlers attended services in the presidio chapel or crossed the river on a single-log bridge to the church in Mission San Antonio de Valero. If they wished, they could trudge to Mission San José without having to cross the river.

When the church finally was completed in 1749, it was dedicated as the Church of Nuestra Señora de la Candelaria y Guadalupe, expressing the traditional devotion of the Canary Islanders to the Virgin Mary under the title "La Virgen de la Candelaria" (Candlemas, celebrated on February 2). The devotion of San Antonio's settlers to the Virgin Mary as "Our Lady of Guadalupe," a practice dating back to 1531 in Mexico, was reflected in the second patron's name in the commemoration.

The first church had a bell tower on its south side, a dome arching over the sanctuary with its altar where mass was said and sermons delivered, and a wing on each side that formed the transept as an extension of the space for the parishioners attending services. With its cupola over the sanctuary and its single tower, it looked somewhat like Mission San José does today. The newer church, completed on October 6, 1873, still contains parts of the old. The walls of the sanctuary under the dome are the walls of

Bats lived near human beings in San Antonio even before they found nesting places at the Spanish missions in the 1700s. A two-story stone building in Military Plaza—used for the district courtroom and later as the recorder's courtroom with an adjoining jail—was known as "the Bat Cave" in the late 1800s. On days when the court was in session, long T-shaped sticks were used to bump and expel the bats resting above the canvas ceiling. Taking advantage of the large numbers of bats in San Antonio, Dr. Charles A. R. Campbell developed in the early 1900s a large bat roost to encourage the winged animals to live in areas where mosquitoes threatened to spread malaria. He built a roost at Mitchell Lake south of town and at several sites in the populated area. His work was recognized internationally as a way of eradicating mosquitoes and collecting guano for fertilizer. In 1910, Campbell persuaded the Bexar County Medical Society to condemn the killing of bats, and in 1914 the City passed an ordinance prohibiting their killing. The last of Campbell's bat roosts can be seen today in the Hill Country on the property of Marshall Steves in Comfort. (Fred Himes illustration)

the original church of about 1750. Its single bell tower was on the north side. A shortage of funds prevented erection of the second bell tower—on the south side of the entrance—until around 1890.

In 1903, when new bells were placed in the cathedral, the bell that rang in 1831 for James Bowie's wedding to Ursula de Veramendi; the bell rung by a sentinel posted by Lt. Col. William Travis to warn of the approach of Santa Anna's Mexican army; the bell that called the Rangers of Jack Hays to saddle their horses and assemble for their retaliatory forays; the bell that tolled over the years for hundreds of the town's celebrations, was set aside. But you can still hear its voice from a spire of the Immaculate Heart of Mary Catholic Church, built in 1911 on South Santa Rosa, not far from the cathedral.

Architects describe San Fernando Cathedral's style today as "a fine example of Gothic Revival." Some believe that San Antonio architect François Giraud, who designed the extensive renovation begun in 1868, was influenced by the cathedral of Notre Dame in Paris, with its twin towers, triple portals, central rose window, and coupled tower arches.

The Spanish Governor's Palace

In Plaza de Armas (Military Plaza) behind the San Fernando church, the soldiers were quartered and the captain had his house, the *Comandancia*, which later was used as the Spanish Governor's Palace. This is the site of the fortified presidio, moved there in 1722 after some four years at its first location closer to San Pedro Springs. Today, what remains of Plaza de Armas is the oldest site in the state continually occupied by Texans.

Military Plaza is almost completely filled by City Hall and its parking places, but still remaining on the west side of Military Plaza, beside Commerce Street, is the long, white, one-story building—the centuries-old "Spanish Governor's Palace."

It is evident that the stout stone structure has withstood the centuries, but one wonders why such a relatively small, one-story building could be called a palace. Over its entry is the original keystone, with its carving of the imperial double-headed eagle of the Hapsburg coat of arms. It bears the inscription: "*Se acabo 1749*" (Finished in 1749), and the monogram "*Viva Jesús.*"

Although after 1700 the Spanish king was no longer a member of the family that had ruled much of Europe for centuries, the Hapsburg coat of arms had become a cherished symbol of royalty recognized by all who had lived in Spanish lands. Almost everyone in Texas at the time, including many of the Indians, knew

Adina De Zavala, with (left to right) Nellie Lytle and Frances Donecker, at the entrance of the abandoned Spanish Governor's Palace in 1926. "Miss Adina," as she was known, led the first organized effort to save and restore the five ruined former Spanish missions, including the Alamo; arranged in 1897 to memorialize the heroic Ben Milam annually at his grave site; and, beginning in 1917, promoted public support of funding for restoration of the Governor's Palace, constructed in the 1740s. The Spanish Governor's Palace was opened with great ceremony on March 4, 1931. Today, it presents an enlightening view of a fine Spanish Colonial home. (Photo courtesy Institute of Texan Cultures)

that the Spanish governor in San Antonio, or his representative, spoke on behalf of the king's government.

The building came to be called a "palace" both because of its royal connections and because, like the Veramendi House—sometimes called Veramendi Palace—it was one of the most luxurious and commodious home in the town. Despite the efforts of Adina De Zavala and others to save it, the Veramendi House, where a vice governor of Texas and Coahuila had once lived and Ben Milam had been killed, was razed by the city in 1910.

Most of the walls of the Governor's Palace are nearly three feet thick. Anchored in the wall beside the entry is an iron ring used there in earlier centuries for tethering horses. Inside this restored Spanish Colonial mansion—alive with the authentic furnishings of its time—are rooms designed for both daily living and entertaining, including an entrance hall, a ballroom, bedrooms, kitchen, and a fountained patio. The mansion reflects the genuine devotion to authenticity of those who restored and refurbished it. The appointments evoke the comfortable atmosphere of a Spanish frontier mansion of the 1700s and 1800s. In restoring the building, even the flagstone floors were carefully selected. They came from sidewalks in older sections of the city, some of them markedly worn down over the years by thousands of footsteps.

In the 1860s, the building was used for a time as a public school, but by the early 1900s it had become neglected and, before becoming entirely dilapidated, was at times a junk shop, a wholesale banana store, and a saloon. At the insistence of preservationist Adina De Zavala (who in the 1890s also had initiated the effort to save the neglected Alamo and the four other deserted missions), women of the San Antonio Conservation Society and others, the city purchased the property in 1929. In 1930, after extensive historical and archaeological research, the palace was restored by builder Guy C. Holder from the plans of architect Harvey P. Smith. It was dedicated in March 1931 in a colorful celebration that included Patrick Cardinal Hayes of New York and Texas Governor Ross S. Sterling.

The Spanish governors in Texas generally were military officers, usually in the grade of colonel or lieutenant colonel, although there were times when captains served temporarily as governors. The power of the governors of the various provinces in New Spain flowed from the king through his personal representative, the viceroy. When the Interior Provinces were established, a commandant-general in Chihuahua supervised the governors of the six provinces, which extended from the Sabine River in Texas to the Pacific Ocean.

In the province of Texas, there were only three real settlements in the late 1700s and early 1800s. They were Nacogdoches, far to the east near Louisiana; La Bahía, on the San Antonio River some 35 miles north of San Antonio Bay near the Gulf of Mexico; and San Antonio de Béxar, capital of the province.

For decades, the Spanish governors of Texas lived opposite the French post of Natchitoches in Louisiana at Presidio Nuestra Señora del Pilar de los Adaes. They had been assigned there in 1721. San Antonio de Béxar did not become the headquarters for Spanish governors of Texas until 1773, when the Crown moved the governor's residence west.

Throughout New Spain, the presidio officers were appointed by the governors. In 1773, San Antonio and La Bahía (Goliad) became the easternmost presidios in a line of military posts that stretched from the Gulf of Mexico to California.

The Spanish governor of Texas was responsible for managing a vast area east of the Nueces River—for example, monitoring the settlements and other regions throughout his province and communicating with his superiors through letters and visits, directing his presidio forces, dealing with thousands of hostile Indians, and working with the missionaries. While Béxar was under Spain, a governor usually became involved directly in local civic affairs.

An authority on early Spanish and Mexican records of the American Southwest, Henry Putney Beers, wrote in 1907 that "the governor made land grants, issued licenses, considered appeals from the alcalde courts, supervised fiscal matters, and administered laws and decrees. He occupied a building on the military plaza in San Antonio that served as his residence, office, and judicial headquarters."

On June 24, 1781, Governor Domingo Cabello issued a decree that gives a rare insight into how a governor viewed his responsibilities, as well as a vignette of life in San Antonio at that time. It also is among the earliest historical references to "the royal government in the main plaza" as differentiated from the presidio section, where it could be assumed the office of the Royal Presidio of San Antonio de Béxar was located.

In the customary fashion, the governor's decree began with a listing of his titles and chief responsibilities.

> Don Domingo Cabello: In charge of Royal Affairs, Governor and Commander-in-Chief of the military posted in the Province of Texas, its missions, territories and borders; Captain in charge of the Cavalry Company at the Royal Presidio in San Antonio de Béxar, and Inspector General of all the military assigned to said province.
>
> Inasmuch as today is the feast of St. John, and since also on the feasts of St. Peter, St. James, and St. Ann, citizens, including women, traditionally celebrate feastdays by holding parades on horseback down the town's streets; and because these festive outings often turn into horse racing, creating dangerous situations, and causing a variety of accidents and mishaps; and because I see it as my duty to protect the citizenry from danger, I command the following:
>
> All citizens, regardless of class, social status, or profession, who wish to indulge in horse racing must refrain from doing so in the streets of the town and of its presidio. Henceforth, horse racing will only be permitted in the unpopulated outskirts of town, in the main plaza by the royal government house, or in the military plaza behind the church.
>
> Under no circumstances is horse racing to ever occur in the streets of this town, nor of its presidio.

Violators will be arrested by patrols which I will appoint for that purpose. Youths caught racing their parents' horses will have them confiscated. If caught racing borrowed horses, they will endure twenty-five lashes. Men eighteen years and older caught racing their own horses will also have them confiscated. Furthermore they will be sentenced to one month in jail, doing hard labor on the government building project, in shackles and without pay or sustenance. An alternative penalty will consist of a fine for the value of the confiscated horses.

So that these banns come to the attention of every citizen, and so that no one can claim ignorance, I command that this ordinance be posted in all the customary places designated for public notices.

Given at this Royal Presidio of San Antonio de Béxar, on the twenty-fourth day of June, 1781. For lack of a notary, as well as of officially stamped notarial paper, I have issued and signed this on ordinary paper in the presence of attendant witnesses, with whom I officiate. In witness whereof I attest: Domingo Cabello.

Beneath the signature of the governor were those of José Placido de Monzón and Manuel Flores y Valdez.

San Antonio's Florida Governor

Standing to the left of the entrance of the Spanish Governor's Palace is a statue of an extraordinarily tall Spanish military officer of a bygone era. The bearded man wears an ankle-length cape and on his left hip, a large sword. At the statue's base is a small plaque that reads:

"The Conquistador" by Enrique Monjo, sculptor. Given to the people of San Antonio as a symbol of the close ties of Spain and San Antonio. November 10, 1977.

The gift was arranged by the Spanish Consul General in Houston, Erik Martel. Martel, a descendant of the Marqués of San

Fernando, later became the Spanish Consul General in Miami. He had the statue shipped to the Spanish Governor's Palace in San Antonio, where it was uncrated and erected in a courtyard inside the building. The Spanish Ambassador to the United States unveiled it at a reception on November 10, 1977. It remained there for more than a year before it was placed, without ceremony, outside on the front walk where it now stands.

It was not long before someone noted that the costume of the sculptured figure was not the military accouterment worn by the Spanish expedition leaders who came to Texas in the 1600s and 1700s. Those explorers and colonizers had not come as "Conquistadors" or military conquerors of the scattered Indian populations of Texas. Research showed that the statue was of Juan Ponce de León, who had conquered Puerto Rico in 1509, "discovered" Florida in 1513, and was killed there eight years later by the Indians while trying to subdue them. Ponce de León had been appointed the governor of "The Island of Florida" by King Ferdinand V in 1514.

John Leal, recently the Bexar County archivist and in the mid-1970s a curator at the Spanish Governor's Palace, recalled that he learned in 1979 that the Consul General at Houston had first seen the statue in Spain at the studio of the sculptor, his friend Enrique Monjo. It had been commissioned by someone in Florida but payment for the work and for its shipment was long overdue.

The Spanish Consul General immediately saw a way to help his friend the sculptor—while simultaneously commemorating the origin of the Spanish presence in Texas—by titling the statue "The Conquistador" and arranging for the government of Spain to purchase it for donation to the people of San Antonio.

So that is why a former Spanish governor of Florida—Ponce de León, companion to Christopher Columbus on his second voyage to the New World, fabled explorer who sought in vain the Fountain of Youth, who lived two centuries before San Antonio was founded—stands today, ageless, near the entrance to the palace of the Spanish governors of Texas.

Moses Austin and Main Plaza's Casas Reales

Between the Spanish Governor's Palace and City Hall stands a larger-than-life statue of Moses Austin, father of Stephen F. Austin who, after his father's death, established the first Anglo-American colony in Texas. The statue commemorates Moses Austin's visit to Governor Antonio María Martínez two days before Christmas in 1820. Austin had come to seek permission to bring a colony of 300 Anglo-American families to settle in Texas. The governor rejected his request without ceremony and told him to leave the city.

Fortunately, as Austin walked away and across the plaza he met a man he had known in New Orleans, a Hollander born in Dutch Guiana named Philip Hendrik Nering Bögel, who called himself Baron de Bastrop. He was multilingual, had acquired experience in surveying and colonization in Spanish Louisiana and Texas, was in the freighting business and a member of the town council of Béxar. He enjoyed high standing among the townfolk and the governor.

After three days of discussions between Moses Austin and Baron de Bastrop, they met with the governor and presented a formal document that had been approved by the town council. The governor endorsed the proposal, and the seeds of the Anglo-American colonization of Texas were planted.

The ten-foot-tall bronze statue of Moses Austin in Military Plaza is the work of San Antonio sculptor Waldine Tauch, a protégé of Pompeo Coppini, who created the monumental Cenotaph in the plaza facing the Alamo. Although the Moses Austin statue was dedicated on May 25, 1939, with great ceremony—led by representatives of the Governor's Palace Board of Directors, the San Antonio Conservation Society, the Canary Islanders, the Battle of Flowers Association, and the Daughters of the Republic of Texas—some historians say the statue should be in Main Plaza, not Military Plaza. Their reason is a belief that Moses Austin met the governor in the *Casas Reales*, the royal government houses on Main Plaza—not at the Governor's Palace.

The Casas Reales occupied the eastern side of Main Plaza, now across Dwyer Avenue between Market and Commerce streets. A

Stephen Fuller Austin, born in Virginia on November 3, 1793, was the founder of Anglo-American Texas. (San Antonio Express-News file art)

building with several sections housed the seat of government used by the *ayuntamiento* as well as by Texas governors at various times. Here were the first courthouse, city hall, and jail in Texas. This was the second capital of Texas—the first being in Los Adaes, now in Louisiana near Robeline.

There seems to be no documentation of the exact location of the meeting of Governor Martínez and Moses Austin in 1820, although assumptions have been made to suggest that the Casas Reales was the place.

In 1807, U.S. Army Capt. Zebulon Pike was the house guest of the Spanish governor in San Antonio, Antonio Cordero y Bustamante, in what seems likely was the "palace" in Military Plaza. Pike wrote that several large social functions were held while he was there. Governor Cordero and a visiting governor from Nuevo León, Simón de Herrera, joined in the festivities. On one evening, said Pike, "after supper we went to the public square, where might be seen the two governors joined in a dance with people who in the daytime would approach them with reverence and awe."

The Casas Reales, the royal houses of Béxar, comprised the official seat of government, first under the Spaniards and later under the Mexicans. In the 1840s, the Texans called it the "Council House." It was the scene of the bloody Council House Massacre in 1840 after a misunderstanding between Indians and Texans. In its earliest days, the complex included a small jail, as well as a clock that could be seen from Main Plaza, and a sturdy timber device to which miscreants were fastened for public floggings—a common practice in those days. Part of the building remains today east of Main Plaza on the corner of Dwyer and Market streets, reconstructed and used as a book store. Before it became Market Street, the road passing the jail was called Calle del Calabozo or Jail Street. (Fred Hines illustration)

The exact location of the Austin-Martínez meeting is less important than the fact that they met and that initial approval was given by a Spanish official for settling Anglo Americans in Texas. When the Moses Austin statue was dedicated in Military Plaza in 1939, little was left of the Casas Reales, which had been abandoned and the courthouse moved to Military Plaza around 1850—and the east side of Main Plaza was mostly a parking lot beside a crowded bus stop. Hardly an ideal place for a statue of Moses Austin.

Today, a bookstore stands on the corner of Market Street and Dwyer. An old drawing of the Casas Reales shows a one-story structure in that location. It is most noteworthy for its clock— which was the only means for most of the citizens to tell time— and its whipping post, leaning against the south side of the building, where scoundrels guilty of relatively minor infractions, such as indecent conduct, could be given up to 100 lashes.

Whipping was not an unusual form of punishment in those days—even under Stephen Austin at San Felipe, who once had some horse thieves given fifty lashes each and had one-half of the head of each shaved. In San Antonio, the town council passed a law in 1761 ordering that anyone trifling with a member of the opposite sex would be pilloried, lashed 200 times with a bullwhip, and banished from the community. In Nacogdoches in 1783, using indecent language in public was punishable by 100 lashes and expulsion for a year. For vagrancy and idleness, the punishment was 60 lashes and expulsion.

Travis Park

Travis Park, which has offered a pleasing green vista for guests of the St. Anthony Hotel since 1909, has been bordered by churches since the 1800s. It was described briefly in the city directory published in 1877:

Our public squares and plazas form a most interesting feature of our city. By a wise provision, incorporated in our municipal laws by the Spaniards, these plazas can never be alienated or diverted to any other purpose. These breathing places of the city are a great convenience to teamsters and farmers, who bring their produce here for sale.

The Military Plaza, the Main Plaza and the Alamo Plaza are already pretty well surrounded by business houses, hotels, etc. Travis, or Maverick Park, the munificent gift to the city of the late Samuel A. Maverick, has been fenced in, laid out in walks, and planted in shade trees. Adjacent to this beautiful park are the St. Mark's Episcopal Cathedral, the Jewish Synagogue, and the Baptist church, and a number of elegant private residences.

Travis Park Methodist Church

In 1883, the Travis Park Methodist Church was built on the southwest corner of Travis and St. Mary's streets, but the Methodists had been active in San Antonio for nearly forty years—since April 1844, when the first Protestant service in the city was conducted jointly by Presbyterian minister John McCullough and Methodist minister John Wesley DeVilbiss in the old county clerk's office. A plaque on a building near Soledad Street and Main Plaza—beside the bridge on Commerce Street—marks the site.

Later, for a time, DeVilbiss used the parlor of the Veramendi House to hold services. After that he temporarily used a room in the Council House on Main Plaza. He obtained a good bell and set

---

San Antonio Was Quick to Adopt Air Conditioning

The St. Anthony Hotel, at 300 East Travis Street, was the first hotel in the United States to have air conditioning. It was installed when the building was completely remodeled in 1935-1936. According to the Carrier Corporation, San Antonio also had the first fleet of air-conditioned buses—sixty-one in all—in 1946. The twenty-one-story Milam Building, nearby at 115 East Travis, was the tallest reinforced concrete building in the world when it was built in 1928, and later, the world's first all-air conditioned skyscraper.

---

it up on a lot he had purchased in La Villita. He would ring the bell and then cross the river to meet his congregation in the Council House a quarter of a mile away.

Having learned that the title to the La Villita lot was invalid, the Methodists were finally able, in 1853, to find a place on Soledad Street to build their own church, and thirty years later they built the new church across from the St. Anthony Hotel. It became the Mother Church for the many Methodist churches of San Antonio and for years was the center of Methodism in the Southwest.

Storied St. Mark's

Most historic of the early Anglo-American churches in San Antonio is St. Mark's Episcopal Church beside Travis Park on East Pecan Street. A future United States president was married there, and the names of many Texas heroes are on its rolls, but the church is probably remembered most for its association in history with Lt. Col. Robert E. Lee, who became commander of the Confederate Army during the Civil War, and who had gained much of his military experience during his years in Texas as a field officer.

During the United States' war with Mexico, Lee was with Gen. John E. Wool's army from San Antonio to Buena Vista during 1846 and 1847 and with Gen. Winfield Scott's forces from Vera Cruz to Mexico City in 1847. As Scott's chief of staff, he won three brevets—major, lieutenant colonel, and colonel—all because of conspicuous gallantry in the field. Long before he had been honored at the highest levels of American military leadership, Col. Lee was warmly appreciated in San Antonio. Everyone seemed to remember him, at least those who wrote their memoirs, and they told their grandchildren about him. The cornerstone for St. Mark's was laid in 1859, but the church was not completed until 1875. While he was commanding the Department of Texas in 1860, Lee was active in supporting the congregation and the building program, which later was interrupted by the Civil War.

During the war, the congregation met in various places, in schools and rented halls and in the Presbyterian Church on Commerce Street. In 1874, the church was designated a cathedral of

*This engraving of St. Mark's Church was titled "Episcopal Cathedral" in
The Alamo City Guide written by Stephen Gould in 1882 and
published in New York. The guide included a detailed history of St.
Mark's Parish. The first service in the historic church was on Easter Day,
1875. The booklet describes the church beside Travis Park as
"constructed of cream-colored limestone from local quarries, and is
from plans by elder Upjohn, a celebrated architect, late of New York."
Richard Upjohn was one of the foremost church architects of the
nineteenth century.*

the Missionary Diocese of West Texas, even though the building
had not yet been completed. In the next years, membership grew
and soon included a large number of the best-known Anglo-American names in San Antonio's history.

Land for the church had been donated in 1858 by Vance and
Brothers and Samuel Maverick, who had already deeded the land

Mary A. Maverick, born in 1818 in Alabama, was the wife of Samuel A. Maverick, a leading Texas pioneer. She reared five children and was unusually supportive to a man who was gone a great deal of the time on surveying trips in the untamed frontier of West and South Central Texas. One of her greatest and most lasting contributions to Texas was the memoir that she prepared from her diaries of 1842 through 1857. It was completed in 1881 and developed for limited publication by her son George in 1896. These plus family correspondence that she saved provide one of the most valuable historical documents one can find to learn about San Antonio a century ago. Long active in St. Mark's Episcopal Church, Maverick died in 1898. (Fred Himes illustration)

for Travis Park to the city. After Sam died in 1870, his wife, Mary Ann Adams Maverick, continued for twenty-eight years to devote herself to her family, St. Mark's, and commemoration of Texas history. The bell that rings out over the vestry door in a small bellcote at St. Mark's was once a bronze cannon at the Alamo. In memory of her husband, Mary Maverick donated the cannon, which had been found on the property Samuel Maverick had bought on the northwest corner of the Alamo grounds. In 1874, at Mary's expense, the cannon was cast into a bell by the Meneely Foundry in New York. It weighs 526 pounds.

On a side of the bell is the Texas star with the word "Alamo" in the center. Above the word is the date 1813, the year the green flag of the Republican Army of the North flew for a time over Béxar—what some historians call "the First War of Independence." Below the word "Alamo" on the bell is the date 1836, the year of

Samuel A. Maverick, born in South Carolina in 1803, served the Texans as a fighter during the revolution against Mexico in the 1830s. Like many other land surveyors in Texas at that time, he acquired a great many certificates of land ownership. The Comanches called the surveyor's compass "the thing that steals the land," and surveyors were in constant jeopardy. He was a member of Capt. Jack Hays' Rangers. Maverick and his wife started a dynasty of outstanding descendants, both men and women. He left a legacy, besides his family, of political and material contributions to his hometown. While in the state legislature, he ensured rights for citizens of all ethnic backgrounds. He gave the city Travis Park and the site for the much-needed railroad. Samuel A. Maverick died in 1870 and is buried in San Antonio's first City Cemetery, on the city's East Side. (Fred Himes illustration)

that heroic battle. Inscribed on the opposite side is a Christian prayer.

In his autobiography, Dr. Hugh Young recalled his near-drowning in the river, now memorialized at St. Mark's:

> When I was four years old I clearly remember playing on the bank of the San Antonio River back of our home with my chum, George Dashiell and Della, a Negro girl who looked after us. We had started to run up the bank toward the house when I slipped on pebbles and plunged into the river. Della, terrified, tried to fish me out with a stick; failing, she ran to the house and called Mother, who dashed down and when she arrived at the river saw me whirling by in the rapids below the quiet hole into which I had fallen. Mother dived into the swirling tide, succeeded in grasping my clothes, and was carried down herself until

Madison Square Presbyterian Church, organized in 1882, is on the corner of Camden Street and Lexington Avenue. Located on Madison Square, it was served conveniently by the Alamo and San Pedro Springs streetcar line, two blocks away. The handsome Gothic structure is a reminder today that this was a fine neighborhood in the late nineteenth century. (Author's collection)

stopped by a wooden post, the remains of an old bath house lower down the river. To this she clung until we were rescued by neighbors. I am told that I was apparently lifeless. . . .

So grateful was Hugh Young's father when he learned that his son had been saved that he had a stained-glass window donated to St. Mark's Cathedral depicting Pharaoh's daughter fishing Moses out of the water. The beautiful memorial is near the front of the church on the left, third window back.

Perhaps the quietest wedding ever held for a future president of the United States occurred in the 1930s on short notice at St. Mark's. Attended only by several friends and no relatives, the ceremony was conducted at 7:30 P.M. on Saturday, November 17, 1934. The bride was Claudia Alta Taylor of Karnack, in northeast Texas, known to an admiring world today as Lady Bird Johnson. The groom was Lyndon Baines Johnson, born in Stonewall in the Texas Hill Country in 1908, who in 1963 became the thirty-sixth president of the United States.

Milam Park includes not only historical sites and a children's playground, but an artistic central gazebo donated to the city by the state of Jalisco, Mexico. In the background is the largest mural of its kind in the United States—artist Jesse Trevino's "Spirit of Healing," showing a guardian angel bending over a young boy holding a glowing dove. The forty-by-ninety-foot mural, unveiled on October 7, 1997, is on the front wall of the Santa Rosa Children's Hospital. It is lighted at night. Composed of about 150,000 pieces of cut ceramic tile, the creation took three years in planning and construction. (Photo by author)

Woodlawn Lake, in the foreground, was called West End Lake before the city acquired it and the surrounding property of sixty-two acres for park purposes. In its earlier days it had been a choice hunting spot, and later offered good ranch and dairy land. Peacock School for Boys was founded nearby in 1894; after educating 15,000 students, the twenty-acre facility was deeded in 1973 to the Salvation Army as the Peacock Center. The church in the background is the Shrine of the Little Flower at 906 Kentucky Avenue. It was built in 1931 from more than half a million dollars collected throughout the United States. A replica of a church in France, it is dedicated to St. Therese of Lisieux, a nineteenth-century Carmelite nun who became known worldwide as "the Little Flower." (San Antonio Express-News photo)

11

101 Stories at Alamo Plaza

The story that brings most people to Alamo Plaza, of course, was written in February and March of 1836 by heroic fighters in one of the most stirring battles in the history of the Americas, but there are many lesser-known stories there.

There is the one about the Japanese monument near the giant oak in the convent yard, with its poem engraved in Chinese about two Asian "Alamos"—and another about how the giant oak got there. And the one about the mother and great aunt of two great Texas patriots who lies at rest in the Alamo church sacristy as millions walk by unknowingly. And there is the story of how Samuel Maverick arranged through a friend to have his house built on the old mission grounds of the Alamo. And the one about Will

---

America's Four Most Colorful, Most Romantic Cities

I know nothing more beautiful in the United States—except perhaps the wheat fields near Spokane—than the approach by airplane to certain cities like San Antonio. They rise from the other plains like amber cloud shapes, their skyscrapers, seemingly so incongruous, take on the protective coloration that surrounds them, in a vast area of flatness, they rise like vertical projections of the earth they rest on. . . . San Antonio is, next to San Francisco, New Orleans, and possibly Boston, the most colorful, the most "romantic" city in America.

—John Gunther, *Inside U.S.A.*, 1947

Rogers' criticism of San Antonio's ill treatment of the Alamo in the 1920s; and the story of the first demonstration of barbed wire.

San Antonio's Japanese Monument

Most of the three million people who visit the Alamo every year probably give little thought to the small monument standing under two pecan trees in the convent courtyard. There, for more than eighty years beside the battered remains of the old convento, the stone shaft and its plinth from Japan escaped serious deface- ment during the bitter war between the two nations.

Chinese writing inscribes the face of the gray granite shaft that stands about five feet high and rests on a brown stone. Above the chiseled characters appear the English words: *TO THE MEMORY OF THE HEROES OF THE ALAMO* and at the foot of the shaft it says: *Prof. Shigetaka (Juko) Shiga, Tokyo, San Antonio, Texas, September 1914.*

Dr. Shiga preferred to use formal Chinese characters for the monument. More of these appear on the monument's back, and there you can read this statement in English: *Stone from the native province of Suneemon Torii, The Bonham of Japan; in the province is Nagashino, The Alamo of Japan.*

Shigetaka Shiga, a university professor in Tokyo in the early 1900s, had been moved emotionally by the story of the heroism at the Battle of the Alamo and had noted similarities between the Texas battle and the Battle of Nagashino, a famed battle that took place in the 1500s near Shiga's birthplace. Among other similarities, both battles featured young commanders (William Barret Travis and Sadamasa Okudaira) as well as heroes (James Bonham and Suneemon Torii) who sneaked through enemy lines to seek help and returned to participate in the fighting.

Professor Shiga, who lectured in the United States, wanted to do something to help develop better relations between the two countries, so he decided to have a monument made in Japan on which he would tell in poetry the story not only of the battles in Texas and Japan, but also of the Chinese defenders in the eighth-century Battle of Suiyang during the An Lushan Rebellion. The granite shaft rests on a stone taken from the battlefield site at Nagashino near the grave of Suneemon Torii. A translation of Professor Shiga's poem by a professor at Our Lady of the Lake University, Dr. Margit Nagy, has been placed beside the monument.

At a ceremony on November 6, 1914, Dr. Shiga, San Antonio city officials, and more than 100 prominent Texans including descendants of the Alamo defenders saw the Daughters of the Republic of Texas take possession of the engraved shaft that stands in the convent courtyard. In Dr. Shiga's hometown of Okazaki is a similar marker—a stone also found near the grave of Torii and also engraved with the poem that appears on the granite shaft at the Alamo.

The Giant Oak in the Alamo Courtyard

The giant live oak in the Alamo courtyard on the north side of the church, with its massive limbs bent low to the ground, seems to most visitors to have lived there since the historic battle. In 1994, Charles Whall told how, eighty-two years before, his father had loaded the young tree onto a special mule-drawn wagon at the Classen ranch north of San Antonio and made a five-hour journey to the Alamo.

Charles recalled how, as a six-year-old, he had sat on the walls of the long barracks with his brother and sister and watched as his father and three workers spent three to four hours digging a ten-by-ten-foot hole for the tree. He said they found no artifacts in the soil—only parts from Model T Fords, discarded there from a nearby garage.

Mother of Patriots is Buried in the Alamo

The mother and great aunt of the only two Texas-born signers of the Republic's Declaration of Independence is buried inside the Alamo. She was the wife of Juan Manuel Ruíz, one of the Béxar ranchers remembered for helping to supply beef-on-the-hoof to Gen. Bernardo de Gálvez's Spanish military forces supporting the revolution of the American colonies against the British from 1779 to 1782. One of her sons was the Texas patriot José Francisco Ruíz—and statesman José Antonio Navarro was Ruíz's nephew. Ruíz's son, Francisco Antonio Ruíz, was alcalde (mayor) of San Antonio at the time of the Battle of the Alamo.

Although her husband had been buried in San Antonio's church of San Fernando in 1797, Manuela de la Peña Ruíz declared firmly in her will that she should be buried in the church of Mission San Antonio de Valero. A wry family tradition says it was because "she didn't want to drown" in one of the recurrent floods that sometimes soaked the floor of the parish church in Main Plaza. She was laid to rest in the sacristy—to the left as one exits the Alamo church—on May 18, 1834, where she lies today, another reminder of the deep Tejano ties to the battle for independence.

A descendant of these great Texans, San Antonian Adolph Herrera, born in 1913, recalls the times around 1918 when he went with his grandfather to pray briefly and place fresh flowers at the burial places of Juan Manuel Ruíz and José Francisco Ruíz inside San Fernando Cathedral, and Manuela de la Peña Ruíz in the Alamo church.

The Mavericks' Home at the Alamo

Since before the Texas Republic—and to this day—the Maverick family, more than any other, has influenced San Antonio. It is one of the rare families on Earth that has contributed two words to the English language. One of these, an eponym, filled a special need and has joined the world's literature.

Samuel Maverick was one of the largest landowners in Texas in the mid-1800s. Because he paid little personal attention to the cattle on one of his landholdings, many of them went unbranded and, roaming free, were assumed to be "Maverick's" by the neighboring cattlemen. "Maverick" now means independent; nonconformist.

The other word, "gobbledygook," means the complicated language used sometimes by high officials—words "too long on Latin, too short on communicating." When Maury Maverick, Sr., coined this "turkey gobble" word during World War II, he was chairman of the Smaller War Plants Corporation in Washington.

The house of Samuel and Mary Maverick in Alamo Plaza was on former property of Mission San Antonio de Valero. In 1849, the Mavericks moved temporarily into what they described as "an old Mexican house" already on the property and made arrangements for building the two-story house shown here. Mary Maverick wrote in her memoirs about their first home on the plaza: "This house was situated on the lot now formed by the West line of Alamo Plaza and the South line of Houston Street. At that time, and for some years thereafter, Houston (Paseo) Street was not in existence." (Daughters of the Republic of Texas Library photo)

From the 1800s, successive generations of Mavericks have produced civic leaders, politicians, soldiers, preservationists, and writers. The most famous among them have been nonconformists—and their most recent member, Maury Maverick, Jr., for many years a columnist for the San Antonio *Express-News*, has described himself as "retired civil-liberties lawyer, former Texas legislator, and former university instructor in political science." His pithy columns provide an uncommon and valuable perspective.

This benign dynasty of civic benefactors began when Samuel A. Maverick, a South Carolinian, a graduate of Yale, and a lawyer, came to San Antonio de Béxar in September 1835, took an active part in the battle for Béxar that same year, was a signer of the Texas Declaration of Independence in 1836, served in the House of the Texas Republic as a representative from Béxar, was mayor of San Antonio in 1839 and 1840, and was one of the commissioners representing the secessionist states who negotiated with Maj. Gen. D. E. Twiggs for the surrender of United States military forces in San Antonio in 1861. The census of 1860 listed Samuel A. Maverick as "land agent" and rated him the wealthiest person in Bexar County, with real property valued at $177,000, personal property at $13,000, and eighteen slaves.

He desired more than anything to live as near the Alamo as possible, where many of his friends had laid down their lives. In 1849, he persuaded the city surveyor, his friend François Giraud, to survey a site at the northwest corner of the former mission. Giraud obligingly cut off a northwest corner of the mission site and the entire corral area on the northeast, and made the boundary the inner wall of the buildings around the mission walls instead of their outer line. This provided space within the former Alamo grounds for Maverick's exclusive personal use.

Maverick built a two-story house on the northwest corner of the old Alamo mission. Mary liked the house especially because it was spacious and on higher, "more healthful" ground than their former home on the northeast corner of Main Plaza. The Maverick house and its land on Alamo Plaza were later replaced by the

Maverick Hotel on Alamo and Houston streets, across from the post office. The Maverick Hotel was followed at the same site by the Maverick Bank, the first five-story building in San Antonio.

A Little-Known San Antonio Mural

On the north side of Alamo Plaza is the United States Post Office and Federal Building. It was completed in 1937 to replace the spectacular, castellated Romanesque Post Office and Federal Building designed by James Riely Gordon and constructed in 1889. Not many people know that in the vestibule inside the main entrance is a remarkable fresco mural by the noted artist Howard Cook. It is titled: *San Antonio's Importance in Texas History.*

Cook had been awarded the contract for the mural after a national competition. His pen drawings and woodcuts had appeared in leading magazines of the day, and he had been given a Guggenheim Fellowship that enabled him to live with his wife in Taxco, Mexico, while he created a fresco mural for Hotel Taxqueño. For the San Antonio fresco, Cook painted the mural on fresh plaster, using a mixture of dry colors and distilled water. The 750 square feet of work surface took two and one-half years from planning to completion, with Cook and his assistants working full-time after he came to San Antonio. The plaster work consumed more than five tons of sand and cement, as well as yards of slaked lime.

Cook said of the mural:

> My true aim in the subject matter was to present the underlying spirit of the people and the forces which had built up the first Republic and later the state of Texas. I had a definite conviction that I would not permit a parade of empty historical costume or a static compendium of patriots.
>
> From the Federal offices, the Judges' bench, the engineers' and janitors' departments, and civic organizations, came the men and women who would live day by day with the murals. They generously helped and encouraged me

with solution of research problems and often posed for me.

What Will Rogers Really Said

Will Rogers, the newspaper columnist and humorist of stage and screen, wrote a historic comment after he had visited the Old Trail Drivers Convention in San Antonio in 1926. His words have been widely misquoted and misinterpreted ever since. He said:

> I have run into a good many pleasant things in my jaunts, but the other day I hit San Antonio—what used to be before Progress hit it, one of the three unique cities of America.
>
> It is a great old town, is San Antonio, even if they have got a filling station in connection with the Alamo. You have to sacrifice something to Progress, but I never thought it would be the Alamo.
>
> I had the most wonderful day there I think I ever had.

For years, publicists have been saying that Will Rogers once called San Antonio one of the *four* unique cities in the United States. Some even have attributed the statement to the famous writer O. Henry, who set a number of his short stories in San Antonio.

Some who misquote Will Rogers say he actually named "the three other cities." These, they say, are San Francisco, Boston, and New Orleans. In truth, he seems by his statement to have withdrawn San Antonio from his unnamed list of three unique cities, and the reason he gave for that was the ugliness of the Alamo compound and its surroundings that one can observe today in photographs taken at that time. At one time, on the north end of Alamo Plaza, the large signs of the Clifton George Company automobile dealership and Ford Motor Company seemed to dominate the entire former mission compound.

Today, it is evident that the Daughters of the Republic of Texas have greatly improved the appearance of the plaza and the former

"Above is an admirable illustration OF THE **HISTORIC ALAMO**, as it is at present, together with the Convent Building, adjoining the Alamo proper, as modernized and converted into a mammoth Business House, by the late Honore Grenet . . . .

Strangers are cordially welcomed here and shown the various

points of interest about the historic buildings . . . . .

This Mammoth Store has a business second to none in this City.

DEALING IN

Groceries, Provisions, Drygoods, Queensware, Boots AND Shoes,

Whiskeys, Wines, Beer, Cigars, Tobacco AND Country Produce.

The location is on Alamo Plaza---with the Street Cars passing every few minutes during the day, until late at night. This makes it one of the most eligible business sites in San Antonio".

In 1878, Honoré Grenet used the two-story Alamo convento building as a grocery, clothing, tobacco, and liquor store, converting the former mission church into a storehouse. He covered the stone structures with a wooden facade that he believed gave the appearance of a fort. When Grenet died, his estate issued the handbill above to advertise the buildings for sale. The property was bought in 1884 by a grocery firm called Hugo & Schmeltzer. At Adina De Zavala's request, the owners promised her historical society first option to buy if they ever planned to sell it. In 1903, her strategy paid off. She had recently welcomed Clara Driscoll into her organization, and Miss Driscoll, from a wealthy family in Corpus Christi, advanced money that resulted in the Daughters of the Republic of Texas' obtaining custody of the property. They have operated it since 1905 for the State of Texas. In 1913, influenced by a faction opposing preservationist Adina De Zavala, Lieutenant Governor William H. Mayes issued a decree—while Governor Oscar B. Colquitt was out of the state—to permit the demolishing of the upper floor of the convento. (Daughters of the Republic of Texas Library photo)

One evening in 1887, when Steve Waterhouse took his lady friend
Beatrice Brinklow to the Opera House in Alamo Plaza to see the great
Edwin Booth in Hamlet, he drove his rented buggy, pulled by a team
named Prince and Nellie. As described by Joseph Gallegly in his novel,
The Adventures of Steve Waterhouse, Steve thought "the cloppity-
cloppity-cloppity-clop of the horses' hoofs on the wooden blocks" as
they rode out on Alamo Plaza "was a pleasant sound to hear." Hellie,
the young man Steve had hired as his horse-holder, jogged behind the
buggy. Steve recalled the scene at the plaza circle:

"Here the crowd of vehicles was as great as you could imagine.
Cabs, broughams, barouches (although but a pair of these), landaus,
phaetons (numerous), dogcarts, buckboards, surreys, gigs, carriages
and buggies all fought with one another to be in the same place at the
same time. Cabbies swore (some in sweet, melodious Irish tones; others
in impure Castillian); fine ladies expressed contempt; old men in
buggies threatened. . . . Seeing what a mix-up we would get into if we
went any further ahead, I fetched a compass to my left, driving quite up
against the Alamo itself, and along in front of the Menger Hotel, in a
short time reaching a point not thirty yards from the main doors of the
Grand Opera House, in front of which I stopped, and helping Beatrice
from the hack, gave orders to the mozo, Hellie." (Fred Himes
illustration)

mission grounds by arranging the purchase of the property surrounding the Alamo and landscaping the area. Now it is the white shaft of the Cenotaph that draws your attention.

The Church Building Used as a Fort

Across the river from the main part of San Antonio—with its presidio, villa, parish church, and two plazas—was Mission San Antonio de Valero. At least one Franciscan priest from the Apostolic College of Santa Cruz de Querétaro in Northern New Spain (i.e., Mexico) was always there pursuing his calling of teaching the Indians to become useful Spanish citizens as well as Christians. The missionaries were assisted by a few soldiers. For many

In 1888, Alamo Plaza, with its former mission church and greatly altered two-story convento that had been made into a wholesale grocery, was graced by the Alamo Beer Garden, Saloon, Restaurant. Humorist Alex E. Sweet wrote in 1883 that a visitor to the town found that every shop and store near the plaza was named "Alamo." After visiting five Alamo saloons, the visitor was escorted by a policeman to a lock-up in one of the rooms of the Alamo, "the only building in that part of town that did not have the word 'Alamo' plastered on it as big as a circus poster." (Daughters of the Republic of Texas Library photo)

By 1922, the smaller shops next to the Alamo had been replaced by the Standard Motor Sales Company and a store selling United States Tires. Not only could you buy an automobile beside the Alamo but also the gasoline to run it. Standing in front of the Alamo are delegates of the Brotherhood of Locomotive Firemen and Enginemen at their 29th Convention on June 4, 1922. (Photo by E. O. Goldbeck. Gift of T. Gordon Mattingly. Courtesy Daughters of the Republic of Texas Library)

years, only one precarious footbridge joined the two communities. They seemed to have no need for closer communication.

A separate town, first called "Pueblo del Alamo" and later "Alamo City," eventually grew up around the mission. It included the neighborhood known as "La Villita" that had arisen around the houses of the soldiers, many of whom had married local Indians. Later, in the mid-1800s, it was the home of many newly arrived Germans.

The mission church and adjacent buildings at the Alamo might not even exist today had it not, after its abandonment, become a military headquarters in 1803 for a cavalry unit recruited at the town of El Alamo near Parras, Mexico—and more than thirty years later, a fort used by both the Mexican forces in 1835 and the Texians in 1836. It was from the "Alamo soldiers," who were quartered for many years at the former mission, that the Alamo got its name. As cavalry troops, they were known as a "flying" unit, with the full title of *La Segunda Compañia Volante de San Carlos de Alamo de Parras*.

A new parish was established for the community, called *El Pueblo de San José y Santiago del Alamo*.

"Bob Wire" in Alamo Plaza

One of the most historic events ever staged in Texas took place in Alamo Plaza in 1876. The plaza had been selected as the site because it was near the Menger Hotel where stockmen stayed, and offered wide-open space, virtually free of human activity. This was to be the location of the sensational demonstration by "Bet-a-Million" Gates and Pete McManus to prove the extraordinary value to cattlemen of barbed wire. It was the product of the I. L. Ellwood Manufacturing Company in DeKalb, Illinois.

An eyewitness account of what happened when John Warne Gates came to San Antonio was reported by W. D. Hornaday in the *Express* on February 28, 1910, only thirty-four years after the event. Hornaday interviewed Pete McManus, by then a respected San Antonio businessman, soon after his retirement from many years of selling barbed wire. McManus told how he and Gates had come to San Antonio in 1876 to demonstrate the practicality of barbed wire for fencing. He said, according to the *Express*:

> We made our first demonstration upon Alamo Plaza for the benefit of a crowd of cattlemen who were gathered there from different parts of Southwest Texas. At that time Alamo Plaza was a mudhole. Mr. Gates and I set up the posts and strung four strands of barbed wire, making a corral of considerable size. Some of the cowboys were skeptical, and Gates and I were jollied a good deal as we went about our work of preparing for the test. A bunch of range cattle were driven into the corral and the ranchmen expected to see them go through or over the fence, but the wires held them without trouble.
>
> Mr. Gates and I gave other demonstrations of the practicality of the fencing material and took some good orders for the wire. That was really the beginning of the barbed wire industry. Mr. Gates saw that it was a good thing and he began its manufacture.

In 1876, John Warne ("Bet-A-Million") Gates and Pete P. McManus staged a demonstration in Alamo Plaza that changed the history of Texas perhaps as much as did the coming of the windmill to the West. They put up the barbed wire in the plaza, then drove some range cattle into the corral and agitated them into milling excitedly about. The ranchers staying in nearby hotels were astonished to find that the thin barbed wires held the cattle securely. (Drawing courtesy José Cisneros and Trinity University, San Antonio)

The production of barbed wire in the Illinois plant jumped in one year from less than three million pounds to nearly thirteen million—and then skyrocketed.

A book titled *Bet a Million!* by Lloyd Wendt and Herman Kogan tells how Gates—a lifelong gambler—got his nickname in London; how he became the nation's largest barbed wire manufacturer; helped found the Texas Company (Texaco); and developed Port Arthur, Texas. His American Steel and Wire Company became the world's first billion-dollar corporation, United States Steel. He rivaled the Wall Street financier J. P. Morgan. Internationally famous, Gates died at age fifty-six in Paris on August 9, 1911, and after a funeral in the American church in Rue de Berri, his body was transported by ship to New York, where he was buried with great honor in Woodlawn Cemetery.

In their biography of "Bet-A-Million" Gates, Wendt and Kogan speak often of Pete McManus. This "affable Irishman" was the traveling salesman who inspired Gates to leave his hardware store and wife in Turner Junction, Illinois, when he was just twenty-one, and to begin selling barbed wire "to make big money." Gates had been sent by the wire manufacturer to assist McManus in San Antonio.

It seems evident that the official plaque beside City Hall, saying Military Plaza was the site of the historic demonstration, is not only incorrect and misplaced, but is misinforming all who read it. Military Plaza was always filled day and night with hay wagons and vendor stands, and had no space for a corralled cattle demonstration. The plaque was rushed to approval to meet a deadline of July 30, 1971, for a convention in San Antonio of the Texas Barbed Wire Collectors Association. Under close examination in Austin, there seemed to be little evidence to support the idea that Military Plaza was the site of the demonstration. Not until May did the president of the association write with a great sense of relief to the Texas State Historical Survey Committee that he finally had discovered "the missing link." It was a recollection of "an old trail driver" of Alpine, Texas, who reported that he remembered a time fifty years earlier, in March 1878, when he had stopped briefly in San Antonio and had seen barbed wire being sold by "John Gates on the main plaza between the Southern Hotel and the Cathedral."

But according to his biography, John Gates was far from San Antonio in 1878, two years after his famous demonstrations, busily engaged in building a steel empire. Perhaps the error will be corrected someday and a Texas State historical marker will be placed in Alamo Plaza to memorialize the event that led to the wide use of barbed wire and a new way of producing beef cattle. Along with the windmill, barbed wire changed the West forever.

Making Memories at the Menger

The arrival of the first railroad in San Antonio on February 19, 1877—the Galveston, Harrisburg and San Antonio (also known as the Sunset Lines and later as the Southern Pacific)—was the beginning of an immense change in the city's fortunes. Commerce expanded enormously.

For two days, and far into the night, San Antonio celebrated the momentous event with revelry, torchlight parades, and speeches—both in the plazas and over on Bowen's Island, then a beer garden and pleasure resort, where the Tower Life Building now stands. From the balcony of the Menger Hotel, Texas Governor Richard Bennett Hubbard addressed the crowd overflowing into Alamo Plaza. Prominent in the great throng were San Antonio Mayor J. M. French and Thomas W. Peirce, president of the railroad.

It was more than a San Antonio celebration—hundreds came from Galveston and Houston. The plaza rocked with the festivities. There were marching military units and bands, the 7th Cavalry, and citizens with torches escorting the officials to the Menger Hotel for the public reception honoring the arrival of the 'iron horse.'

When celebrities, as well as stock raisers and other businessmen, came to San Antonio, the Menger was the place to stay. The arrival of the Sunset Lines coincided with an addition of forty-five rooms to the Menger's east side and in 1882 the hotel was expanded again. For more than a century, and to this day, the Menger has hosted generals, presidents, ex-presidents, presidential candidates, military heroes, cattlemen, tycoons, famous athletes, artists, authors, and actors—and plain people.

It was established in 1859 by William A. Menger; a cooper in Germany, he started a barrel factory in San Antonio after he arrived in 1847. With brewmaster Carl Stein, he began manufacturing beer in 1855, attracting out-of-towners who wanted to stay a day or more. To meet the demand, the hotel was built nearby, expanding the boarding house that was operated by his German-born wife, Mary Baumschlueter Guenther. Later, Menger hired Charles Degen as his brewmaster.

The indefatigable five-foot-tall Menger established a policy of self-sufficiency. The hotel had, and still has, a water supply from a capacious artesian well. Its beer and wine were stored in caverns beneath the building, which still exist. Menger beer was cooled by water from an acequia that once flowed past the Alamo and through the hotel. When the technology for manufacturing gas arrived in San Antonio in 1879, Menger installed machines to fuel 100 lights.

Of first importance from its earliest days were the Menger's popular locally brewed beer and good food—served in style on the premises or packed for lunches to carry along in the days before roadside restaurants. Mrs. Menger set the original standard for good cooking—plain, at first. The hotel became famous for its dinners of wild game, including turtles from the San Antonio River. Later, in the 1890s, such delicacies as "*shad roe a la Portugaise, salamis* of prairie chicken with *crepes* Monte Carlo, roast duck with hominy, and Menger mince pie" were served in the Colonial Room. Chefs from Europe had brought cuisine that Texans found both exotic and tasty.

The world's attention was focused on the Menger Hotel's culinary skills in 1992, when the *Wall Street Journal*, *Time* magazine, and the *Economist* wrote about presidential candidate Bill Clinton's enthusiasm for the Menger's mango ice cream, which he asked for when he arrived in San Antonio. He had first tasted it there in

1972, when he was with presidential candidate George McGovern's campaign. The ice cream has been on the menu for a least a century, and it is said that at first the mangoes came from a tree in the hotel courtyard.

The Menger courtyard has been especially favored from its beginning. Visitors from the East, as well as Texans, rhapsodized over its beauty. A Fort Worth writer observed in *Bunkers Monthly* in 1928 that "the Menger *patio* of a moonlight evening . . . is one of the very choice spots in the universe. . . ." In earlier years, one could see wild game hanging there; later, venison, wild turkey, wild geese, and quail were kept cool in the cellars beneath the hotel. The courtyard was eventually made into a tropical garden, featuring two alligators to fascinate the guests. Today, it offers a swimming pool.

The Menger's glittering balls, carefree cotillions, and masquerades were reported excitedly in the newspapers, but it was far more than a favorite place for parties. It was not uncommon for an Army wife staying at a frontier fort to come to the Menger to have her baby, and more than one man and woman spent their declining years and last days there.

Richard King of the great King Ranch spent much time at the hotel in his last years. He had begun accumulating his enormous holdings in 1853 with the purchase of 15,500 acres for $300. He and his family later expanded it to 614,000 acres, stocked with tens of thousands of cattle. He died at the Menger in 1885, and the funeral services were held in the Menger parlor.

Joaquin Miller, the popular rage of London as "the Byron of Oregon," stayed at the Menger when he stopped on a lecture tour in 1897. The eccentric "Poet of the Sierras" was enthusiastically received. But the poet who created an even greater stir at the hotel and throughout San Antonio was Oscar Wilde, who visited in 1882. The *San Antonio Light* covered his visit in great detail. The "Apostle of Aestheticism," said the *Light*, was dressed in a "drab velvet jacket." He had a "white waistcoat, blue cravat, white lace ruffles about his neck and sleeves, light drab knee-length trousers, scarlet stockings and black slippers with large silver buckles." His long black curls hung to his shoulders.

Wilde gave a lecture at the Turner Theatre on "Decorative Art" and then went sightseeing. Later, in New Orleans, he told a reporter of the *Picayune* about San Antonio's missions. "These old Spanish churches with their picturesque remains and domes and their handsome carved stone work, standing amid the verdure and sunshine of a Texas prairie, gave me a strange thrill of pleasure."

The Menger has been enlarged and renovated numerous times in its more than a century of life. In 1992, a $9 million renovation added to its space and decor. Today, one can stay overnight there or stroll through the storied lobby and patio and visit the elegant dining room and ballroom and the bar where Teddy Roosevelt and some of his Rough Riders raised hopeful toasts. The Menger has been designated by the National Trust for Historic Preservation as a "Historic Hotel"—one of "a unique family of fine hotels recognized for architectural preservation and unsurpassed standards of hospitality."

Roosevelt's Rough Riders

Theodore Roosevelt stayed at the Menger in 1892, en route to a hunting trip at Ike Pryor's ranch near Uvalde. This ardent outdoorsman who was later to be the U.S. president (from 1901 to 1909) signed the register again in 1898 when he was in town to help train the "Rough Riders," so named by a *San Antonio Express* reporter on May 3, 1898.

Theodore Roosevelt wrote in his book *The Rough Riders* that he and the other officers disliked their nickname at first, but changed their minds after generals of the division and brigade began calling their organization—the First United States Volunteer Cavalry—"the Rough Riders."

In San Antonio, one often hears that at the Menger Bar—a replica of a bar in the House of Lords in London—Teddy Roosevelt recruited troops for his Rough Riders. Although there is no evidence of his recruiting, he did go there more than once, and so did some of his officers and men.

It should be noted that after the U.S. Congress authorized the raising of three cavalry regiments for use in what came to be known as the Spanish-American War, the response of volunteers was overwhelming. Those wishing to be in Roosevelt's cavalry unit flocked to San Antonio to the volunteer cavalry's headquarters on what is now Riverside Golf Course on Roosevelt Avenue near Fair Avenue, where they were organized and trained. There was no need to recruit soldiers at the Menger but some volunteers surely found their way there. Roosevelt said that "the difficulty in organizing was not in selecting, but in rejecting men."

In the year preceding the Spanish-American War, Roosevelt had been assistant secretary of the Navy. He wrote later that, although his political party was in opposition, "I had preached, with all the fervor and zeal I possessed, our duty to intervene in Cuba, and to take this opportunity of driving the Spaniard from the Western World."

After the United States declared war on Spain on April 24, 1898, in support of Cuban independence forces and spurred by the destruction of the U.S. battleship *Maine* in Havana Harbor with 260 killed, Roosevelt volunteered for service and was commissioned a lieutenant colonel directly under the commander, Col. Leonard Wood. They were given permission to accept volunteers primarily from the four Territories of that time—New Mexico, Arizona, Oklahoma, and Indian Territory, but they did accept others. Many came from Texas, and many of these had been Texas Rangers.

Enthusiasm to volunteer was amazing. Men enlisting as ordinary soldiers came from Harvard, Yale, Princeton, Columbia, and other universities, as well as from elite clubs such as the Somerset of Boston and the Knickerbocker of New York. College athletes, city clerks, rugged cowboys, and even Indians volunteered, but the vast majority were what Roosevelt called "Southwesterners, a splendid set of men."

Troop E, formed in Santa Fe, New Mexico, had six sign up as a body on the same day. They made up the entire composing room of the local newspaper, *The New Mexican*, which, not surprisingly, missed an edition.

The Rough Riders, with their 1,000 men, 1,200 horses and mules, plus equipment, departed San Antonio in two trains on

Sunday, May 29, 1898, headed for Tampa, Florida, to join other U.S. military forces for war in Cuba. Departure was from the depot of the San Antonio and Aransas Pass ("the SAP") Railroad on Alamo and Flores streets (razed in 1939). Their send-off by San Antonio's city fathers and the townfolk the evening before was spectacular. Professor Beck's band played a concert climaxed by the musicians firing pistols in the air. The Rough Riders joined exuberantly in the gunfire. Some 2,000 rounds were fired amid cowboy whoops, while bandsmen and civilians scurried for cover. Someone cut the electric light source, and in the darkness everyone rushed into town to continue celebrating.

At the time of their departure, Col. Leonard Wood had been in San Antonio about three weeks, having arrived on May 6, and Teddy Roosevelt, who had arrived on May 16, had spent less than two weeks in the city before heading for adventure in Cuba.

12

Celebrations — A Colorful Blend of Cultures

San Antonio's people—a constantly growing mixture of national and ethnic groups—have always taken time away from the routine of their lives to rejoice and make merry at every opportunity, and for whatever seemed like a valid reason. From the early days of the Hispanic majority, through the days when the Germans were in the ascendancy, until the period when the Anglos were most numerous, the fun-making and joyous entertainments have continued. From processions to oompah bands to rodeos and country dancing, San Antonio has always been, as Liz Carpenter says, "a town where all the people know how to live."

235

Still Discovering this 280-Year-Old City

San Antonio's unique cultural montage—with its large variety of ethnic groups living together compatibly as nowhere else in the world—is beginning to attract wider attention nationally. San Antonio is truly "a mix of influences," affecting all forms of its human creativity.

According to Frank Scheck, writing in the August 2, 1997 *Christian Science Monitor*, the culture of San Antonio is sufficient reason alone to base a trip to the eighth largest city in the United States. In an article titled, 'Move Over, Santa Fe, For Arty San Antonio,' the author says the city has more culture than many realize. 'It is a polyglot of ethnic cultures, reflected in a synergistic arts scene that is as hot as the sweltering summer temperatures that grip the region.'

'Forget the Alamo!' said a long headline in *The Washington Post* of August 17, 1997, 'today's San Antonio has little to do with that symbol of doomed Anglo imperialism. It's a thriving capital of Hispanic culture, and a magnet for multicultural tourism.' Staff writer Gary Lee fell ravingly in love with Tejano music in San Antonio, saying that 'as musical trends go, Tejano is hotter than a mouthful of jalapeños,' and concluding that it epitomizes the city's fusion of national traditions. He wrote: 'Born in the cactus-covered towns straddling the border, Tejano is to music what Tex-Mex is to food: a mix of styles from both countries. The lyrics, sagas of heartache, new love and hot emotions, closely resemble those of American country music. But the instruments, an assortment of drums, horns, vocalists, stem more from the Mexican tradition. I was struck by the finely tuned mix of English and Spanish in which Tejano shows are conducted. And the accordion, a constant in every Tejano band, was borrowed from the polka music favored by German immigrants who settled heavily in southwest Texas in the mid-1800s. This mix of influences, I came to realize, is what San Antonio is all about.'

Tejano food, music, dance, amusements, traditional dress, and other art—both folk and professional—have been embodied in San Antonio's fiesta customs from its earliest days as a community. The spirit of Mexican fiesta music, dance, and costume is exemplified each year on the River Walk at the Arneson River Theater. Every Tuesday, Friday, and Saturday during the summer months, Fiesta Noche del Rio is presented there beside Rosita's Bridge—named for Rosita Fernández, who, as a beautifully costumed singer and dancer, has for decades represented San Antonio's Hispanic culture and who was dubbed "San Antonio's First Lady of Song" by Lady Bird Johnson when she was First Lady of the United States.

Fiestas are a tradition in both Spain and Mexico. The people of Spain—from whom the Texas Hispanics have inherited much of their appreciation for the fullness of living—have used fiestas to embrace the soul of life from its beginning to its inevitable end. Thousands of fiestas are held each year in Spain. Every town and village has an annual fiesta for its patron saint. In addition, the primary days of the religious liturgical calendar throughout the year call for even more fiestas.

In Mexico, fiestas are an ancient tradition. According to the Mexican Department of Tourism, some 5,000 to 6,000 fiestas are held there each year. Before the conquest of Mexico by Spain, religious fiestas were for the pagan deities, and since then they have been for Christian saints. According to folklorist Frances Toor:

> Even after four centuries, the Catholic fiestas have some pagan elements and preserve some of the primitive color and beauty in dances, costumes, and decorations.
>
> The fiesta-makers are humble folk. A fiesta is their highest expression of community life. Everyone cooperates, giving unselfishly of his means and time. It is also their highest artistic expression because they bring to it the best they are able to create—dances, music, drama, costumes, fireworks, and all the ritual arts.

The Tejanos of San Antonio continue to celebrate both religious and civic holidays whose beginnings predate the first days of the Republic of Texas in 1836. There was a time, now long gone, when San Antonians celebrated some religious holidays with horse races in the downtown streets and with bullfights in Franklin Square after the morning religious services. Now also gone are the days of cockfights in Main Plaza that prompted shocked exclamations from visitors from the United States, although, at times, a goodly number of Anglos could be seen among the spectators.

Tejanos celebrate enthusiastically all of San Antonio's holidays—national, Texan, or local—including the mammoth annual commemoration of the Texan defeat of the Mexican army under the command of that country's president, Gen. Santa Anna, on April 21, 1836, beside the San Jacinto River near today's Houston. They also celebrate some holidays of Mexico.

Most spectacular are the Tejano celebrations of religious holidays, such as Good Friday, when great crowds participate, while costumed men and women re-enact the last days and hours of Christ's suffering—Roman soldiers harassing the cross-bearing "Christ" as he drags his heavy burden slowly from Market Square to the front of San Fernando Cathedral where, amidst the throngs of people, he is attached to the cross that then is raised to a vertical position. This observance of *Vía Cruces*, the Way of the Cross, is one of several presented in San Antonio, most notably at the Guadalupe parish.

Annually, for nine days before Christmas, Tejanos have re-enacted the search by Joseph and Mary for a sheltered birthplace for Christ in dramas called *Las Posadas* presented in many neighborhoods. With the city's growth, posadas have moved to the churches. The most publicized re-enactment is the annual *Gran Posada*, a dramatized procession with some 200 participants. It begins at Farmers Market and passes through El Mercado, and past the Spanish Governor's Palace, City Hall, and the County Courthouse to San Fernando Cathedral. Every December, the San Antonio Conservation Society sponsors a colorful evening, Las Posadas, along the River Walk, and, as a sequel, it sponsors *Los*

Pastores (the Shepherds) at Mission San José each January. The Guadalupe Players of Our Lady of Guadalupe Church present a "churchyard drama of conflict, heavenly intervention and jubilation."

Another special day is the Blessing of the Animals on January 17, or the nearest Sunday. Also traditionally celebrated are June 13, the feast day of Saint Anthony of Padua, the patron saint of San Antonio, and the five-day period beginning on St. John the Baptist Day, June 24, and ending on Saints Peter and Paul Day, June 29.

When Col. Robert E. Lee was serving in San Antonio in 1858, he wrote to his wife that seeing "the Mexicans" cavorting about the town on horses to celebrate St. John's Day on June 24 made him wonder about the suffering of the animals in the heat. He wrote: "I did not know before that St. John set so high a value upon equitation."

Our Lady of Guadalupe

Guadalupe Day, December 12, is a glorious occasion for many San Antonians. A few years ago, the former rector of San Fernando Cathedral, Father Virgil Elizondo, began presenting a televised religious program broadcast to twenty-six cities nationwide and into parts of Central America and Mexico on the Univision Las Americas Network. The program continues annually to honor *La Virgen de Guadalupe*, Our Lady of Guadalupe. The televised celebration is called *Las Américas Saluden a su Madre* or "The Americas Salute Their Mother."

It does not take long, when looking at the professional and folk art of Tejanos—including their inner-city murals—to perceive that Our Lady of Guadalupe plays a vital role in their minds and in the most mundane aspects of their everyday lives. Tejano culture cannot be understood without learning what to unbelievers is an incredible story that began in 1531 in Mexico. It is the story of Our Lady of Guadalupe, and the widespread and fervent belief that has made *La Virgen de Guadalupe*, the mother of Jesus, a very visible figure in many facets of Tejano life.

According to tradition, the Virgin appeared to Juan Diego on Tepeyac Hill several times and asked him to tell the local bishop to construct a chapel on the site. The bishop asked Juan to give him some sign that his story was true, so the Virgin told Juan Diego to pick a bouquet of roses that were growing nearby even though they were out of season. He carried the roses to the bishop in his cloak, and as he unfolded it, the Virgin's image was revealed printed on the cloak. The bishop authorized the construction, which another prelate completed.

After years of investigation, the Vatican declared the apparitions authentic, but Catholics are not required by church teaching to believe, as a matter of faith, in their authenticity. Papal recognition was given to Our Lady of Guadalupe in 1754, when Benedict XIV proclaimed her the patroness of all New Spain—all the Americas—and declared December 12 her feast day.

Puzzling to many, Juan Diego's cloak is still intact and bears the so-far scientifically unexplained image of the Virgin. It is enshrined over the altar of the modern Basilica of Our Lady of Guadalupe in Mexico City. Pope John Paul II made a visit to Our Lady of Guadalupe parish in San Antonio one of his primary stops, and a place for an address, when he came in September of 1987.

Cinco de Mayo and Diez y Seis

Tejanos nourish vivid memories of triumphs in the homeland of their forefathers—and all other San Antonians seem to enjoy what could be good reasons for joining the merrymaking. Two of Tejanos' favorite civic observances are *Cinco de Mayo*, celebrated on the fifth of May, and *Diez y Seis de Septiembre*, "Sixteenth of September," also called only "*Diez y Seis*." Celebration of *Cinco de Mayo* usually goes on for three days, with feasting, dancing, and colorful traditional costumes.

On May 5, 1862, near the city of Puebla, seventy-eight miles from Mexico City, 6,500 French soldiers approached a defensive force of some 5,500 Mexican soldiers and civilians. The French were en route to Mexico City, sent there by Emperor Napoleon III to establish an empire in the region. After the battle, Gen. Ignacio

Seguín Zaragoza (who, incidentally, had been born at Presidio La Bahía, near today's Goliad, Texas, and was related to the Seguíns of San Antonio) wrote to his president, Benito Juárez: "It is 4:30. The French Army was defeated. Our troops have defeated them."

The victory in 1862 delayed by one year the French conquest of Mexico and helped thwart Napoleon's grand plan for a permanent empire there—an event that would have drastically changed United States history. On June 19, 1867, Ferdinand Maximilian—who had been for a brief time the Emperor of Mexico—and two of his Mexican generals, Miguel Miramón and Tomás Mejía, were executed by order of returning president Juárez.

Mexican Independence Day, celebrated on September 14, 15, and 16, is somewhat like the American Fourth of July. San Antonio's Tejanos have traditionally celebrated it with enthusiasm. To the people of Mexico and their descendants, it commemorates the beginning of the revolution in September 1810 that ended when Col. Agustín Iturbide took control for Mexico of the formerly Spanish-ruled capital on September 27, 1821.

The revolution had been ignited by a parish priest in the village of Dolores, Guanajuato, who expressed the deep-souled feeling of large numbers of Mexicans that the Spanish government had become too oppressive to be tolerated. The priest, Miguel Hidalgo y Costilla, a *creole* (born in Mexico of Spanish parents) was allied with another creole, Capt. Ignacio Allende, commander of the local militia. They planned to proclaim Mexico's independence from Spain. For these patriots, the reasons were compelling.

The European crisis—Napoleon's incarceration of the Spanish King Ferdinand VII and enthronement of Joseph Bonaparte—placed the Spanish American colonies in a dilemma. To whom did they owe allegiance? The Spanish colonials in administrative positions decided to protect their own interests; the creoles avowed they could govern Mexico for their absent monarch. During the night of September 15-16, 1810, Father Hidalgo rang the church bell and called the villagers together. When they had assembled, he cried out his historic *Grito de Dolores*—a sorrowfully

In one of the annual Good Friday re-enactments of the "Way of the Cross," including the crucifixion of Jesus Christ, Manuel Albarado is placed on a cross at San Fernando Cathedral by Roman guards. As always, the re-enactment began at El Mercado, with the trial followed by a solemn procession down Dolorosa Street to the Cathedral. (San Antonio Express-News photo)

impassioned cry for freedom. He is said to have shouted: "Long live Our Lady of Guadalupe! Long live Independence!" And it is said that his listeners responded with: "Death to the *gachupines!"* (Natives of Spain, who held many privileges to themselves alone because of the place of their birth, were called *gachupines* by creoles and others less privileged in the New World.)

Father Hidalgo's anguished cry, his *grito,* is echoed every year at 11 P.M. September 15, the eve of Mexico's Independence Day, by the president of the Republic of Mexico and by state governors and mayors in every city and town in Mexico. It also is repeated each year at the Mexican Cultural Institute in Plaza Mexico at HemisFair Park.

The grito used today by Mexican officials is:

¡Viva la independencia!
¡Viva la libertad!
¡Viva Mexico!
¡Viva Mexico!
¡Viva Mexico!

San Antonio's Ten-Day Fiesta: How It Began

On April 28, 1890, the San Antonio *Daily Express* published a report from Mexico City whose significance in the definition of San Antonio's future self-image no one at the time could have foreseen. The story began with the headline: FLOWER FEAST— *The Famous Fete of Nice Reproduced in Mexican Capital.* Here is an excerpt from the translation:

The flower feast, or combat of flowers, commenced at four o'clock this afternoon [Sunday, April 27]. The arrangements by Aldems, Valledo and Barn were the most perfect. It was calculated that 100,000 people were on the promenade of La Reforma and Avenida Juarez. Nearly 500 carriages of sightseers unadorned, 1,000 horsemen, besides over forty adorned with flowers and ribbons, were out. The feast fully

An article in the San Antonio Express *of March 26, 1911, discussed
the first Battle of Flowers Parade in San Antonio, which had occurred
twenty years before, on April 24, 1891. The feature writer said that
"this first battle was purely a social event, only friends and neighbors
and the descendants of the Texas veterans participating, and for that
reason there was much enthusiasm and gaiety. . . ." Only natural
flowers were used and the most spirited exchange of flower flinging
took place in Alamo Plaza where the parade split into two lines with
the ladies' carriages driven in opposite directions around the plaza so
they could pelt each other as they passed. The writer said that "among
the attractive turnouts which has lived in the memory of all was that of
Mrs. W. W. King. Her beautiful span of yellow Arabian horses . . .
[drew] a handsome carriage which was elaborately trimmed with
Marechal Nell roses. Yellow ribbons were used for the lines." (Drawing
courtesy of José Cisneros and Trinity University, San Antonio)*

equaled those of Nice. The amount of flowers was enormous, of which four carloads came from Jalapa. . . .

San Antonio readers of the story were treated to a detailed description of floats and their artistic floral decorations; the distinguished citizens and their families and members of foreign legations; the forty cavaliers on horseback, and the exciting spectacle of the carriages and landaus accompanied by outriders. Not surprisingly, the float entered by the Spanish government was awarded first prize.

The idea of a battle of flowers, as performed in Nice and in Mexico City, fit well into a tradition of parades that San Antonio had inherited from its significantly large German populace. Since June 1882, the Germans had been holding their annual *volksfests* citywide, day-long celebrations attended by thousands of out-of-town Germans who joined their San Antonio friends to parade, picnic, and enjoy music, orations, and fireworks.

Even long before that, San Antonians paraded in what they called "processions." In 1829, for instance, in the annual Diez y Seis celebration, committees and subcommittees organized festivities and collected donations for a great celebration—a mass at San Fernando church, processions of the citizens through the streets, a pealing of bells, and gun salutes, speeches, music, food, and later a great ball at the town hall.

Apparently, even in the 1880s San Antonians were celebrating the Texan victory at San Jacinto. Maria Aurelia Williams, who became Mrs. John Herndon James, was born in San Antonio in 1859 and lived in the city until 1937. In her memoirs, *I Remember*, she wrote:

> For many years . . . it was the custom of the young people of San Antonio to join in the worldwide revelry in acknowledgment of the coming of spring on the date of the anniversary of the San Jacinto battle, April 21, thus patriotically uniting the joyousness of the new growing

year with the celebration of independence gained. This revelry far ante-dated the first set festival.

The deep feeling of need for a spring carnival had been nurtured in the hearts of Europeans since medieval times. Even before Christianity, the Romans celebrated the rebirth of nature at springtime. In Italy, France, and Spain, carnival time came in the last days and hours of the pre-Lenten season when Christians prepared to go without meat during Lent, thus the Medieval Latin term *carne vale*, "flesh farewell." Not only European cultures, but the scores of cultures in Mexico have centuries-old traditions of festivals in endless variety, including outlandish costumes and face-painting.

By 1891, a number of San Antonians had been thinking for a long time about the need to celebrate in some spectacular way both the Texans' historic defeat of Mexican forces at San Jacinto and the heroism of the men who died at the Alamo. April 21, the date in 1836 of the great victory, would be the day of a battle of flowers parade.

When news came that President Benjamin Harrison was scheduled to visit the city on April 20, 1891, the *Express* suggested on April 8 that the entertainment for the distinguished guest be combined with a flower carnival. On April 13, as it had the year before, the newspaper ran an article describing the battle of flowers celebration in Mexico City. That same day, a group of prominent women met at the San Antonio Club on an upper floor of the Grand Opera House to plan a very special observance.

Most commonly mentioned in all accounts of the first leaders of the Battle of Flowers celebration, along with Mrs. H. D. Kampmann, whose husband owned the Menger Hotel, was Mrs. Ellen Maury Slayden, wife of U.S. Congressman James Luther Slayden. Yet a number of women and men—all associated with the exclusive San Antonio Club—were involved. According to their plan, the flower-pelting would be played out on the streets encircling the new park that had been constructed in Alamo Plaza by Anton Friedrich Wulff the previous year and beautified with roses and palm trees.

Because of an unusually heavy rain on the day of the president's arrival, the parade had to be postponed, but an eager crowd squeezed inside the Grand Opera House to hear President Harrison deliver his remarks from the stage. The parade was held four days later, on April 24.

Most of the stores on Commerce and Houston streets and Alamo Plaza had closed their doors by five o'clock that afternoon. The *San Antonio Light* reported that "streetcars and carriages poured their thousands into these streets and on the plaza, and around Alamo Plaza every balcony and housetop, every door and window and other points of vantage were packed and covered with people. The plaza was one dense mass of humanity and a close estimate places the number of sightseers and participants at 15,000. The procession contained over 100 carriages and other vehicles, all gaily decorated and many containing decorations of real artistic merit."

The *Express* reported that by 5:30 P.M., "the finishing touches" had been given the carriages, and the horsemen and women were mounted and eager to ride. They were followed by the cyclists on decorated bikes. Led by a military band, the parade moved westward on Houston Street, then to Jefferson and on to Martin, then to Navarro, and from Navarro to St. Mary's, to Commerce, to Main Plaza, and back through Commerce Street to Alamo Street and Alamo Plaza. There, the parade marshal, Gustave A. Duerler, divided the procession in two parts going in opposite directions so that in passing they could pelt each other, as well as bystanders, with flowers. After an hour of this, the marshal gave the signal to end the battle, and all were asked to withdraw. They used real flowers in those days, but after an early frost once made paper flowers necessary, artificial blossoms were used thereafter.

The Battle of Flowers Parade, associated with San Jacinto Day, has been held virtually every year since 1891—with numerous refinements added and the one-day celebration extended to ten. In some war years, the parade was not held, but San Jacinto Day has always been observed. Fiesta in San Antonio in the 1990s is a huge citywide party in which three mammoth parades are

featured and eighty to 150 events are staged by institutions, organizations, neighborhoods, and ethnic and religious groups all over
the city with parades, food and concession booths, music, and
fireworks.

Downtown, dozens of brightly uniformed marching bands lift
the spirits, and special color is added by military men and women
from five large military installations, the martially uniformed Texas
Cavaliers, and the mounted and costumed men and women of the
San Antonio Charro Association, which during the week also puts
on a spectacular *charreada*, an exciting Mexican rodeo. More than
50,000 volunteers and eighty-plus nonprofit organizations participate in the great fiesta, with over a million people enjoying
the ten days and evenings of revelry.

The Battle of Flowers Parade, traditionally held on a Friday—
which a great part of the city treats as a holiday from school and
work—is said to be the fourth largest in the United States and the
only large one run entirely by women. Organized by the Battle of
Flowers Association, the two-hour parade has some 150 to 180
entries, including thirty-five marching bands and more than
thirty-five colorful floats bedecked with members of the Fiesta
royalty.

Atop special floats, elegant young women—the Queen and
the princesses and duchesses of her court—wear gowns more
elaborate than any worn in Las Vegas or the Follies in Paris and as
ornate as in any royal court on Earth. Their design each year
follows a different theme. Weighing at least forty pounds and
trailing trains three to four times as long as their wearer's height,
the gowns cost anywhere from $5,000 to $25,000; some have been
rumored to cost as much as $60,000. They can represent twelve
months of work under skilled direction—developing and render-
ing designs in luxuriant applique, embroidery, elaborate bead-
work, and glittering rhinestones inspired by decorations on rare
porcelain and jewelry, and other creations patterned after lavish
costumes of European and Asian nobility throughout history.

A solemn departure from the festivities is the annual Pilgrimage to the Alamo, when more than 1,000 members of civic, mili-

tary, patriotic, and school organizations place wreaths and flowers while an unseen speaker tells of the thirteen-day siege and reads the names of the 189 who died there.

Royalty—King Antonio and the other smartly uniformed men and the lavishly gowned ladies—vie for the honor of taking part in the annual festivities. It also is difficult, expensive, and an honor to be selected as the Ugly King, *El Rey Feo.*

The Queen and her entire court, consisting of princesses, duchesses, dukes, prime minister, the lord high chamberlain, and even the pages, have been chosen by the Order of the Alamo since 1901. To reign as Queen of Fiesta is the highest honor San Antonio society can bestow on one of its debutantes. The Order of the Alamo was founded in 1909 by John Carrington, a businessman from Virginia who later founded the Texas Cavaliers. It is these two organizations that determine who will occupy the thrones of the primary Fiesta royalty—other than the Ugly King and his court.

El Rey Feo is selected by LULAC, the League of United Latin American Citizens, in an annual competition for the man who can raise the greatest amount of money for scholarships for deserving Hispanics. The Ugly Kings, after their small beginning in 1947, were not incorporated into the official activities of Fiesta until 1980. These prominent civic and business leaders—usually Hispanic—have raised as much as $210,000 in a single year for scholarships—some $3 million over the years. More than 500 scholarships have been awarded.

Since 1959, through the cooperation of the city government and the Greater San Antonio Chamber of Commerce, the overall coordination of the many organizations and events of the ten-day Fiesta has been handled by the Fiesta San Antonio Commission.

As many as 200,000 spectators line the banks of the San Antonio River on a Monday evening to watch the Texas Cavaliers' River Parade with its more than forty highly decorated river floats, half of them including live music. On the following Friday, some 225,000 people witness the Battle of Flowers Parade, and on Saturday night, perhaps 340,000 see the three-hour, illuminated Fiesta Flambeau Parade, with its fifty local, Texas, national, and international marching bands, twenty-three horse units, and fifty-six floats.

The Texas Cavaliers were formed in 1926 "to keep alive the memory of the pioneers," to sponsor an annual Pilgrimage to the Alamo, and to "preserve the Texas tradition of horsemanship in this age of automobiles." Dashingly accoutered in specially designed uniforms, the cavaliers rode horses in the parades until 1952, when they made the decision to walk. That was the practice until 1941, when the Cavaliers launched the first River Parade.

The River Parade

In Henry Graham's *History of the Texas Cavaliers*, which the group published in 1976, he writes that the idea of the river parade came to a group of San Antonians who visited Mexico City's float-

---

The "Phantasmagoric" River Parade

Jan Morris, the British travel writer, recorded the following account of her dazed puzzlement with San Antonio's citywide fiesta-week doings in *Granta 10* in 1984: "What phantasmagoric gully was that stream beneath our windows, lined along its curling course with what inconceivable multitudes? What shapes were those on the water passing by, those drifting baubles of light and color, those gesticulating figures weirdly dressed? Whose flags were these, thick across every street, and what manner of people, these somber men with Mickey Mouse balloons?

"From what exotic divisions did these generals come, with their massed medals of unimaginable campaigns, their drooping epaulets and their theatrically gilded caps?

"The talk of the town seemed a kind of gibberish to me. Of Ugly Kings and Fabergé Courts, of Cavaliers and Coronations, of curtseying instructions and sixty-thousand [dollar] dresses. The whole city seemed seized in an arcane ecstasy all its own, jumping up and down with the excitement of it, discussing nothing else."

---

ing gardens of Xochimilco. "The gaily flower-bedecked boats and barges plying the canals there inspired an idea among the Cavaliers," Graham wrote. "Why not liven up the King's Entry and have him introduced as part of a river parade?" He believed that the inspiration for both the Battle of Flowers and the River Parade had Hispanic origins.

A Variety of Fiestas

Celebrations blossom throughout the city during the big fiesta. The Mexican *charreada* is filled with exciting rodeo events sponsored by the San Antonio Charro Association. There are St. Mary's University Fiesta Oyster Bake, A Taste of New Orleans at Sunken Garden Theater, and others. One of the most popular celebrations is Cornyation, presented at Beethoven Hall, which makes irreverent fun of the more serious traditional Fiesta ceremonials; its sovereign head was King Anchovy XXXII in 1997. A three-day German-style party with music and dancing is put on each year as "Hermann's Happiness" by the Order of the Sons of Hermann in Texas. It is a charitable fund raiser. The annual King William Fair draws more than 80,000 to the parade, feasting, and funmaking. It attracts thousands of children.

A Night in Old San Antonio

Among a number of large fiestas held throughout the city during the annual Fiesta San Antonio, NIOSA is the most spectacular. It is a "block party" crammed into several small sections of La Villita. Thousands have fun there during four evenings. Each night it is packed with as many as 25,000 happy people milling past or tarrying in the pungent, rising smoke of cooking *fajitas* and the fragrant ethnic food and refreshment of more than 200 booths, while listening or dancing to the music of bands playing melodies of a dozen cultural or social genres. Thanks to 16,000 volunteers each year, everything is devoted to carefree merrymaking—the visceral spirit of the carnival—perhaps best characterized by the *cascarones*, the gaily colored eggshells filled with confetti for sale by the thousands to revelers who enjoy breaking them over the heads of friends.

Staged since 1948 by volunteers from the San Antonio Conservation Society and by others they enlist for help, NIOSA is in itself a reflection of the history of San Antonio. Its fifteen sections tell something of the city's enchanting story: Mission Trail, Villa España, Haymarket, Mexican Market, South of the Border, Frontier Town, Sauerkraut Bend, Irish Flats, French Quarter, Main Street USA, Chinatown, Arneson Theater, Clown Alley, Tin Pan Alley, and International Walkway.

In 1995, the Conservation Society revealed that its NIOSA celebration had grossed more than $5 million in the previous three years. It is from these funds that the Society finances the preservation of many valuable historic properties for the enjoyment of San Antonians and visitors and for its continuing historical education programs.

In 1997, an estimated 3.3 million people attended the nearly 200 Fiesta events sponsored by eighty organizations, bringing more than $300 million into the city. Thus, each year San Antonio renews itself as it pays tribute to the tragedy, heroism, and triumph in its past, considers life's perspectives, alternatives, and prospects, and looks hopefully to the new season.

"Highland" Country Music

To many visitors, the real flavor of San Antonio today is found in the country music dance halls. The first Anglo Americans to settle in Texas in significant numbers came from an area that geographers call "the upper south," mostly from Tennessee, Kentucky, Arkansas, and North Carolina. Many of these people were from the backwoods or the mountains. From 1836 to 1860, more immigrants came from "the lower south," from the Gulf coastal states of Alabama, Georgia, Mississippi, and Louisiana. Just before the Civil War, in 1860, there were about as many "lower southerners" in Texas as "upper southerners." Trinity University linguistic specialist Dr. Scott Baird explains that "the lowlands southern dialect one often hears in San Antonio is distinctive because speakers do not pronounce the final 'r,' especially after vowels." On the other hand, he says, the cowboy or 'kicker' culture speaks mainly "highlands southern." Highlands Southerners gave us country western music, bourbon, and the pronunciation of the sound 'r.'

Dancing was the principal public entertainment of men and women on the frontier of Texas. The happiest occasions—weddings, birthdays, special celebrations, and the entertainment of important visitors—were marked by a dance. When dances were held at ranches, the "floor" sometimes consisted of canvas wagon covers laid out on flat ground outdoors. Dances often were the best way for single men and women on the frontier to meet—and many a marriage had its beginning there. Early accounts of life in Texas describe exuberant dances, late hours, "floor stompings"—from the early days in Austin's colony, to San Antonio's Texas Republic days, and throughout the times of the soldiers, cattlemen, and cowboys.

Today, a typical dance hall offers not only the graceful schottische but the exciting polka, the lilting Texas waltz, and the shuffling two-step as they have been danced for decades. So deep-rooted is this tradition in the Texan mystique that there is seldom a honky-tonk or dance hall without at least one good-sized Texas flag displayed on a wall or ceiling or both.

In country music dance halls in San Antonio and its environs, it is easy to imagine oneself living in another time. For more than half a century, the John T. Floore Country Store, on the outskirts of San Antonio in Helotes, has drawn hundreds of folk from miles around every week to dance to country music. It has a half-acre, open-air concrete dance floor beside the enclosed hall for the many evenings when the weather permits outdoor dancing—from Easter to December.

Often, in the 1940s through the 1960s, before he became nationally famous, country music star Willie Nelson played his guitar and sang with a band at Floore's Country Store. He still tells of his strong ties to the place where he got his start and tries to play there about once a year. Live bands play for dancing on Friday and Saturday—and every Sunday is Family Day, with children and adults enjoying free dancing to live country music.

A little north of San Antonio in Leon Springs, a new entertainment complex is centered on an 18,000-square-foot dance hall that faces two innovative restaurants designed by Phil Romano, founder of the Fuddruckers national hamburger chain—Macaroni Grill and Nachomama's—plus Rudy's Country Store. Leon Springs Dancehall has live music three nights a week. Among the most authentic-looking "old Texas" dance halls near San Antonio is a barbecue place whose weather-beaten appearance belies its tongue-in-cheek name—the Cibolo Creek Country Club. It presents live music—often more eclectic and alternative than country—on Fridays, Saturdays, and Sundays.

A more traditionally colorful honky-tonk—the real thing—is a stone's throw away, across the creek in the old German village of Bracken. The Hangin' Tree Saloon reverberates to an authentic Texas image with live music every weekend. Two of the most typical Texas country dance halls or honky-tonks with the nostalgic feel of the old West are not far from San Antonio. One that especially pleases the visitors to nearby Bandera, the "Cowboy Capital," is Arkey Blue's Silver Dollar in a not-very-large basement with sawdust on the floor and an owner who has been providing live music there on weekends for more than twenty years.

The popular Gruene Hall is at the village of Gruene (pronounced Green) beside the Guadalupe River, four miles north of downtown New Braunfels. It is known as the oldest dance hall in Texas and offers a resilient wooden dance floor and rousing country music in an ancient white frame building. Each week, San Antonio's newspapers list dozens of places with live music for dancing.

The Old West Still Lives

San Antonio is never more in touch with its cattle-raising past—the "Western mystique" it loves—than during the more than a week in winter when some 3,500 trail riders from outlying towns and ranches brave the elements day after day. In 1997, they converged on San Antonio for a parade downtown on the morning of February 1 before the annual Rodeo and Stock Show began. Volunteers serving breakfast for San Antonians getting into the spirit of the rodeo fed 40,000 gathered outside Central Park Mall on

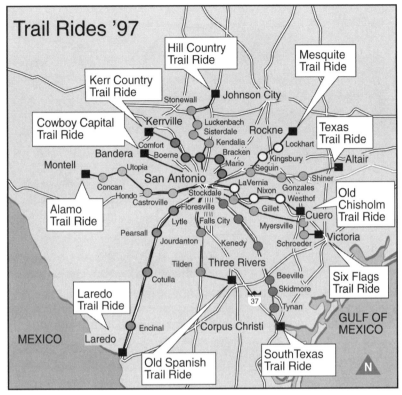

Trail Rides '97

Express-News graphic

January 24 for the free Cowboy Breakfast. Music and a celebrity cow-chip throwing contest added to the traditional revelry.

Each year, riders come from a dozen Texas areas, and each trail ride has a name. The South Texas Trail Ride comes from the Corpus Christi area on the Gulf of Mexico, Laredo Trail Ride from the Laredo area on the Mexican border, Old Spanish Trail Ride from near Three Rivers, Six Flags Trail Ride from Victoria, Old Chisholm Trail Ride from Cuero, Texas Trail Ride from Altair, Mesquite Trail Ride from Rockne, Hill Country Trail Ride from Round Mountain, Kerr County Trail Ride from Kerrville, Cowboy Trail Ride from Bandera, and Alamo Trail Ride from Montell.

Recalling the trail drives every year is especially appropriate in San Antonio, the southernmost big town on the famous

Trail riders converge on San Antonio from every direction at the beginning of the annual stock show and rodeo on the last days of January and early February. These riders are en route from Bandera in February 1992, and the prominence in the background is Polly's Peak, named for the legendary José Policarpo Rodríguez (1829-1911). Polly raised a large family on Privilege Creek, a few miles east of Bandera. He became famous among the U. S. Army soldiers and Texas Rangers as a scout, guide, hunter, Indian fighter, and surveyor. He was also a rancher who became a successful Methodist-Episcopal preacher. The stone church he built on Privilege Creek, known as "Polly's Church," is still in use. (San Antonio Express-News photo)

Chisholm Trail, which was followed north in the 1870s by the cattle drivers through Austin, Waco, Fort Worth, and Red River Station in Texas and on to the railheads in Kansas—and as far north as Montana.

The annual San Antonio Stock Show and Rodeo is held at the Joe and Harry Freeman Coliseum. Brothers Joe and Harry and other businessmen, such as Morris and Perry Kallison, got the Bexar County Coliseum built in 1949. With a seating capacity at that time of 7,320, it opened to the public on October 19, hosting the Ringling Brothers and Barnum & Bailey Circus.

The Coliseum houses the administrative office of the San Antonio Livestock Exposition, Inc., which stages the great rodeo every February, combined with a horse and livestock show. There are as many as seventeen rodeo performances during the sixteen-day event, and 127,000 fans may attend on a single day.

At rodeo time, San Antonians celebrate the heritage of the cowboy, horse culture, and livestock-raising. It is the time for the grand presentation of a variety of choice livestock and livestock products such as wool and mohair; the horse show competition; the calf scramble for boys; the junior livestock show and auction; the livestock auction; nationally known entertainers; and the rodeo performances featuring champion competitors in bronco and steer riding, roping, and other ranching skills.

Horse-lovers also visit the San Antonio Rose Palace in a seventy-two-acre ranch-style setting near Boerne, where every month throughout the year there are saddle horse or horse breeder shows plus team roping and dressage competitions in the largest such arena in Texas. Permanent boarding and training facilities for horses adjoin the main complex. The Rose Palace also offers rodeos in its two covered and two outdoor arenas. Each covered arena's floor space exceeds 40,000 square feet.

Although she was surely thinking in universal terms, Pulitzer-prize winning historian Barbara Tuchman could have had San Antonio in mind when she wrote:

> Happily, man has the capacity for pleasure too, and in contriving ways to entertain and amuse himself, has created brilliance and delight. Pageants, carnivals, festivals, fireworks, music, dancing and drama, parties and picnics, sports and games, the comic spirit and its gift of laughter, all the range of enjoyment from grand ceremonial to the quiet solitude of a day's fishing, has helped to balance the world's infelicity. *Homo ludens,* man at play, is surely as significant a figure as man at war or at work.

13

History Preserved and Expanded

Some of San Antonio's most appealing attractions once served distinctly different functions. The striking architecture of the San Antonio Museum of Art was designed for a brewery in the 1800s. The ancient quarries that provided the stones to build old San Antonio and Fort Sam Houston's Quadrangle walls and tower have been transformed into the Sunken Garden Theater and areas of the San Antonio Zoo. The San Antonio Botanical Center was once part of the city waterworks, and the Southwest Craft Center was a school run by nuns from New Orleans and Galveston for young women of Texas.

Commerce Street, looking east from Soledad Street toward Alamo Street, before automobiles and before the city began widening it from Main Plaza to Alamo Street in 1912. By 1915, the distance between buildings on each side had been increased to sixty-five feet, with a forty-foot roadway and sidewalks 12½ feet wide. Buildings were either cut back or moved back. The five-story Alamo National Bank Building on the southwest corner of Commerce and Presa was lifted onto heavy wooden beams and moved back twelve feet; today this building has three additional stories. The large clock mounted on its standard in 1878 in front of E. Hertzberg Jewelry Company at 227 West Commerce has been preserved by the San Antonio Conservation Society and now can be seen at the corner of Houston and St. Mary's streets. (Daughters of the Republic of Texas Library photo)

SAN ANTONIO, TEXAS. HOT WELLS BATH HOUSE. 10

From 1901 to 1925, Hot Wells Hotel brought excitement to the people of San Antonio as they read in the newspapers about the famous visitors to the luxurious health spa, as well as the doings of the local folk who attended swimming parties, domino parties, concerts, lectures, and balls. Construction was begun in 1900 by the Texas Hot Sulphur Water Sanitarium Company, and owners soon claimed the offerings were superior to those at Hot Springs, Arkansas, and Carlsbad, Germany. Ladies from the city would travel by buggy or electric trolley car to Hot Wells to buy ostrich feathers from the adjacent farm that also held ostrich races. There was a menagerie at the park that included a black bear and a mountain lion donated by Judge Roy Bean. The venture never was successful after the 100-room hotel building burned in 1925, although some buildings were used at times for dining and tourist courts until 1977. Nearby, not far from Mission San José, Georges Mélies, brother of a pioneer French filmmaker, established Star Film Ranch and made some seventy silent motion pictures in 1910 and 1911. Then, from 1912 to 1916, filmmaker Patrick S. McGeeney's Lone Star Company made films about San Antonio's charms in a studio using the Mélies set near San José. Although several entrepreneurs over the years planned to restore the old hotel, an arson fire in October 1997 totally destroyed all that remained of the once-grand spa. (Author's collection)

San Antonio Museum of Art

In 1884, John H. Kampmann, building contractor and financier, opened the Lone Star Brewing Company and operated it until 1892 when his company sold it to Adolphus A. Busch, the well-known St. Louis brewer. The brewery prospered until the national and state Prohibition laws of 1918 ended its beer operations. The company continued at the Jones Avenue location—for a time producing a soft drink called "Tango" that made "the palate dance with joy" and later milling cotton there for a few years. The last occupant of the buildings, until they were vacated in 1925, was the Lone Star Ice and Food Company.

The major buildings left behind on West Jones Avenue by the original Lone Star Brewery had been built through the combined talents of E. Jungenfield and Company with San Antonio's James Wahrenberger and Albert F. Beckman. They constructed the attached two- to five-story buildings, unified by the eye-catching crenelated projections, that are today the renovated and transformed San Antonio Museum of Art. Now, the "German-built" Lone Star Brewery building, which opened on March 1, 1981, as an art museum, houses a widely renowned collection of Hispanic folk art; ancient art from Egypt, Greece and Rome; Asian art; and American paintings and sculpture from colonial to contemporary.

Buckhorn Hall of Horns, Fins, and Feathers

The highly marketable "Lone Star" name was assumed in 1940 by the Champion Brewing Company, which was located on the river south of town, but in July 1996 the brewing operation was moved to Longview in East Texas. Two popular tourist attractions on the grounds remain open but as of this writing are scheduled for relocation.

The Buckhorn Hall of Horns, Fins, and Feathers houses one of the largest horn collections in the world. Many of the hundreds of antlers there used to be in the Buckhorn Saloon in downtown San Antonio. A popular gathering place in the late 1800s and early 1900s, the Buckhorn Saloon was started in 1881 by Albert Friedrich on Dolorosa Street across from the old Southern Hotel on Main Plaza. He later moved it to the corner of Houston and Soledad streets.

For three decades, cowboys, traders, trappers, and cattlemen brought unusual horns from the valleys and prairies of Southwest Texas to the Buckhorn Saloon to sell or to trade for whiskey or beer. That bit of the Old West disappeared in the 1920s, when the famous Buckhorn was suppressed by Prohibition and had to be moved to the corner of Houston and South Flores streets, where it began offering only the refreshments of a soda fountain as the Buckhorn Museum and Curio Shop. The enormous and ornate working bar at the Lone Star Brewery's Hall of Horns has been a reminder of another age.

The O. Henry House

The other attraction at the former Lone Star Brewery is the O. Henry House. It contains memorabilia of the famous short-story writer who collaborated briefly with Henry Ryder Taylor, a British journalist, on a satirical newspaper called *The Rolling Stone*. The house, in which O. Henry (whose real name was William Sydney Porter) worked from time to time when not in Austin, was moved from its original location on South Presa; its future location is uncertain.

Yturri-Edmunds House and Ogé Carriage House

Virtually across the way from the brewery, just off Mission Road, is the Yturri-Edmunds Historic Site. Restored in 1990 by the San Antonio Conservation Society, the property has a Mexican-style ranch house built in the early 1800s, and a grist mill, once powered by the Pajalache Acequia, which was used for grinding grain. On the site also is the Ogé Carriage House, constructed about 1881 and moved not long ago by the Conservation Society from the King William area, where it was too near high water.

The Witte Museum

Nature is preserved and displayed where it can be studied close up at San Antonio's Witte Memorial Museum—a museum of regional history and natural science. Among the Witte's many acquisitions, including a variety of special works of Southwest art, are the artifacts of Indians of the region, a mineral collection, and displays of Spanish arms.

In addition to its presentations of ancient Texas civilizations and regional flora and fauna, the Witte has historic buildings on its grounds that have been moved from downtown San Antonio and restored. Worth visiting are the authentically restored homes of José Francisco Ruíz, one of two native Texans to sign the Texas Declaration of Independence on March 2, 1836, and John Twohig, pioneer San Antonio merchant, patriot, and philanthropist, known as the "Breadline Banker" because of his charitable customs. His two-story stone home was erected in the 1840s beside the river near St. Mary's church. The Ruíz House was used as the first public school quarters in San Antonio around 1801. It stood at what is now 420 Dolorosa Street, facing north on Military Plaza.

A new attraction in 1997 is the spectacular, castle-like H-E-B Science Treehouse—a four-level, 15,000-square-foot center for science exhibits and activities for all ages.

Next to the Witte Museum, on the north, is the Texas Rangers Museum, also known as the Texas Pioneers, Trail Drivers, and Texas Rangers Memorial Building. It contains memorabilia of the trail drivers who drove cattle from South Texas to Kansas and farther north, the Texas Rangers, and other Texas pioneers. At its front is Gutzon Borglum's Trail Drivers Memorial, a bronze cast of a preliminary model by the famous Mount Rushmore sculptor. The full-scale piece was never executed.

Some say there might not be a Witte Museum today had it not been rescued by snakes. In the Great Depression, which began in 1929 when the museum was just getting well started and was in dire need of money, it saved itself by starting a reptile display that included demonstrations with rattlesnakes and even the serving of rattlesnake meat to eat. There was a time during that period when the Witte had only $2.47 in its treasury, and when it had difficulty raising $750 to build a flimsy enclosure for what its organizers decided to call its Reptile Garden. This later was made into a circular, roofed enclosure with a large inner pit and stone walls.

The idea had come from W. C. (Bill) Bevan, the editor of "Snakelore" in *Outdoor Magazine*, who needed a better-paying job. He moved to the museum area and lived with a pet boa constrictor in a donated streetcar.

The Reptile Garden, claimed by some to be the first of its kind in the country, received donations of reptiles at first and then began buying them. Unexpected benefits of this new expertly handled collection of venomous snakes were the fruitful experiments conducted there to collect and test poisonous snake venom. The tests became a center of interest for the Anti-Venin Institute of America.

The Witte charged ten cents for admission to see the snakes and alligators. It paid fifteen cents a pound for rattlesnakes—and many small farmers, strapped for cash, were happy to have this source of income. In 1934, when the "snake-fry" was begun, it attracted national attention. During World War II, the Witte's Reptile Garden was a favorite place for soldiers to visit. Eating rattlesnake meat cooked on a skillet over a campfire was very popular with visitors to San Antonio. Usually the meat was served as bite-size tidbits, but for a time you could buy "rattleburgers." The last "fry" was held on September 14, 1950.

Alamo Cement Company Quarries

The ancient quarries now in Brackenridge Park, where the Spaniards and Mexicans had cut blocks of stone for the Alamo and other early buildings, have been given a variety of new roles in San Antonio's history. The stone used first by the Alamo Cement Company came from those quarries. The chimney for the cement company's kiln, as well as some of the workers' houses, can be seen there today. In 1908, the company moved to a site beside the railroad tracks in the Alamo Heights area, a suburb then outside the city limits.

Within its nearly 500 acres, the company began excavating a deep new quarry and established not only a large plant but also a

Gutzon Borglum (1867-1941) was based in San Antonio when he began designing and sculpting models of three of the enormous heads of presidents Washington, Jefferson, Lincoln, and Theodore Roosevelt to be carved into the stone sides of Mount Rushmore in South Dakota. Borglum lived in San Antonio intermittently from 1923 to 1938. His studio in Brackenridge Park, a former pumphouse for the rivermill race, is today an architectural firm's office near the Brackenridge Golf Course parking lot. Borglum also lived and worked for a time in rooms at the Menger Hotel, where visitors reported chips of stone covering the floor. When his son, Lincoln, was a student at Lukin Military Academy in San Antonio, he and his friend Allen Day transported in an automobile three of the modeled heads to South Dakota for use in the Mount Rushmore National Memorial. Borglum was once commissioned by the Prime Minister of Poland, the great pianist Ignace Paderewski, to sculpt a statue of President Woodrow Wilson, which he completed in his Brackenridge Park studio. (Institute of Texan Cultures photo)

village for its workers called Cementville. The village church, St. Anthony's, can be seen on Peter Baque Road today.

After seventy-eight years near Alamo Heights, Alamo Cement Company moved in 1986 to Green Mountain Road off Loop 1604. In its place today are the gently rolling greens of an eighteen-hole golf course, the Quarry of Lincoln Heights. Nine holes lie within the deep quarry. Behind the golf course, a great new mixed-use development has been arising—Lincoln Heights, consisting of upscale residential, business, and shopping areas. And closer to U.S. 281 is the new Alamo Quarry Market—a center for stores and restaurants, specialty shops, and entertainment venues.

The Art of Dionicio Rodríguez

Besides the buildings that remain to remind us of the gigantic cement plant (several now transformed into restaurants and retail shops) are samples of the concrete structures created by Dionicio Rodríguez, a master of *faux bois*, which appear to be made of branches and trunks of trees. His remarkably durable and realistic art also can be seen elsewhere in San Antonio—for example, a pedestrian bridge built about 1929 in Brackenridge Park, and the ample, one-of-a-kind bus stop shelter at the corner of Broadway and Patterson.

San Antonio Zoo

After the ancient limestone quarries of Brackenridge Park were vacated by the Alamo Cement Company, they became settings for the Japanese Tea Garden, as well as the vast, open-air Sunken Garden Theater (Alpine and North St. Mary's), and the San Antonio Zoological Gardens and Aquarium in the 343-acre Brackenridge Park.

The park includes picnic areas, playgrounds, bike paths, paddle boats, a golf course, riding stables, and what is claimed to be "the world's longest miniature railroad"—which once actually experienced a real holdup. Founded in 1899, the park was named for banker and philanthropist George W. Brackenridge, who had deeded it to the city.

If one could call a permanent public place for display of animals a zoo, then one could say that San Antonio's zoo existed in the early 1870s, when Sidney Lanier wrote about "the aviary, the Mexican lion, the two bears, the wolf, the coyote and other attractions" in San Pedro Park. From 1910 to 1915, it was a municipally owned zoo. In 1914, George Brackenridge donated some elk and buffalo for display, and the city zoo was moved to Brackenridge Park. By 1929, the San Antonio Zoological Society had begun developing the zoo we see today—an accredited member of the American Zoo and Aquarium Association.

With 3,400 animals representing 700 species, displayed over twenty-three acres, it has one of the largest collections in the country. It is the largest in the Southwest and among the leaders in the world. The bird collection also is notably large—and reptiles, amphibians, fish, and invertebrates are well represented in the botanically rich setting through which the San Antonio River flows.

San Antonio Botanical Center

San Antonio Botanical Center was once a key site in the city's first water supply system. In the late 1870s, the powerful flow of the river had begun to weaken—mostly because of the drain of drilled wells. It was clear then that water would eventually have to be piped to homes and businesses.

The Water Works, constructed by a private company, was approved by the city of San Antonio on July 5, 1878. The outline of its reservoir is still visible in a walled outdoor theater near a small lake at the Botanical Center. It was an ingenious arrangement that carried water from the San Antonio River uphill past the Broadway and Funston streets intersection to the reservoir near the summit above the eastern end of Mahnke Park. From there it could flow downhill through pipes carrying the water to the homes that would use it. A water raceway had been built across a large bend in the stream near the head of the river to a pumping plant in Brackenridge Park. From the river level at the upper end of the raceway to the location of the pumping plant

The Lucile Halsell Conservatory at the San Antonio Botanical Gardens is a complex of five greenhouses specializing in tropical and exotic plants from around the world. The thirty-eight-acre garden center offers year-round displays of diverse Texas landscapes. (San Antonio Express-News photo)

was a drop of eight to ten feet. As a result, the water going down the raceway had sufficient force to operate a large turbine connected to the plunger of a pump. The pump then forced the water up to the reservoir on the hill at an elevation of 787 feet, from which it flowed by gravity down through the company's water mains.

The thirty-eight-acre Botanical Center, on a hill overlooking the city, presents diverse Texas landscapes all year round. Included are a biblical garden, a garden specially designed for the blind, and the Lucile Halsell Conservatory—a spectacular towering glass complex of five greenhouses featuring tropical and exotic plants from around the world.

Southwest Craft Center

Another of San Antonio's distinctive groups of buildings is the Southwest Craft Center on the site of the former Ursuline

Academy, just behind the new Central Library. The original academy building was constructed of *pisé de terre* or rammed earth. The Ursuline Order of nuns had begun in Italy in 1535 and spread in Europe. French nuns had been sent to San Antonio from New Orleans and Galveston in 1851 to start the first "permanent" school in San Antonio. Through its 141 years, it graduated many young women who had come from all over Texas and from Mexico. The academy was moved in 1961 from its original location to Vance Jackson Road, where the sisters taught high school only. Enrollment declined, and the school was closed in 1992.

The buildings at the old location on Augusta Street were saved from destruction by the San Antonio Conservation Society. After holding it a few years, the society sold the property to the Southwest Craft Center, a nonprofit organization that today offers the buildings and a gifted staff as a community resource for education in arts and crafts. In 1971, the buildings were designated a State Historical Landmark. The tree-shaded grounds beside the river offer the opportunity for lunch at the Copper Kitchen and browsing at the gift shop filled with locally made handcrafts and other art, as well as a view of the old buildings of the Ursuline Academy, with its cavernous chapel now used for community meetings and theatrical events.

Graves of Heroes and Fighters

The Alameda, named for the Spanish word for the cottonwood trees that lined its sides and now called East Commerce Street, was for many years one of San Antonio's principal streets. It was part of the Camino Real, the King's Highway, the Spanish royal road from Mexico to Louisiana. In its early days, East Commerce stretched east to Powder House Hill, where military units stored explosives.

When electric streetcars began serving the area in 1884, they ran on the "Cemetery Line." After heading east through St. Paul Square, the streetcars reached the burial grounds, some of which belonged to the city and some to various religious, fraternal, national, or ethnic groups.

In 1877, there were seven cemeteries in the area, including the military one that became the city's first National Cemetery. For those who like to explore the resting places of historic or notorious people, San Antonio's cemeteries on old Powder House Hill are rich in the numbers of gravesite markers bearing names famous in state and local history. The City Cemetery and others are located near East Commerce Street and New Braunfels Avenue.

In the old Federal Cemetery at 517 Paso Hondo Street, near the intersection of New Braunfels and Commerce, lie veterans of the U.S. war with Mexico, the Civil War, Indian Campaigns, the Spanish-American War, and World War I. The new National Cemetery was begun in 1937 at Fort Sam Houston.

14

Our Military Heritage

More battles have been fought in and around San Antonio than any city in the United States. One, of course, was at the Alamo—among the most memorable conflicts in American history. The Battle of Medina had more casualties than any battle in the history of the United States west of the Mississippi. The history of South Texas is steeped in the blood of heroes.

Fighting around San Antonio began in the 1700s when the Indians attacked Spanish expeditions as they moved into the area, and from time to time over the years blood was shed on both sides when Indians would ride into San Antonio to steal horses. The fighting between Spaniards and Indians continued for a century, and it did not stop during the period of Mexican control or later, for many years, when Texas was in the hands of the Anglo Americans.

In the early 1800s, loosely organized mounted armed troops from the United States came to drive out the Spanish forces that controlled Texas. Later, when Mexico had achieved independence from Spain, armed Americans attacked the Mexican government forces in Texas. Finally, in 1835 and 1836 the armies of the Mexican government were defeated and the Republic of Texas established.

Meanwhile, the fighting against the Indians—often with many casualties—went on even after the 1870s. The forts across West Texas, supplied mostly from San Antonio, marked the outposts for that long war between the original inhabitants of the country and the people who had come from Europe by way of the United States and Mexico.

Military Museums

San Antonio's unique military heritage is evident in the museums to be found at Fort Sam Houston, and at both Brooks and Lackland Air Force bases. Admission to all is free. The Quadrangle at "Fort Sam" is the site of Apache chief Geronimo's captivity; it is centered by the famous clock tower, and today is the home of free-roaming deer, peacocks, rabbits, and ducks. Nearby are the Pershing House, the Gift Chapel, and MacArthur Field, site of the first military flight.

The Army Medical Department Museum is the best of its kind in the nation. Of more general interest is the Fort Sam Houston Museum with its collection of memorabilia cataloging the Army's presence in San Antonio from 1845.

Edward H. White II Memorial Museum (Hangar 9) at Brooks Air Force Base is housed in the oldest aircraft hangar in the Air Force, built in 1918. More than half the museum is devoted to aerospace and tells the history of flight medicine and manned flight in the atmosphere and the space beyond. It is named for Air Force Lt. Col. Edward H. White II, son of a retired Air Force general, who was born at Fort Sam Houston. On the Gemini-Titan

4 Mission June 3-7, 1965, which he piloted, Edward White was the first American to venture outside a spacecraft in orbit. He died in 1967 in the Apollo 1 launch-pad fire at Cape Canaveral.

At both Lackland and Kelly Air Force bases, visitors can see static displays of a variety of aircraft.

Medal of Honor Winners

Soldiers have served and retired—have lived and died—in San Antonio for 280 years. Their names are found on monuments, but many names, if found at all, are mostly on humble, weather-beaten stones. Many represent heroes, the heroism forgotten. A few have been awarded the Medal of Honor—the highest recognition for valor in action with an enemy.

The earliest action in history for which a Medal of Honor was awarded occurred in San Antonio. Corporal John C. Hesse of the Union forces spirited away the U.S. flag at the time Maj. Gen. David E. Twiggs surrendered all U.S. military property in Texas to the Confederacy in 1861. Hesse took the flag to Washington, D.C. He was honored "for rescuing the colors of his regiment." Years later, when such awards were reviewed, his was revoked.

Some holders of the Medal of Honor, beginning with two from the Indian Wars, are in San Antonio cemeteries. A San Antonio native who was awarded the Medal of Honor for World War I heroism, David Barkley, was discovered later to be the Army's first Hispanic Medal of Honor holder, for his mother was of Mexican descent. On April 6, 1921, his body lay in state in the Shrine of Texas Liberty, only the fourth to be so honored at that time. The others were Army Maj. Gen. Frederick Funston, a former commander at Fort Sam Houston, who after his sudden death in 1917 was replaced by Brig. Gen. John J. Pershing; Nettie Houston Bringhurst, last surviving daughter of Sam Houston, on December 6, 1932; and Clara Driscoll, who helped preserve the Alamo, July 19, 1945. Most recently, on November 19, 1995, Marine Corps Staff Sgt. William James Bordelon, who was posthumously awarded the Medal of Honor for his actions on November 2, 1943, in the invasion of Tarawa, was honored at the Alamo.

San Antonio's most decorated World War II veteran, Cleto L. Rodríguez, who died in 1990, had earned 20 medals, including the Medal of Honor. Ivanhoe Elementary School was renamed Cleto Rodríguez School in 1975, and in 1991 a portion of Highway 90 was named Cleto Rodríguez Memorial Expressway. He died on December 7, 1990, and is buried in the Fort Sam Houston National Cemetery.

Two other Texas Medal of Honor winners, Lucian Adams and José López, were honored on August 9, 1994, when the City of San Antonio authorized the renaming of portions of Interstate Highways 37 and 10 in memory of the two heroes.

A Military Retirement Center

Not surprisingly, because of San Antonio's nearly subtropical climate and relatively low cost of living, the city has become one of the leading retirement areas in the country for both military and nonmilitary personnel. Of special importance to retirees from every walk of life are the exceptionally good medical facilities in the city. San Antonio was rated by *The Retired Officer Magazine* in September 1993 as the best of ten locations in the United States in which military retirees could live. As for civilians, San Antonio was rated second best location in the country for retirement in one book, and among the ten "undiscovered" retirement havens in the United States by another.

Fort Sam Houston

When the United States entered World War I in 1917, large numbers of new soldiers came to Camp Wilson, later designated as Camp Travis. There, adjoining Fort Sam Houston, men of the 90th Division were assembled in temporary buildings and trained for overseas duty.

Today, Fort Sam is the home of the Fifth U.S. Army. It is also headquarters for the U.S. Army Medical Command, the single manager of all of the Army's medical, dental, and veterinary services in the United States. The Fifth Army is responsible for the training and mobilization readiness of U.S. Army Reserve units in twenty-one states west of the Mississippi River (not including Minnesota) and coordinating military support to civil authorities in times of disaster. It also oversees National Guard units in that region of the country.

Famous Generals—Pershing, MacArthur, Eisenhower

Fort Sam Houston and San Antonio have seen more than a few extraordinary military men become world-renowned leaders. One was Brig. Gen. John J. Pershing, who was sitting in his office in the Quadrangle on April 6, 1917, the day America entered World War I. He was named Commander in Chief of the American Expeditionary Forces in France and rose rapidly in grade, eventually becoming General of the Armies.

"I feel as if I were coming home after being away a long time," wrote Douglas MacArthur in 1930. "You know, I lived here for

Townspeople Enjoyed Military Socials

In 1892, Richard Harding Davis wrote:

Fort Sam Houston at San Antonio is one of the three largest posts in the country, and is in consequence one of the heavens toward which the eyes of army people turn.

It is only twenty minutes from the city, and the weather is mild throughout the year, and in the summer there are palm trees around the houses; and white uniforms—which are unknown in the posts farther north, and which are as pretty as they are hard to keep clean—make the parade ground look like a cricket field.

They have dances at this post twice a month, the regimental band furnishing the music, and the people from town helping out the sets, and the officers in uniforms with red, white, and yellow stripes.

A military ball is always very pretty, and the dancing hall at Houston is decorated on such occasions with guidons and flags, and palms and broad-leaved plants, which grow luxuriously everywhere, and cost nothing.

five years and went to school at the old West Texas Military Academy. That was when the school was just across from the army post [Fort Sam Houston], where I lived. Then again, I was here in 1911 [as an Engineer Corps captain] stationed at the Post."

As a lieutenant in the Wisconsin 24th Infantry in the Civil War, his father, Arthur MacArthur, was awarded the Medal of Honor for his heroism in leading a charge to the top of Missionary Ridge in Chattanooga, Tennessee. At the end of the war, he was known as the "Boy Colonel of the West." He was twenty-three and a lieutenant colonel.

When Arthur MacArthur was stationed as an assistant adjutant general at Fort Sam Houston in the Quadrangle in the 1890s, his son was making a name for himself as a leader in the San Antonio military academy now called Texas Military Institute. (A century old, TMI is now in new buildings on the edge of the Hill Country near Camp Bullis.)

Later, Douglas MacArthur would earn the Medal of Honor, as had his father, making the two the only father-son holders of the medal. And eventually he would carry the rare title of "General of the Army," having become one of the eight five-star generals in United States history. No one, of course, other than Gen. John J. Pershing has been awarded the highest rank of General of the *Armies*.

After attending the military institute in San Antonio, Douglas MacArthur went on to the U.S. Military Academy at West Point. He became a commander of the 42nd (Rainbow) Division in World War I and in the 1930s Field Marshal of the Philippines. Later he held successive positions as Superintendent of the U.S. Military Academy and then commander of the combined U.S. Army Forces in the Far East (USAFE). He was one of the signers of the World War II peace treaty with Japan and Supreme Commander of the United Nations forces in the Korean War in the early 1950s.

In his *Reminiscences*, published in 1964, MacArthur looked back on his long career. He wrote that when his father was transferred from Fort Sam Houston in 1896, "It was a wrench to leave San Antonio. My four years there were without doubt the happiest of my life. Texas will always be a second home to me."

The Supreme Allied Commander in Europe in World War II, a five-star General of the Army and later the 34th president of the United States, Dwight David Eisenhower spent time in San Antonio. During his first tour at Fort Sam Houston, Eisenhower had met his wife, Mamie Doud, who came with her family regularly from Denver, Colorado, to winter in San Antonio. Many years later, on October 14, 1952, when President Eisenhower visited San Antonio, he said:

> Coming to San Antonio for my birthday is like coming back home. I guess there isn't a city or town in the whole world that holds more happy memories for me. Here I was stationed as a youngster in the army, and also in later life. Here too, I won my first and most important victory. For it was here that I met my Mamie for the first time and we became engaged to be married. Here, too, our first son was born. When a man gets to be sixty-two years old, he likes to count over the real values that have gone into his life. Many of the things that have made mine worthwhile had their beginnings right here in this grand old city of San Antonio.

The names of more than a dozen major players in American history can be found in the story of Fort Sam Houston. In addition to Civil War generals and heroes of the Indian wars were men who became famous in World War I, the Philippine Insurrection, and World War II.

Beginning of the Air Force

Another name in the pantheon of Fort Sam patriots was "Benny" Foulois, this country's foremost military pilot in the early days, who laid the groundwork for the American airpower that would contribute so much to winning World War II. As Maj. Gen. Benjamin D. Foulois, he was chief in the early 1930s of the Army's Air Corps, the air service that later became the independent United States Air Force.

U.S. aviation got its real start as a functional flying operation from its beginning on the fields beside Salado Creek—the "Mounted Drill Ground" in the northeast section of the Fort Sam Houston reservation where a small hangar was built. Not only the first training flights of Lt. Benny Foulois, but the first military aerial reconnaissance flights and the first airplane seat belts were initiated there. Reconnaissance flights were made along the Rio Grande in support of U.S. patrols in March 1911.

Brooke Army Medical Center

One of the largest and newest military hospitals in the world, a teaching facility, Brooke Army Medical Center (BAMC) is on the post. It was named for Brig. Gen. Roger Brooke, a medical doctor and former commander of the old station hospital. The medical center, which was opened in 1996 with the transfer of its mission from the old hospital, has consolidated medical care into one modern, 1.47-million-square-foot complex. The hospital has 450 inpatient beds.

U.S. Army Institute for Surgical Research

This facility, the largest burn research unit in the world, continues to pioneer lifesaving advances in burn care, involving new developments such as improved fluid resuscitation, topical antimicrobial chemotherapy, and treatment of acute renal failure.

Other Fort Sam Facilities

Also at Fort Sam Houston are the Academy of Health Sciences, a training detachment of the 507th Medical Company (Air Ambulance), the 41st Combat Support Hospital, and the 485th Medical Detachment. Non-medical units are the headquarters of the Fifth Recruiting Brigade (Southwest), a U.S. regional support group, and major elements of the 49th Armored Division of the Texas National Guard.

Kelly Air Force Base

Kelly Air Force Base, in southwest San Antonio, was established in 1917 at about the time the United States government declared war on Germany and her allies of the Central Powers, and entered World War I.

On April 9, 1917, three days after the declaration of war, Eddie Stinson—a civilian aircraft instructor and member of the famous San Antonio flying family—and three other pilots flew four aircraft from Fort Sam Houston to a cottonfield that would be called Kelly Field. The site had been selected by Major Benny Foulois because of its level terrain, good artesian well sources, and proximity to railroad facilities.

Tent hangars had been built there a few days before the first flight to house the aircraft, and on their first night the pilots made their beds on the ground next to their aircraft. From then on, Kelly Field grew rapidly, first with tents and soon with substantial buildings—hangars, barracks, mess halls, officers' quarters, warehouses, machine shops. Although in April 1917 the Army's entire air force (the Aviation Section of the Signal Corps) consisted of only thirty-five pilots, 1,987 enlisted men, and fifty-five training planes, it grew with amazing speed.

And who was the man for whom the field was named on July 30, 1917? He was English-born George Maurice Kelly, a second lieutenant, who on May 10, 1911, was landing a Curtiss biplane he had been flying over Fort Sam Houston. As the plane touched the ground, it lost a brace from one of the wheels and then bounced into the air and veered toward the tent camp of the 11th Infantry. In a maneuver to avoid hitting the camp, Lieutenant Kelly banked the careening plane sharply away and plowed into the ground to his death.

He was the first of many Army pilots killed in training. He is buried in the National Cemetery on Powder House Hill near Gen. John Bullis, the great Indian fighter and leader of the highly effective Negro-Seminole Indian mounted soldiers of the U.S. Army.

Kelly Air Force Base is the oldest continuously active air base in the United States Air Force. It was established only fourteen years after Orville and Wilbur Wright made their first flight at Kitty Hawk, North Carolina, on December 17, 1903. Kelly soon became the largest flying field in the country, sending hundreds of trained officers and enlisted men to serve overseas in World War I. In a single month, August 1917, sixty-seven organizations were formed. In December 1917 alone, 1,289 officers and 32,812 enlisted men arrived. By the end of 1918, there had been 5,182 officers and 197,468 enlisted men at Kelly Field.

Famous Kelly Officers

Two of the officers at Kelly—Generals Fechet and Spaatz—later rose to the top to command the entire military air arm of the Army, which in 1947 became the United States Air Force. Col. James E. Fechet commanded Kelly Field from September 5 to October 2, 1918. It was under Fechet that Brig. Gen. Frank P. Lahm established Randolph Field, the "West Point of the Air," at San Antonio on June 20, 1930.

When Kelly Field was organized in May 1917, it had three squadrons: Third Aero Squadron, Fifth Aero Squadron, and Provisional Aviation School Squadron. The commander of the Fifth Aero Squadron was Capt. Carl Spaatz. After distinguished combat flying in World War I, Spaatz served in many key assignments. He was commanding officer of Kelly Field from October 1920 to February 1921. In World War II, Spaatz served in both the European and Pacific theaters of war. He was commanding general of the U.S. Strategic Air Forces in the Pacific and supervised the final strategic bombing of Japan, using B-29s, including the atomic bomb missions on Hiroshima and Nagasaki.

In February 1946, Spaatz became commander of the Army Air Forces, and in September 1947, President Harry S. Truman appointed him the first Chief of Staff of the new United States Air Force, a service co-equal with the U.S. Army and Navy.

A number of Kelly Field pilots went on to become world famous. One was Charles Augustus Lindbergh, later acclaimed internationally when he made the first solo flight across the Atlantic from New York to Paris in a Ryan monoplane on May 20-21, 1927. Lindbergh had learned to fly "the military way" at Brooks and Kelly fields in San Antonio. He was commissioned second lieutenant in the Army Air Service at Kelly Field on March

14, 1925. When he died in 1974, Lindbergh held the Medal of Honor, awarded by the Army Air Corps for his heroic transatlantic flight. He had served the military in many ways as a civilian in World War II. In April 1954, he was appointed a brigadier general in the United States Air Force Reserve—another great American with unforgettable ties to San Antonio and Kelly.

Kelly's Future

In 1996, Kelly Air Force Base, with some 1,600 military personnel and more than 10,000 civilian employees, was San Antonio's single largest employer. It had been in 1995 the largest industrial center in the entire Southwest, public or private, according to the San Antonio Chamber of Commerce. At the U.S. Air Force Air Logistics Center at Kelly, some 61 percent of the civilian employees were Hispanic.

Kelly's base perimeter runs for nineteen miles, encircling more than 3,924 acres. Its runway is unusually long—11,550 feet. For years, it has been one of the Air Force's largest maintenance depots, the home of the San Antonio Air Logistics Center of the Air Force Materiel Command. Among the major organizations with headquarters at Kelly are the Air Intelligence Agency, the Information Warfare Battlelab, Air Force News Center, Defense Commissary Agency (Midwest Region), the 433rd Military Airlift Wing (U.S. Air Force Reserve), and the 149th Fighter Wing (Texas National Guard).

At Kelly, highly specialized mechanics have for years cared for the gargantuan C-5 Galaxy and the gigantic new C-17 that can carry major Army battle vehicles. They have supported 6,000 aircraft of thirty-three types, as well as all Air Force nuclear ordnance.

However, all that could change in the next few years because on June 22, 1995, the independent Defense Base Closure and Realignment Commission (BRAC) voted to discontinue the aircraft repair depot at Kelly. Some of the jobs will not be finally ended until the phaseout is completed in July 2001, when San Antonio Logistics Center will be closed and Kelly realigned with Lackland AFB. Meanwhile, the closure has been a stunning blow to the city's economy as well as to the lives of thousands, and vigorous plans are under way to convert the base and its skilled employees to private commerce and industry. In August 1996, an international company, EG&G, headquartered in Massachusetts, was selected to oversee the implementation of steps toward the 2001 base closure and to plan redevelopment of the installation for maximum employment. A new subsidiary of the company, EG&G Management Services of San Antonio, will handle the program.

Brooks Air Force Base

In his last official act as president of the United States, John F. Kennedy dedicated several new buildings at Brooks Air Force Base to be devoted to research in the medicine of flying in the atmosphere and in the space beyond—in aerospace. That was on November 21, 1963, the day before he was assassinated in Dallas. In his remarks, President Kennedy said:

> I have come to Texas today to salute an outstanding group of pioneers—the men who man the Brooks Air Force Base School of Aerospace Medicine and the Aerospace Medical Center. It is fitting that San Antonio should be the site of this Center and this School as we gather to dedicate this complex of buildings.
>
> For this city has long been the home of the pioneers in the air; it was here that Sidney Brooks, whose memory we honor today, was born and raised. It was here that Charles Lindbergh and Claire Chennault and a host of others who in World War I and World War II and Korea, and even today, have helped demonstrate American mastery of the sky, trained at Kelly Field and Randolph Field, which form a major part of aviation history.
>
> And in the new frontier of outer space, while headlines may be made by others in other places, history is being made every day by the men and women of the Aerospace Medical Center without whom there could be no history.

President John F. Kennedy with (left to right) San Antonio mayor Walter W. McAllister, Sr., and Texas Governor John B. Connally at his dedication of several new buildings at Brooks Air Force Base on November 21, 1963—his last official act. He was assassinated the next day in Dallas, where Governor Connally suffered serious gunshot wounds. (Joe V. Maldonado photo)

Brooks Air Force Base, the first balloon and airship school in the American military forces, was founded in 1917. A Primary Flying School for aircraft was established by the Army Air Service there in 1922. Among several graduates who became famous was Claire L. Chennault, the World War II hero in the Pacific rim who organized and commanded the American Volunteer Group known as the "Flying Tigers"—fighter pilots who harassed the Japanese air units for years. They were a group of American volunteers who went into action in China shortly after the Japanese attack on Pearl Harbor. On December 20, 1941, they downed four Japanese bombers near Kunming.

Another famous graduate of Brooks was Nathan F. Twining, Air Force chief of staff in 1953 and chairman of the Joint Chiefs of Staff in 1957, the first Air Force officer to serve in that position. Two others from Brooks who became top generals and chiefs of staff of the Air Force were Hoyt S. Vandenberg and Thomas D. White. Three other early chiefs of staff who took training there were Curtis R. LeMay, John P. McConnell, and John D. Ryan, who spent time at Kelly Field. All these generals had distinguished themselves during World War II.

Brooks Field was named for Lt. Sidney J. Brooks, Jr., a native San Antonian and former reporter for the *San Antonio Light*. He was killed in a plane crash at Kelly Field No. 2 on November 13, 1917. In 1941, an Advanced Flying School was established at Brooks, and for fourteen years after World War II it was the site of a succession of tactical and reserve flying activities. In the summer of 1959, the base became the headquarters for the Aerospace Medical Center.

Human Systems Center

Today, Brooks is the headquarters of the Human Systems Center of the Air Force Materiel Command. Its mission is to protect and enhance human capabilities and human-systems performance for both individuals and command forces, including those of Department of Defense and allied nations.

Armstrong Laboratory

Among the major units at the aerospace base is the Armstrong Laboratory, one of four Air Force "super laboratories." It provides the science and technology base and direct support needed to enhance human performance in Air Force systems and operations in aerospace. It is the nation's most advanced center for the science and technology of protecting humans in the environments of both the atmosphere and the space beyond. The laboratory conducts research and development in the fields of biodynamics, biocommunication, radiation-directed energy bioeffects, plus many other studies.

U.S. Air Force School of Aerospace Medicine

Another major operation at Brooks, the U.S. Air Force School of Aerospace Medicine, is a major provider of educational programs related to aerospace medicine for Air Force, Department of Defense, and allied nations personnel.

Lackland Air Force Base

More than four million Americans throughout the United States are familiar with San Antonio because they took their basic training at Lackland Air Force Base, the largest training installation in the Air Force, better known as the "Gateway to the Air Force." Many thousands of basic trainees get brief glimpses of the city after completing six weeks of rigorous physical and academic training.

Not only basic trainees but also officer trainees have come to Lackland. Today, most of them come from Air Force Reserve Officer Training Corps (ROTC) cadets and a small number who have been awarded direct commissions. More than 93,800 men and women were commissioned at Lackland over the years until September 22, 1993, when the Officer Training School's last class of cadets became second lieutenants and the school was moved to Maxwell AFB, Alabama, home of the Air University.

Lackland Air Force Base traces its beginning to June 26, 1942, when the War Department detached from Kelly Field the area lying west of Leon Creek, making it the San Antonio Aviation Cadet Center. This area had been used by Kelly before 1941, first as a bivouac and bombing range for aviation cadets and later as an Army Air Forces Preflight School.

The training center was given a number of different names over the years until 1947, when it was named for the person who had originally recommended a reception and training center there. Brig. Gen. Frank Darwin Lackland, former commandant of the Advanced Flying School at Kelly Field, died in 1943. Because training is one Air Force mission that will never come to an end, the "Gateway to the Air Force" seems likely to continue in the years ahead to be also the "Gateway to San Antonio."

Defense Language Institute

Thousands of foreign military personnel from 100 countries have learned about San Antonio while being trained at Lackland. Many have been assigned to Lackland's Defense Language Institute English Language Center. Some 2,000 foreign students, military and civilian, have come annually in past years to stay two to eight months.

Inter-American Air Forces Academy

After Hurricane Andrew destroyed the facilities of the Inter-American Air Forces Academy at Homestead AFB, Florida, on August 24, 1992, it was moved to Lackland. Both Lackland and Kelly Air Force Bases provide permanent facilities for the academy, which conducts professional, technical, and management training in Spanish to military forces and government agencies from some twenty-five Latin American nations and the Caribbean. The Inter-American Air Forces Academy graduates approximately 660 students a year.

Wilford Hall Medical Center

Air Force patients referred from around the world are treated at Lackland's 59th Medical Wing, Wilford Hall Medical Center, the largest hospital in the Air Force. It is one of the most advanced hospitals in the Southwest, performing not only open-heart surgery but liver, kidney, corneal, and bone marrow transplants as well as advanced cancer therapy and neurosurgery. It is the Air Force's sole AIDS referral center and the site for important work in treatment and research on AIDS. Some 24,000 patients a year are admitted to the 585-bed hospital. At the same time, it serves more than a million outpatients yearly.

With the $6.4 million expansion of the center's emergency department completed in 1996, plus the new Brooke Army Medical Center, San Antonio's two military hospitals had what are believed to be the best and most up-to-date emergency facilities on the planet.

The Center is named for Maj. Gen. Wilford F. Hall, a pioneer aviation surgeon in the 1930s who developed hospital-like interiors and medical procedures used for special air transport and later founded the American Board of Aviation Medicine.

Randolph Air Force Base

Before there was a United States Air Force Academy in Colorado Springs, Randolph Field, as it was then called, was known widely as the "West Point of the Air." Schools there trained cadets to become officers. That was before the Army Air Corps had become the Army Air Forces under the War Department, and some seventeen years before the United States Air Force became a separate military department.

When the base was dedicated on June 20, 1930, a crowd of 15,000 people swarmed onto the installation to witness the greatest fly-by of aircraft in American history—233 aircraft. Thus began a great flying training center that continues to this day.

The installation's unusual layout is centered on the 148-foot-tall water tower camouflaged with ornamental precast concrete grillwork and a blue and gold mosaic tile dome. Its 500,000-gallon water tank and the administrative offices at its base have been used since October 5, 1931. Called the "Taj Mahal," it was the work of 1st Lt. Harold Clark, a trained architect who envisioned a "perfect Air City." His plans for the training center were approved

The Administrative Building at Randolph Air Force Base, known as the Taj Mahal, holds a 500,000-gallon water tank in its tower and a 1200-seat theater as well as offices. Designed by San Antonio architects Atlee B. and Robert M. Ayres, it was inspired by nineteenth-century Mexican churches, and the blind tracery of its tower shaft has its roots in the architecture of Moorish Spain. (Charles Cyr photo)

enthusiastically by Brig. Gen. Frank P. Lahm, who in 1926 could see that space at Kelly and Brooks fields was insufficient for the great amount of flight training required.

Ironically, the field was named for one of the committee members assigned to select a name for it. Capt. William Millican Randolph, a native of Austin, an experienced flyer and member of the name-selection committee, was killed when returning to Kelly Field. He crashed his AT-4 on takeoff from Gorman Field, Texas, on February 17, 1928.

Today, the 12th Flying Training Wing at Randolph Air Force Base graduates some 500 instructor pilots each year from the thirteen-week training program. Among other major organizations on the base are the Air Force Personnel Center and Air Force Recruiting Service. Randolph also supports the Morale, Welfare, and Recreation Center for the Air Force, which has its headquarters off base in San Antonio.

What was for many years known as the Air Training Command became on July 1, 1993, the Air Education and Training Command (AETC). The command united the Air Force's educational and training processes. It oversees undergraduate and advanced flight training, plus other technical training. AETC is also responsible for recruiting and accessing personnel into the Air Force.

In August 1996, Randolph was added to the National Register of Historic Places, with 349 historic structures on the 3,129-acre base named a national historic district. Years earlier, in 1974, Fort Sam Houston and its Quadrangle, Pershing House, and Post Chapel were entered into the National Register of Historic Places.

Early Movie Sites
Movie buffs will recall that aircraft from Kelly Field flew in Hollywood's first motion picture to be awarded an Oscar. Hundreds of soldiers from Camp Stanley and Fort Sam Houston served as extras. *Wings*, a filmed story of heroism and romance during American action in France in World War I—a silent, black and white movie, of course—starred Charles Rogers, Richard Arlen,

and Clara Bow. Gary Cooper drew attention despite the brevity of his debut. The picture portrayed the American air forces providing support to the U.S. Second Division in France, which had suffered 25,000 casualties and 4,000 dead. The world premiere of the Paramount film was held at the Texas Theater in San Antonio. *Wings* was presented the Motion Picture Academy Award for best picture of 1927-1928.

Another patriotic movie, *I Wanted Wings*, starring William Holden, Veronica Lake, Ray Milland, and Constance Moore, was filmed at Randolph Field in 1940. But the first of these military-based films was *The Big Parade*, with World War I battle scenes shot at Fort Sam Houston in 1925. The silent picture was directed by the legendary King Vidor (incidentally, a Hungarian Texan) and starred John Gilbert and Renée Adorée.

A Rare Military Legacy

Over the decades, military men and women from all over America have brought thousands of bright, inquiring minds to the city to fashion a rich legacy of technical, management, medical, and scientific skills and knowledge. Many key federal employees also have brought their expertise to the city, and large numbers have transferred their specialized training to the civilian sector.

In terms of people, the military presence in the San Antonio area is significant. The four Air Force bases and one Army post, plus subunits, require thousands of specialists. The total Department of Defense population includes active duty military personnel and civilian employees, National Guard and Reserve personnel, and retired military and civilian personnel. Some small units of the Navy and Marine Corps are also represented. As of fiscal year 1994, there were 38,500 active-duty personnel, 3,400 military Civil Service and Non-appropriated Funds civilians, and 9,500 Reserve and National Guard personnel. In addition, there were 85,000 military and civilian retirees and survivors.

At the same time, the presence of highly technical military organizations has elevated the learning, expertise, and income level of many thousands of San Antonio civilians employed by the government. This has been most significant in its influence over many decades in shaping the lives of Hispanics and other non-Anglos as well as of Anglos. Moreover, the city is enriched technically by the unparalleled facilities of the research centers and laboratories in the area—both military and civilian.

15

Breaking from the Past

As early as 1909, the idea of having a world's fair in San Antonio prompted discussion among businessmen. They began then to consider a fair to memorialize the 200th anniversary of the founding of San Antonio, but not until 1958 did anyone effectively present the idea for an international fair. This time, the fair would commemorate the 250th anniversary of the city's founding. Retailer Jerome K. Harris suggested to the Chamber of Commerce, of which he was an officer, that an international fair, to be called "Hemis-Fair," be organized to show "our affection and appreciation of Mexico." As time went on, the fair's theme was expanded to include the Americas—North, South, and Central—"the confluence of civilizations" in the Western Hemisphere.

Henry B. Gonzalez, a Democratic congressman under President Lyndon B. Johnson, together with Gov. John B. Connally, was among the powerful influences needed to stage the world's fair, HemisFair, in 1968. A number of useful buildings remained after the fair, among them the Henry B. Gonzalez Convention Center. Gonzalez is shown here as Grand Marshal of the 1984 Paseo Navideño Parade in San Antonio. (San Antonio Express-News photo)

U.S. Congressman Henry B. Gonzalez took up the cause, as did Governor John B. Connally, for whom San Antonio was a second hometown next to nearby Floresville. Hill Country Texan Lyndon B. Johnson, then president, also helped. Mayor Walter W. McAllister, Sr., lent powerful support. Under the initial leadership of lawyer and banker Bill Sinkin, some 300 local businessmen pledged their support, and in 1962 the San Antonio Fair, Inc., was founded. Marshall T. Steves, Sr., became its president in 1964 and remained so until it closed.

Thirty-three countries, including those in the Organization of American States, plus the state of Arkansas, joined the United States and Texas in celebrating what was called "the Confluence of Civilizations." Governor Connally, commissioner general of HemisFair, described the Fair as "an exciting creation of world-wide significance, born of the common heritage binding the Americas midst the historic surroundings of San Antonio."

When it opened on April 6, the exposition's 92.6 acres at the foot of the Tower of the Americas were filled with pavilions for governments and industries plus theaters and other buildings for entertainment. Fiesta Island was a place for rides and games. Site planners provided elevated walkways and footbridges. Spectators watched the water-ski show from the great grandstand, then rode the monorail or the skyride or boarded a boat for a lagoon cruise.

Making Room

An entire neighborhood was virtually razed to make room for the new downtown San Antonio. Except for thirty-five structures that were saved, the new HemisFair buildings replaced historic homes and businesses, meeting places, St. Michael's Catholic Church and its school, Rodfei Sholom Synagogue, and the neighborhoods of Poles, Germans, Mexican Americans, Chinese, African Americans, and other ethnic groups.

After the area to be transformed had been selected by the San Antonio Urban Renewal Administration, the federal government allocated $12.5 million for the purchase of the site. Urban renewal officials described the area as

> filled with pecan, loquat, hackberry and elm trees and numerous historic structures in varying states of repair. It also included San Antonio's skid row, several substandard boarding house conversions, various light industrial, ware-housing uses incompatible with the primarily residential neighborhood.

More than 570 structures were razed, according to urban renewal records. These included 247 single-family homes, 140 industrial and commercial buildings, forty-five public buildings,

The Human Cost of Progress

Among the remnants of the homes, churches and businesses razed for HemisFair lurked shadows of broken dreams. As Michael Middleton has said, "Every city exists uniquely in the mind of each individual who knows it." San Antonio author and screenwriter Claude Stanush recalls that he was born fifty feet from where the Tower of the Americas stands. His grandfather's two-story house on South Street had stone walls "thick as a fort's, so that it would stand for generations." He remembers that when the HemisFair grounds were prepared, his grandfather's house was listed as a historic structure, and promises were made to preserve it.

"We all know what happened to some of those promises," he recalls. "My family and I watched with sad hearts as the big iron ball crashed into those massive stone walls, again, and again and again, until finally they crumbled and fell in a heap."

Frank Toudouze refused to move after his property had been condemned to clear the way for Urban Renewal Project 5 in the HemisFair area. The condemnation, he maintained, was illegal. His home had been in his family for fifty-two years. On April 7, 1966, after sheriff's deputies broke into Toudouze's house, cutting the lock on the front gate and breaking open a screen and the front door, Mr. and Mrs. Toudouze were found sitting in the kitchen. Mrs. Toudouze, tears in her eyes, fingered a rosary, and Frank was playing "May the Good Lord Bless and Keep You" on his harmonica. He kept on playing the soulful tune as the two were led from their home and entered a family automobile to drive away.

Toudouze fought his eviction in court but lost the battle in the State Supreme Court. By that time, his home had been demolished. He never claimed the money he was awarded for it. An administrative assistant at the Bexar County Courthouse told a reporter for the *San Antonio Light* in 1988 that "there was $10,597.58, and it reverted to the state treasury on April 18, 1984."

sixty-eight duplexes, and sixty-nine apartment buildings. There were 768 people— families and individuals—and 275 businesses uprooted. Urban renewal administrators say they "located, acquired and delivered the land in fourteen months." And today, for many who remember the neighborhood of their youth, now leveled, "once familiar scenes appear, like strains of a forgotten melody."

For better or for worse, the way of life of the people displaced by HemisFair was shattered in the name of progress and urban renewal. Archaeologists at the University of Texas at San Antonio still regret the fact that when the area was cleared, little archaeology was done on what they term "this very sensitive area of downtown San Antonio."

The Many Benefits

This, the first world's fair in the Southwest, changed San Antonio profoundly. It brought new life to the River Walk, channeling its waters past the new Chamber of Commerce building on Alamo and Commerce, and on to the new Convention Center—whence, twenty years later, it would be extended to Rivercenter, a major shopping and entertainment mall. To bring the river to HemisFair, bridges were built on dry land, then beneath them a river channel was excavated so the water could flow eastward freely.

An estimated $14 million was spent in private investment along the river, and new hotels and motels sprang up around the city. Total construction activity between 1966 and the close of the fair totaled $490 million, including $71 million on the fair site. Funding for the fair came from city, state, and federal funds as well as private sources.

The twenty-one-story, 500-room Hilton Palacio del Rio on South Alamo was built in 202 days by construction contractor Henry Bartell Zachry. Seven miles away, the twelve-foot by nineteen-foot bedrooms were cast in concrete, given wiring and plumbing lines and connections, and completely decorated, down to the last light bulb. Then the thirty-five-ton rooms were moved to the hotel site where a tall crane lifted each one into place, beginning at the fifth floor.

At times, crews stacked an average of eighteen to twenty rooms a day; the last one was emplaced on December 22, 1967. Meanwhile, elevators, stairways, restaurant, swimming pool, coffee shop, banquet hall, and private club were being built. The hotel opened for business on March 30, 1968, less than a week before the fair began.

New entrepreneurs, some from other states or countries, came to town, stayed, and prospered. A number of today's successful local businesses got their jump-start as the city began breathing new life in the late 1960s.

The world's fair, declared such by the Bureau of International Expositions, lasted six months—from April 6 to October 6. About six million people came.

What Is Left Today

The list of buildings and centers standing today in the Fair area is long: the Chamber of Commerce, the Henry B. Gonzalez Convention Center, the Tower of the Americas, the University of Texas Institute of Texan Cultures, the United States Courthouse, the Federal Building, the International Conference Center, Plaza Mexico, the Lila Cockrell Theater of the Performing Arts, and buildings for extension schools of the National Autonomous University of Mexico (Universidad Nacional Autónoma de Mexico), and Texas A&M University Engineering Extension Service. The site of the historic HemisFair Arena, used by the San Antonio Spurs basketball team and other events for decades, has given way to a much-enlarged Convention Center.

The crowning landmark of San Antonio, the Tower of the Americas, dominates San Antonio's skyline as an enormous exclamation mark. It says: "The cultures of our past are the foundation of our future!"

In 1968, only two towers in the world—one in Paris and another in Dortmund, Germany—had loftier observation decks than the Tower of the Americas. It is 579 feet above grade level, and the top of its mast is 750 feet high—200 feet taller than the Washington Monument. Three high-speed elevators, in addition to two 952-step stairways, can take visitors to the revolving restaurant and the observation deck, which offers a 360-degree view of the city and environs. Adjoining it are the HemisFair Urban Water Park and the Mexican Cultural Institute, which exhibits contemporary works by artists from Mexico and Central and South America.

The convention and tourist business brings nearly seven million visitors to San Antonio each year, surpassing the number of visitors to the two other largest cities in Texas, Houston and Dallas. As San Antonio moves into the twenty-first century, even more changes are evident. HemisFair was the catalyst. It helped make the city the favorite place in Texas to visit. It gave impetus to making the River Walk what it had been intended by its architect, Robert H. H. Hugman. Today, the services sector of the local economy, which includes tourism, is the city's largest source of employment, followed by trade, government, and manufacturing. Within the services sector, the city's hospitality industry provides the major employment. In the government sector, military installations provide only a little more than half the jobs; the remainder come from local government. More than 56,600 jobs in San Antonio are supported by the visitor industry, and its economic value to the city was estimated in 1995 at $3.15 billion.

For better or for worse, the Tower of the Americas in HemisFair Park is the symbol of the new San Antonio—it is physically San Antonio's highest tribute to its past. It is a memorial not only to one ancient neighborhood forever removed, but to all that is meant by historic change in a city's life.

Institute of Texan Cultures

Among the richest legacies of San Antonio's HemisFair '68 was the University of Texas Institute of Texan Cultures. Its dioramas and other displays tell graphically how the native Americans came from Asia and lived in Texas, and how, later, immigrants from other continents came to Texas and settled the land, establishing new lives while preserving their cultures. It demonstrates the costumes, crafts, foods, music, and other art of more than two dozen ethnic and national groups. The institute offers an active education program that reaches throughout the state.

The Folklife Festival

The Texas Folklife Festival is a special four-day party held every August. The fifteen-acre grounds at the Institute of Texan Cultures are the site of this mammoth, exuberant celebration of cultures from all parts of the state.

St. Paul Square

The area around the Alamodome and the renovated Southern Pacific Railroad station used by Amtrak was once alive with commerce and people but became almost paralyzed by the urban renewal programs that cleared away many buildings in preparation for San Antonio's world fair of 1968. Now in the shadow of the new Alamodome, the St. Paul area is slowly coming back as a lively entertainment area.

St. Paul Square was named for St. Paul Methodist Episcopal Church, built in 1870, whose tall steeple can be seen on North Center Street. Although today the church is used for law offices, it was for many years a religious and social meeting center for members of San Antonio's black community.

Because of its railroad depot, built in 1902, the St. Paul Square area was a center for trade, hotels, restaurants, and nightlife. For years the hotels there were the only public places in San Antonio for black musicians such as Louis Armstrong, Count Basie, Marian Anderson, and other visiting artists to stay overnight.

By 1979, both St. Paul Square Historic District and Southern Pacific Depot Historic District had been entered in the National Register of Historic Places. The railroad station is noted for its Mission Revival architectural style, baroque detailing, and interesting interior with stained-glass windows.

Beginning in the 1970s, with city and federal assistance (and invigorated by San Antonio's Alamodome completed in 1993), the 5.6-acre tract known as St. Paul Square has been enjoying a renewed life once thought to be gone forever. Today, developers are planning a major entertainment, shopping, dining, and hotel center in the square.

South Texas Medical Center

San Antonio offers a wide range of medical services, including twenty-three general hospitals and military hospitals, and three level-one trauma centers. Medicine is near the top among the major sectors of the city's economy, and it has the largest medical complex in Texas. On its 700 acres, the South Texas Medical Center encompasses nine major hospitals, two physical rehabilitation centers, and the University of Texas Health Science Center, plus medical offices, clinics, laboratories, research facilities, support organizations, and nursing facilities.

The University of Texas Health Science Center—highly advanced in a variety of specialties—is one of only six sites in the country federally approved for patients to try experimental new cancer drugs never before given to human beings. It has a medical school, dental school, school of nursing, school of allied health sciences, and school of biomedical sciences. Its graduate school of biomedical sciences offers Ph.D. programs in biochemistry, microbiology, cell and structural biology, physiology, and pharmacology. The School of Nursing is the largest in the UT system and has strong nursing Ph.D. programs.

In 1993, its dental school was listed best in the nation in a survey by *U.S. News and World Report*, based on an evaluation among experts of its reputation for scholarship, curriculum, and quality of faculty and graduate students.

Audie Murphy VA Hospital

One of the hospitals in the Medical Center was named for the Texan who was the most decorated soldier of World War II and who afterward made more than forty motion pictures. There is an eight-foot-tall bronze statue of him in front of the Audie L. Murphy Memorial Veterans Administration Hospital. A room containing memorabilia reflecting events in the life of Audie Murphy is near the entrance on the first floor. The hospital has a Research

Service with 28,000 square feet and 158 investigators devoted to research and development studies in a variety of diseases. The 674-bed acute-care facility provides treatment in medicine, surgery, neuropsychiatry, and rehabilitation medicine.

Other Research Park Facilities

The Health Science Center is located on three campuses, covering 175 acres. The two newest of these are the UT Institute of Biotechnology in Texas Research Park and the Robert F. McDermott Clinical Science Building near the main campus. With a total enrollment of 2,400, the center is among the state's leading research facilities.

At the park also is the Cancer Therapy and Research Institute for Drug Development and the Southwest Oncology Group, both involved in research and testing of treatments for cancer. With all these institutes and groups devoting time to cancer research, San Antonio is becoming a principal center for the national effort.

Among other organizations at the Research Park are BioMedical Enterprises, Inc., and SRC Systems, Inc., a software development company for medical management. The biomedical research organizations initially associated with the Texas Research Park are scheduled to be joined by entrepreneurs, corporations, and non-profit institutions related to the biotech industry that will devote themselves to product development as well as research.

An Attractive Site for Corporate Relocations

In recent years, major corporations have moved to San Antonio because of their confidence in the quality of the work force they can draw upon. Among these are Sony Microelectronics and VLSI Technology, Inc., two of the highest-technology semiconductor facilities in the world. Both companies serve a variety of computer users and employ hundreds of extraordinary specialists. Sony's computer chip plant—the company's only semiconductor manufacturing plant outside Japan—is expected to be continuously expanded and upgraded.

Another significant endorsement of the city's viability and great potential for rounded development was the move in 1992 and 1993 of the large corporate headquarters of Southwestern Bell Corporation from St. Louis to San Antonio. On April 1, 1996, SBC Communications, a former Bell System company, and Pacific Telesis Group announced a definitive agreement to merge into a single company to be called SBC Communications, Inc. The merger will create an organization of more than 100,000 employees and income of nearly $3 billion. The entity will serve seven of the country's ten largest metropolitan areas, and the nation's two most populous states—California and Texas. The corporation also has a controlling interest in Teléfonos de México (Telmex), one of the world's fastest-growing telecommunications companies.

As it has from its beginning in 1718—and during the 1890s with its annual International Fair, and in 1968 with its world's fair dedicated to "the common heritage binding the Americas"— San Antonio looks expectantly to mutual benefits from its close ties with the lands south of the border, only some 150 miles away.

16

Enjoying Life

This is a city with an astonishing variety of excellent restaurants that have pleased well-traveled tastes for more than a century—and a city that knows how to entertain. It supports the arts in all their manifestations, including a symphony orchestra and artists of every kind in music, dance, theater, and writing. It has outstanding museums, art centers, theaters, and concert halls. More than 20 museums offer enlightening insights to military life and advances in medicine and aerospace, as well as to the lives of patriots, cowboys, pioneers, trail drivers, ethnic and social cultures, and rare art.

Music

The San Antonio Symphony celebrated its fifty-seventh anniversary in 1997. The Texas Bach Choir is the only one of its kind in Texas, with a forty-five-member group specializing in sacred choral music. The San Antonio Municipal Band plays seven to ten free concerts a year at various sites throughout the city, and the newly formed San Antonio Opera Company is bringing Grand Opera back to the city to increase the quality of life and cultural growth.

Artists and Galleries

The city has become a haven for artists, many of them reflecting the unique multiculturalism of a "San Antonio style." Few realize that this is home to more recognized Mexican-American artists than any other city in the country. The Blue Star Arts Space & Arts Complex in the Southtown neighborhood draws anyone interested in modern art and artists at work. San Antonio Museum of Art will soon be able to show even more of its amazing collection of Mexican and other Hispanic art when it expands into its Latin American Arts Center. Downtown, at 305 Houston Street, the new San Antonio Children's Museum is a place of hands-on learning for both children and adults.

Why Not a Bohemian Rendezvous?

In February 1928, Lawlor McCormack wrote in *Bunker's Monthly, The Magazine of Texas*, edited by the well-known journalist of the time, Peter Molyneaux, and published in Fort Worth, that San Antonio would be the ideal place for a Texas literary colony. He said: "I would not be surprised if some of our younger American writers who affect the custom of congregating in colonies would discover the old Alamo City ere long. And why not? It has as much 'atmosphere' as New Orleans, and is as old, and—in spite of O. Henry's *Fog in San Antone* and the fact that I have all the passion of a native for New Orleans—I'll assert without qualm that it has a much milder and more delightful Winter climate than the Creole metropolis. They are making quite a bohemian rendezvous of the Vieux Carré in New Orleans, and why not San Antonio?"

McNay Museum

One of San Antonio's great works of art is the Marion Koogler McNay Museum, which originally was Mrs. McNay's home. She had influenced two of San Antonio's leading architects, Atlee B. and Robert M. Ayres, in the design of her Spanish Colonial Revival-style house, which was begun in 1927. She died in 1950 and the museum was opened four years later.

The great beauty of the grounds, with a pool shaped like the famous Rose Window at Mission San José, makes it a favorite place for brides to have their pictures taken. Based on Marion Koogler McNay's extraordinary collection of great art—she had studied at the Art Institute of Chicago—the museum is filled with beautifully displayed masterpieces. The exhibition areas have been enlarged over the years to house many fine gifts of art. The McNay has been described as one of the most tasteful and elegant museums in the state.

Steves Homestead

Another former home that has become popular with visitors to San Antonio is the large Steves Homestead on King William Street. It was built in 1876 for the prosperous Edward Steves, owner of a lumber company, from designs of the prolific and talented English architect Alfred Giles. On beautiful grounds, surrounded by large trees, the house is authentically and lavishly furnished in the style of its period. It is operated as a house museum by the San Antonio Conservation Society, which received it as a gift from Mrs. Curtis Vaughan, daughter of Albert Steves, Sr., in 1952 and restored it from nineteenth-century photographs.

The "Enchilada Red" Library

As with many city libraries begun in the early 1900s throughout the nation, San Antonio received funds provided initially by the Scottish-born American industrialist and philanthropist Andrew Carnegie; he donated $50,000 in 1902, with the proviso that the city support the library from its funds. The Carnegie Library was torn down and replaced by the San Antonio Public Library in

1930. A new building called the Main Library was built in 1968 on St. Mary's Street, but it was replaced in 1995 by the spectacular "enchilada red" Central Library at Romana Plaza on Soledad Street. Equipped to serve readers and researchers entering the new century, the new library, along with its seventeen branches throughout the city, fosters community programs and specialized organizations to serve interest groups such as writers, genealogists, and historians.

The spectacular architecture of the new seven-story Central Library with its 500,000 books, a notably rich Texana/genealogy collection, data in the Spanish language as well as English, computerized data system, special children's and elders' facilities, parking garage, and other features make it a stellar attraction for visitors and San Antonians. Ricardo Legorreta of Mexico was the internationally acclaimed architect of the $38 million work of art, which opened on May 20, 1995.

The Hertzberg Circus Collection

In central downtown, the Hertzberg Circus Collection is housed in the building that replaced San Antonio's Carnegie Library at 210 West Market Street. Harry Hertzberg, a San Antonio lawyer, book collector, and lifelong circus fan, acquired an enormous store of circus memorabilia, which he donated to the San Antonio Public Library in 1940. This building has become the wonderful circus museum of today. More than 20,000 items of circusana have been fascinating visitors to the museum for decades. In addition to colorful circus posters of yesteryear, there are a variety of props used by showpeople. Visitors are intrigued by the small coach, tiny violin, and other relics of the diminutive circus stars Tom Thumb and his wife.

Sports

San Antonians are avid sports fans. The San Antonio Spurs basketball team has played to enthusiastic supporters for more than twenty years. The city traces the beginnings of its Texas League baseball team, the San Antonio Missions, back more than 100 years.

It is a farm team for the Los Angeles Dodgers. After twenty-five years in Keefe Stadium at St. Mary's University, the Missions moved in 1994 to the city's new 6,000-seat playing field at U.S. 90 and Callaghan Road, Wolff Stadium, named for former Mayor Nelson W. Wolff. In 1996, a franchise of the International Hockey League came to San Antonio. The Dragons play an eighty-two-game schedule from October to April.

Soccer leagues are to be found all over the city. Seasons are October through April and June to mid-August. The San Antonio Soccer Association, made up of both professionals and amateurs, is affiliated with the United States Soccer Association.

There are thirty golf courses in Bexar County; six of these and a driving range are operated by the city. Many of the privately owned courses are open to the public. Pecan Valley Golf Club is one of America's top public courses, and from 1977 to 1995 was the site of an annual PGA championship, the Texan Open. La Cantera Golf Club, adjoining Fiesta Texas, which opened its 18-hole championship course in January 1995, began sponsoring the championship in October 1996, now named La Cantera Texas Open. The Senior PGA Tour's SBC Dominion Seniors began in March 1996.

Because of its year-around good weather and close-by daily and nightly entertainment, San Antonio is beginning to vie with Scottsdale, Arizona, as a place for "destination golf resorts." Several outstanding courses are in the area, including Hyatt Regency Hill Country Resort near Sea World, La Cantera, the Quarry, and Tapatio Springs in Boerne. The Hyatt Regency Hill Country Resort, opened in 1993, lies among the trees on 200 rolling green acres, once part of the 2,700 acre Rogers-Wiseman Ranch in northwestern San Antonio, and includes a 500-room hotel, an eighteen-hole championship golf course, tennis courts, and a four-acre water park. Restaurants and entertainment, including evening dancing and Sunday brunch, are open to the public.

In every corner of the city there are fans and participants in hunting, freshwater and saltwater fishing, ice skating, swimming, jogging, cycling, and virtually all sports. Motor racing fans can go to any of five nearby speedways.

Horse racing began at Retama Park on Cíbolo Creek, off I-35 at Selma between San Antonio and New Braunfels, in 1995. Its grandstand accommodates 10,000 people. Polo, long a popular sport in San Antonio, is played there. The San Antonio Polo Club, founded in 1920, is one of the oldest still-active polo clubs in the United States.

Nationally Known Amusement Parks

Sea World and Six Flags Fiesta Texas, while not unique to San Antonio, add to the wide variety of entertainment available in the area.

San Antonio's Sea World, the largest marine life park in the world, is actually four parks in one—marine animal park, rides and slides park, water park, and show park. Shows feature world-famous Shamu and champion killer whales, sea lions, dolphins, beluga whales, walrus, otters, and water skiers, while state-of-the-art exhibits include penguins, eels, tropical fishes, and the largest zoological population of hammerhead sharks in North America.

Since its opening in 1988, Sea World has added new attractions including "The Great White," the Southwest's only inverted steel roller coaster; the Lost Lagoon water park, the huge wave pool and towering slides; Shamu's Happy Harbor, a colorful interactive play area for children; and water rides.

Sea World of Texas combines fun with learning through a marine sciences education program that yearly attracts approximately 100,000 participants. Adventure Camps enable students to live in Sea World dormitories and study alongside animal experts. Another educational treat is the Texas Walk sculpture garden, with seventeen life-size bronzes of notable figures in Texas history.

Six Flags Fiesta Texas celebrates the heritage of Texas in five areas: Hispanic, German, Western, nostalgic 1950s, and the Boardwalk. The 200-acre family entertainment theme park offers musical shows, food, rides, water park, and other attractions. The world-famous Rattler roller coaster and "Joker's Revenge" are breathtaking, as is the nightly fireworks and laser extravaganza, "The Lone Star Spectacular." The Ol' Swimmin' Hole, an expanded 1.5 acre water activity area, is a great place for families to beat the Texas heat. The Road Runner Express and DC Comics Super Heroes Live are recent additions.

Historic Corridor

The route from San Antonio to Presidio and Mission La Bahía in Goliad—south along the San Antonio River on Highways 181 and 239—is dotted with fascinating towns embracing stories of yesteryear. "Remember the Alamo! Remember Goliad!"—the battle cry heard from Texans at the Battle of San Jacinto in April 1836— is echoed today at Goliad, with its historic sites going back to the 1700s. The largest single loss of Texan lives during the war for independence in the 1830s—342 men—occurred there during the Goliad Massacre on March 27, 1836. And the first Polish settlement in America, Panna Maria, lies en route to Goliad, just off Texas 123.

The Hill Country

Restful summits of the Hill Country—their live oak trees green year around—can be seen at San Antonio's northern edge. Sailing and other water sports are enjoyed nearby at Canyon Lake and Medina Lake, and farther north in the Highland Lakes. And drifting down the Guadalupe River in large inner-tubes is a diversion that draws thousands. Big water entertainment parks enliven both New Braunfels and San Antonio.

Bandera

In the environs of Bandera, "the cowboy capital of Texas," forty-nine miles from San Antonio, visitors flock to the dude ranches.

The Coast

In Texas, "The Coast" means the Gulf of Mexico, where broad stretches of white sand beaches and plentiful offshore fishing are offered on the 624 miles of Texas' coastline, only three hours away.

Every Texan's 'Other Love'

Whether your residence is Wizard Wells or Waco or Wichita Falls, you have another love always, which is San Antonio. It's kind of like that other woman or other man that you remember from your high school days, that you never quite surrender. And no one surrenders San Antonio, which is one of the memorable cities in the United States.

–Joe B. Frantz (1917-1993), historian, history professor, and former director of the Texas State Historical Association

---

Some San Antonians have second homes and sailboats on the Gulf. Corpus Christi offers many delights worth a side trip from San Antonio, one of them being the permanent home of Spanish-owned replicas of the caravels of Christopher Columbus, the *Niña*, *Pinta*, and *Santa María*. The World War II aircraft carrier *USS Lexington* and the Maritime Museum are also popular attractions for visitor tours.

The exotic life of Mexico is as near as Laredo or Del Rio, only some 155 miles.

Afterword

From the springs at the Head of the River, near the ephemeral town of Avoca, through the green bowers by the old domed cathedral, past the cherished Alamo, beside sidewalk cafes, alongside lost *acequias*, in the shadows of the four missions, we can hear the stories of the Indians and Europeans and Tejanos and Anglo Americans and those who followed.

They lived beside these historic streams with sibilant names—Olmos, San Pedro, Salado, and San Antonio—and the meandering *acequias* from which they drew their water for drinking, washing, irrigating, and milling.

Their stories of the same events are told differently by people in different groups among the variety who engaged in the clash of cultures of which history is made. Yet all these people—even before the day the place was named in 1691—have taken their turns in making San Antonio the Enchanted City of Texas. The story of how it was created goes back more than 300 years—and, always, the streams of life run through it.

In some magic way, by spending time in San Antonio you join your life forever to those historic streams, and among their winding valleys your fond memories will be buried deep.

San Antonio:
If but to say your name
Would be to be there,
I'd say your name
A thousand times, today.

F.W.J.

Where to Learn
More About the City

Here are titles of some of the sources referred to in this book plus suggestions for further reading. Many of the books are out of print, but usually can be found in larger libraries or from dealers in used or rare books. Many others, of course, are available from well-stocked bookstores and through book specialists' catalogues.

A comprehensive list of books and other sources would fill many pages. In fact, several of the books listed below have multi-page bibliographies that could keep you searching for many dozens of books—and reading them for years. One of the best, for example, is the fourteen-page bibliography by Sam and Bess Woolford, *The San Antonio Story* (Austin: Steck Co., 1950), which tells of the city's history from its beginning up to 1950. Some of the books have highly informative page notes at the end, and some have chronologies that help the reader better understand the past. Kenneth W. Wheeler's *To Wear A City's Crown* (Cambridge: Harvard University Press, 1968) is another with an unusually comprehensive bibliography—twenty pages plus twenty-three pages of notes. Although it deals only with the period 1836 to 1865, it discusses important aspects of the city—its urban growth and social and cultural aspirations—that are not often considered.

Two books that carry the history of San Antonio into the 1940s—and both are available from most bookstores—are *The WPA Guide to Texas* (New York: Hastings House, 1940; republished in Austin by Texas Monthly Press, 1986) and Richard A. García's *Rise of the Mexican American Middle Class, San Antonio, 1929-1941* (College Station: Texas A&M University Press, 1991).

The latter book's epilogue treats key aspects of history nearly up to 1991. It has an extensive bibliography and valuable page notes.

Most books that include a period of San Antonio's eventful past confine themselves exclusively to the earliest history or to the period of the revolt of the Texians and Tejanos to free their territory from control by the government of Mexico. Two books that together cover the period from the 1600s to 1836, and that offer an extensive bibliography and many notes, are Jesús F. de la Teja's *San Antonio de Béxar* (Albuquerque: University of New Mexico Press, 1995) and Stephen L. Hardin's *Texian Iliad* (Austin: University of Texas Press, 1994). *San Antonio in the Eighteenth Century*, produced in 1976 by the San Antonio Bicentennial Heritage Committee and printed in San Antonio by Clarke Printing Co., is especially comprehensive for a 154-page book.

But the significant though less tumultuous events that followed the founding, the settling, and the Revolution are not so exhaustively covered. A few books, such as *To Wear A City's Crown,* which covers 1836 to 1865, and J. J. Bowden's *The Exodus of Federal Forces from Texas 1861* (Austin: Eakin Press, 1986) include the Civil War period or the time immediately before. Timothy M. Matovina's *Tejano Religion and Ethnicity: San Antonio, 1821-1860* (Austin: University of Texas Press, 1995) covers about forty years of local history from a special vantage point and also offers an extensive bibliography and many useful notes. Another of these in the post-1836 period is the story of the highly eventful life—from 1836 to 1886—of Dr. John Salmon Ford, which is told by Stephen B. Oates in *Rip Ford's Texas* (Austin: University of Texas Press, 1987).

Biographies, as well as histories of ethnic or national groups, or professions, businesses, industries, churches, schools, arts and other organizations, or nearby cities, counties or regions usually reveal facts about extended periods in the city's history. So do selected bibliographies, some containing theses, prepared by libraries and book dealers. The many books and booklets published by the University of Texas Institute of Texan Cultures to propagate the stories of the state's ethnic and nationality groups provide a rich source of history about San Antonio, as well as the rest of Texas. To get their catalog, call (800) 776-7651.

The classic history of San Antonio, William Corner's *San Antonio de Béxar: A Guide and History* (San Antonio: Bainbridge & Corner, 1890) covers the city's story from its beginning in 1718 almost to the 1900s. Not only does Corner present his own account plus interviews with key oldtimers, but he also includes a history of the city written by the nationally famous poet and musician Sidney Lanier. His chronology covers thirty-eight pages. Mary Ann Noonan Guerra indexed the book and had it republished by Graphic Arts in San Antonio in 1977.

There are a few other exceptions to the long list of Spanish- and Mexican-period books. Besides the more current Woolford book, *The San Antonio Story*, others—such as T. R. Fehrenbach's excellent *The San Antonio Story* (Tulsa: Continental Heritage Press, 1978)—also offer meaty chronologies. Fehrenbach's book covers the period up to about 1978. John L. Davis' insightful *San Antonio: A Historical Portrait* (Austin: Encino Press, 1978) contains mostly photographs and goes to 1970. Cecilia Steinfeldt's *San Antonio Was* (San Antonio: San Antonio Museum Association, 1978), with photos by James Hicks, is loaded with facts and photographs and has an ample bibliography and many page notes. It deals with San Antonio up to 1978. A revised edition of Charles Ramsdell's excellent *San Antonio—A Historical and Pictorial Guide* (Austin: University of Texas Press, 1985), now out of print, can be found in libraries. *Urban Texas, Politics and Development* (College Station: Texas A&M University Press, 1990), edited by Char Miller and Heywood T. Sanders, contains a great deal of interesting information about San Antonio's politics, social history, and physical and economic growth until about 1989.

Of course, various books deal with special aspects of San Antonio's more recent history. Examples are the revised edition of Vernon G. Zunker's *A Dream Come True, Robert Hugman and San Antonio's River Walk* (San Antonio: Vernon G. Zunker, 1994), Jack Maguire's *A Century of Fiesta in San Antonio* (Austin: Eakin Press, 1990), Lewis F. Fisher's *Saving San Antonio: The Precarious Preservation of a Heritage* (Lubbock: Texas Tech University Press,

1996), Nelson W. Wolff's *Mayor* (San Antonio: San Antonio Express-News, 1997), and Maury Maverick, Jr.'s *Texas Iconoclast* (Fort Worth: Texas Christian University Press, 1997).

There are San Antonio tourist guide publications as well as fine specialty books that deal with cooking, self-guided walking tours, local ghosts, or other aspects of the city, including professional photographic and textual coverage, such as *San Antonio, Portrait of the Fiesta City* (Stillwater, MN: Voyager Press, 1992) by Susanna Nawrocki and Gerald Lair, with photos by Mark Langford. *San Antonio Uncovered* (Plano: Wordware Publishing, 1992), by Mark Louis Rybczyk, lists a number of memorable facts and oddities about the city.

One of the best sources of information about San Antonio is the series of books written and published in San Antonio (Alamo Press) by Mary Ann Noonan Guerra: *San Fernando, Heart of San Antonio* (1977), *The Missions of San Antonio* (1982), *The Alamo* (1983), *The San Antonio River* (1987), *Heroes of the Alamo and Goliad* (1987), and *The History of San Antonio's Market Square* (1990). All six books have many illustrations, consist of about sixty pages, and feature chronologies and bibliographies.

Another rich lode of San Antonio lore can be found in two books by Donald E. Everett containing carefully selected local news and feature stories published in San Antonio newspapers from 1845 to 1929. The books are *San Antonio Legacy* (San Antonio: Trinity University Press, 1979), and *San Antonio, the Flavor of its Past, 1845-1898* (San Antonio: Trinity University Press, 1983) In *San Antonio Legacy* is the historic interview in 1910 of Pete McManus by W. D. Hornaday of the *Express*, telling how McManus and John W. ("Bet-a-Million") Gates first demonstrated barbed wire to skeptical ranchers in Alamo Plaza.

From time to time, newer Texas college and high-school textbooks are published containing updated histories of Texas, including San Antonio. Some of these can be worth reading for anyone. Librarians, teachers, and book dealers—both those who sell new books and those who sell used or rare books—can guide you not only to many more books not listed here but also to Texas-related periodicals, including newspapers and magazines. At a library, you can find a treasure of information in back issues of the first-rate *Texas Highways,* the monthly "travel magazine of Texas," and the wide-ranging *Texas Monthly.* Anyone interested in the history of Texas or its current life would probably be interested in reading these regularly.

For an overview of all Texas history in which to find San Antonio's distinctive place, you can do no better than to read T. R. Fehrenbach's magnificent *Lone Star: A History of Texas and Texans* (New York: American Legacy Press, 1983), which takes the history past the 1960s, and *The History of Texas* (Arlington Heights, IL: Harlan Davidson, Inc., 1990) by Robert A. Calvert and Arnoldo De Leon, which goes to 1990. Both books have valuable suggestions for further reading.

One of the best investments you can make, if you are sincerely interested in learning more about Texas history, is to pay $35 to become a member of the Texas State Historical Association. You will receive four thick issues a year of *Southwestern Historical Quarterly,* likely to contain interesting and reliable historical information about virtually any topic in any period of Texas history. The association's address is 2/306 Richardson Hall, University Station, Austin, TX 78712.

If you have the need and a considerable amount of available money, you can order the six-volume *The New Handbook of Texas,* published in 1996. In its more than 23,500 articles compiled by some 3,000 authors, it covers virtually every aspect of the people, places, and events in Texas history. It is cross-indexed and presents source materials and bibliographies. It costs $395, plus taxes and shipping, which adds up to $447.59 for Texans. However, members of the Texas State Historical Association get a 15 percent discount on this, as they do on all books published by the Association.

Here is a list of some other books that offer a better appreciation of San Antonio:

Almaráz, Félix D., Jr. *Tragic Cavalier: Governor Manuel Salcedo of Texas, 1808-1813.* Austin: University of Texas Press, 1971.

_____. *The San Antonio Missions and Their System of Land Tenure.* Austin: University of Texas Press, 1989.

Barnes, Charles M. *Combats and Conquests of Immortal Heroes: Sung in Song and Told in Story.* San Antonio: Guessaz & Ferlet Co., 1910.

Bolton, Herbert Eugene. *Texas in the Middle Eighteenth Century: Studies in Spanish Colonial History and Administration.* Austin: University of Texas Press, 1970.

Burkholder, Mary V. *The King William Area: A History and Guide to the Houses.* San Antonio: The King William Association, 1973.

Bushick, Frank H. *Glamorous Days in Old San Antonio.* San Antonio: Naylor Co., 1934.

Cagle, Eldon, Jr. *Quadrangle: The History of Fort Sam Houston.* Austin: Eakin Press, 1985.

Campbell, T.N. and T.J. Campbell. *Indian Groups Associated With Spanish Missions of the San Antonio Missions National Historical Park.* San Antonio: Center for Archaeological Research, University of Texas at San Antonio, Special Report No. 16, 1985.

Carson, Chris and William McDonald, editors. *A Guide to San Antonio Architecture.* San Antonio Chapter, American Institute of Architects. San Antonio, 1986.

Céliz, Francisco. *Diary of the Alarcón Expedition into Texas, 1718-1719.* Translated by Fritz Leo Hoffman. Los Angeles: Quivira Society, 1935.

Chabot, Frederick Charles. *With the Makers of San Antonio.* San Antonio: Artes Gráficas, 1937.

Chipman, Donald P. *Spanish Texas: 1519-1821.* Austin: University of Texas Press, 1992.

Coppini, Pompeo. *From Dawn to Sunset.* San Antonio: The Naylor Co., 1949.

Crook, Cornelia E. *San Pedro Springs Park: Texas' Oldest Recreation Area.* San Antonio: C. E. Crook, 1967.

Cruz, Gilbert R. *Let There Be Towns: Spanish Municipal Origins in the American Southwest, 1610-1810.* College Station: Texas A&M University Press, 1988.

Cude, Elton, *"The Free and Wild Dukedom of Bexar."* San Antonio: Munguia Printers, 1978.

Curtis, Albert. *Fabulous San Antonio*. San Antonio: The Naylor Co., 1955.

Cutler, Charles L. *O Brave New Words! Native American Loanwords in Current English*. Norman: University of Oklahoma Press, 1994.

Dawson, Joseph G. III. Editor. *The Texas Military Experience: From the Texas Revolution Through World War II*. College Station: Texas A&M University Press, 1995.

De La Teja, Jesús F. *A Revolution Remembered, The Memoirs and Selected Correspondence of Juan N. Seguín*. Austin: State House Press, 1991.

De Leon, Arnoldo. *The Tejano Community, 1836-1900*. Albuquerque: University of New Mexico Press, 1982.

Elizondo, Virgil. *The Future Is Mestizo: Life Where Cultures Meet*. New York: Meyer Stone, 1988.

Fisher, Lewis F. *Crown Jewel of Texas: The Story of San Antonio's River*. San Antonio: Maverick Publishing Co., 1997.

Fox, Daniel E. *Traces of Texas History: Archaeological Evidence of the Past 450 Years*. San Antonio: Corona Publishing Co., 1983.

Fuentes, Carlos. *The Buried Mirror: Reflections on Spain and the New World*. New York: Houghton Mifflin Co., 1992.

_____. *A New Time for Mexico*. New York: Farrar, Straus and Giroux, 1996.

García, Richard A. *Rise of the Mexican-American Middle Class, San Antonio, 1929-1941*. College Station: Texas A&M University Press, 1991.

Garrett, Julia Kathryn. *Green Flag Over Texas: The Last Years of Spain in Texas*. Austin: The Pemberton Press, 1939.

Habig, Marion A. *The Alamo Chain of Missions: A History of San Antonio's Five Old Missions*. Revised Ed. Chicago: Franciscan Herald Press, 1976.

_____. *Spanish Texas Pilgrimage: The Old Franciscan Missions and Other Settlements of Texas, 1632-1821*. Chicago: Franciscan Herald Press, 1981.

Haley, James L. *Texas: From Spindletop Through World War II*. New York: St. Martin's Press, 1993.

Handy, Mary Olivia. *Fort Sam Houston.* San Antonio: The Naylor Co., 1951.

Henderson, Richard B. *Maury Maverick, A Political Biography.* Austin: University of Texas Press, 1970.

Heusinger, Edward W. *A Chronology of Events in San Antonio.* San Antonio: Standard Printing Co., 1950.

Hollon, W. Eugene and Ruth Lapham Butler, editors. *William Bollaert's Texas.* Norman: University of Oklahoma Press, 1956.

Jackson, Jack. *Los Mesteños: Spanish Ranching in Texas, 1721-1821.* College Station: Texas A&M University Press, 1986.

James, Vinton Lee. *Frontier Pioneer.* San Antonio: Artes Gráficas, 1938.

Johnston, Leah Carter. *San Antonio: Saint Anthony's Town.* San Antonio: Naylor Co. 1976.

Jones, Oakah L., Jr. *Los Paisanos: Spanish Settlements on the Northern Frontier of New Spain.* Norman: University of Oklahoma Press, 1979.

Jordan, Terry G. *German Seed in Texas Soil: Immigrant Farmers in Nineteenth Century Texas.* Austin: University of Texas Press, 1966.

Lack, Paul D. *The Texas Revolutionary Experience: A Political and Social History, 1835-1836.* College Station: Texas A&M University Press, 1992.

Lich, Glen E. *The German Texans.* San Antonio: University of Texas Institute of Texan Cultures, 1981.

Long, Jeff. *Duel of Eagles: The Mexican and U.S. Fight for the Alamo.* New York: William Morrow and Company, Inc., 1990.

Lord, Walter. *A Time to Stand.* New York: Harper & Brothers, 1961.

Marks, Paula Mitchell. *Turn Your Eyes Toward Texas: Pioneers Sam and Mary Maverick.* College Station: Texas A&M University Press, 1989.

Meinig, D. W. *Imperial Texas: An Interpretive Essay in Cultural Geography.* Austin: University of Texas Press, 1969.

Middleton, Michael. *Man Made the Town.* New York: St. Martin's Press, 1987.

Nixon, Pat Ireland. *A Century of Medicine in San Antonio: The Story of Medicine in Bexar County, Texas.* San Antonio, 1936.

Olmsted, Frederick Law. *A Journey Through Texas : Or, A Saddle-Trip on the Southwestern Frontier.* Austin: University of Texas Press, 1978.

Patterson, Becky Crouch. *Hondo My Father.* Austin: Shoal Creek Publishers, Inc., 1979.

Poyo, Gerald E. and Gilberto M. Hinojosa, editors. *Tejano Origins in Eighteenth-Century San Antonio.* Austin: University of Texas Press, 1991.

Roemer, Ferdinand. *Roemer's Texas, With Particular Reference to German Immigration and the Physical Appearance of the Country.* San Antonio: Standard Printing Co., 1935.

Santleben, August. *A Texas Pioneer: Early Staging and Overland Freighting Days on the Frontiers of Texas and Mexico.* New York: Neale Publishing Co., 1910.

Schwarz, Ted, with Robert H. Thonhoff, editor and annotator. *Forgotten Battlefield of the First Texas Revolution: The Battle of Medina, August 18, 1813.* Austin: Eakin Press, 1985.

Simons, Helen, and Cathryn A. Hoyt. *Hispanic Texas: A Historical Guide.* Austin: University of Texas Press, 1992.

Thonhoff, Robert H. *The Texas Connection With the American Revolution.* Burnet: Eakin Press, 1981.

Toor, Frances. *A Treasury of Mexican Folkways: The Customs, Myths, Folklore, Traditions, Beliefs, Fiestas, Dances and Songs of the Mexican People.* New York: Crown Publishers, Inc., 1947.

Torres, Luis. *Voices from the San Antonio Missions.* Lubbock: Texas Tech University Press, 1997.

Waugh, Julia Nott. *The Silver Cradle: Las Posadas, Los Pastores and Other Mexican American Traditions.* Austin: University of Texas Press, 1988.

Weatherford, Jack. *The Indian Givers: How the Indians of the Americas Transformed the World.* New York: Crown Publishers, Inc. , 1988.

Weber, David J. Editor. *Troubles in Texas, 1832: A Tejano Viewpoint from San Antonio.* Dallas: DeGolyer Library, 1983.

_____. *The Spanish Frontier in North America.* New Haven: Yale University Press, 1992.

San Antonio Chronofacts

12,000 to 9000 B. C.   Thousands of years before the birth of Christ, hunters and their families followed wild game south from northeast Asia. Some families reached the San Antonio area, camping off and on near the many springs until the Spaniards moved in.

1519   Pilots of the Alonso Alvarez de Piñeda expedition, sponsored by Francisco de Garay, governor of Spanish Jamaica, made the first map of the Texas coast.

1521   Having begun his invasion in 1519, Hernan Cortes' army conquered the Aztecs in the Central Valley of Mexico for the Spanish Crown—leading the way for explorations in Texas during the next century.

1534   "Lost," Cabeza de Vaca and companions stopped near an Indian camp in the San Antonio area.

1691   The "place of San Antonio," called Yanaguana by the natives, was named on June 13, feast day of Saint Anthony of Padua, by Father Damián Massanet and Domingo Terán de los Ríos, first governor of Coahuila and Tejas.

1709   On April 13, expedition leader Capt. Pedro de Aguirre, commander of Presidio Rio Grande, and Fathers Isidro Félix de Espinosa and Antonio de San Buenaventura y Olivares named San Pedro Springs and San Antonio River.

1716   Father Isidro de Espinosa, on expedition under Captain Domingo Ramón, entered the "plain at the San Antonio River" on May 14 and noted that "the San Pedro" was a good site for a mission.

1718   Father Antonio Olivares and Gov. Martín de Alarcón founded San Antonio on San Pedro Creek, with establishment of Mission San Antonio de Valero on May 1, followed on May 5 by a presidio started nearby. Presidio and civil settlement, Villa de Béjar, soon had 300 inhabitants.

1720   Father Antonio Margil de Jesús founded Mission San José on east bank of San Antonio River about 3½ miles south of Mission San Antonio. Later, missionaries moved it to the west bank before 1727 and to its present site in 1740, when they began construction of permanent buildings.

1722   In January the governor of Texas, the Marqués de Aguayo, moved the presidio downstream to the present site of Military Plaza (Plaza de Armas), where today are the Spanish Governor's Palace and the City Hall.

1731   Fifteen families—with four bachelors counted as a 16th— arrived at Béxar from the Canary Islands on March 9 to establish a municipality, Villa de San Fernando, near the presidio for the Spanish Crown. There were fifty-five people. Soldiers and settlers measured off locations from the place marked for the main entrance to San Fernando church. They surveyed land and sites designated for church, public buildings, main plaza, streets, and homes, plus land for recreation and farming. The *cabildo* (city council) held its first meeting on August 1.

1738   Canary Islanders laid cornerstone of church of San Fernando. Completed in 1750, but damaged by fire in 1828. Ecclesiastical authorities placed a new cornerstone in 1868 and completed reconstruction by 1873. Today, walls of the domed sanctuary are those of 1749-1750.

1755   Artisans completed construction of the church at Mission Concepción, which had been transferred to the region as a primitive structure, and established on March 5, 1731, at its present site. It was completed in stone and dedicated on December 8, the feast day of the Immaculate Conception.

1756   Construction of church of Mission San Antonio de Valero, part of the present Alamo, was begun. The first stone church, built in 1744, collapsed. This mission, located on San Pedro Creek in 1718 in simple huts, was relocated twice. Church of Mission San Juan Capistrano, which had been moved as a wooden hut to its present site on March 5, 1731, was constructed of stone, along with a stone friary and granary. The stone church of Mission San Francisco de la Espada replaced the temporary structure built after the mission was moved there on March 5, 1731. Stone friary and aqueduct had been built in 1745. Aqueduct and church still stand.

1807   U. S. Army Lt. Zebulon M. Pike spent ten days in June in San Antonio at Governor Antonio Cordero's home, today restored as "Spanish Governor's Palace." U. S. Government published Pike's report on his explorations in 1810.

1811   Revolutionist Juan Bautista de las Casas arrested the Spanish governor, but was later overcome. He was taken to the capital in Monclova, Mexico, sentenced, shot, and his head severed and sent to San Antonio to be displayed in Military Plaza. For its loyalty to the Spanish Crown, Villa de San Fernando was rewarded by being elevated on October 13 to the rank of a city *(ciudad)*.

1813   Republican Army of the North, made up of rebel Spanish subjects and Anglo Americans, took over San Antonio de Béxar (April 1-August 18) and flew its green flag over the city for several months.

1820   Moses Austin, from the United States, got approval from Spanish governor in San Antonio to start a colony. He died in 1821, and his son, Stephen F., assumed the task and was received by Governor Antonio Martínez in San Antonio on August 12.

1821   Spanish rule of Texas ended, and Mexican rule began, when the revolution, started in Mexico in 1810 by Father Miguel Hidalgo y Costilla, was taken over by Agustín de

Iturbide, whose forces took Mexico City on September 27. Iturbide declared himself emperor.

1824   The Mexican government united the provinces of Texas and Coahuila—with Texas constituting the Department of Béxar, headed by a political chief in San Antonio. Texas was woefully underrepresented in the distant capital. Mexican Federal Constitution of 1824 was patterned partly after the U. S. Constitution and for a time was endorsed by Austin and other Texan leaders for making Texas a state in the Mexican Confederation.

1832   Bexar town council (*ayuntamiento*) wrote a statement of grievances with Mexican government on December 19. *Bexareños* contacted other Texas councils to support the petition. Austin called it "a bold stand for Texas."

1835   "The Battle of Béxar" began on December 5. Ben Milam was killed at the Veramendi house not far from Main Plaza (*Plaza de las Islas*). Texian volunteers defeated the Mexican forces under Gen. Martin Perfecto de Cós, brother-in-law of Gen. Antonio Lopez de Santa Anna, President of Mexico. A treaty was accepted on December 11—remembered as "San Antonio Day."

1836   On March 2, convention delegates at Washington-on-the-Brazos signed the Texas Declaration of Independence from Mexico. On March 6, Mexican soldiers scaled the walls of the Alamo and overwhelmed the outnumbered force of Texians and Tejanos. General Santa Anna had entered Béxar with his army on February 23. On April 21, Santa Anna's army was defeated by volunteers under Gen. Sam Houston in the Battle of San Jacinto near today's city of Houston, ending Mexican rule. In September, after an election and approved Constitution, the Republic of Texas began with Sam Houston as president.

1837   The new Republic of Texas created Bexar County by a congressional act that had been approved on December 22, 1836. On December 14, 1837, the Texas Congress incorporated the city of San Antonio in Bexar County.

1840   "The Council House Fight" broke out with much bloodshed in the former Casas Reales on Main Plaza on March 19, after a misunderstanding between Comanches and Texians. Comanches later retaliated, sacking towns.

1842   Hoping to recover its lost province, Mexico sent Gen. Rafael Vásquez to San Antonio to demand surrender. Arriving on March 5 with 500 men, he hoisted the Mexican flag. He declared new laws and left after two days. Gen. Adrian Woll, a Belgian who became a Mexican citizen, entered the city with an army on September 11 and captured members of District Court and prominent citizens. He departed on September 20, taking vital official records and captives to Mexico.

1846   Although Texas legally entered the Union on December 29, 1845, President Anson Jones of the Texas Republic rescheduled the transfer of authority from the republic to the state in a ceremony on February 19, 1846, when the newly elected governor, J. Pinckney Henderson, accepted the reins of government.

1848   Mexican War (1846-1848), with U. S. forces supplied partly out of San Antonio, ended after capture of Mexico City with treaty signed in a suburb of Guadalupe at a house on Calle Hidalgo. The Treaty of Guadalupe Hidalgo was signed on February 2. The United States acquired Southwest and California—one million square miles.

1856   Corporate bounds and limits of city were changed by council on September 8 to include a square league—six miles square with dome of San Fernando Cathedral as the center.

1857   Wells, Fargo & Company started first transcontinental mail service in the United States. Agents in Alamo Plaza served the San Antonio & San Diego Mail Line. Mail from East Coast came by ship to Indianola and by stagecoach to San Antonio.

1861   A Texas Convention in Austin voted on January 28 to secede from the United States and join the Confederate States of America. Governor Sam Houston refused to sign and was replaced.

The first major loss suffered by U. S. government in the Civil War came in San Antonio on February 16, when Union Maj. Gen. David E. Twiggs surrendered all U. S. Army property in Texas.

1865   Civil War ended in Texas on June 2, and U. S. president appointed Andrew J. Hamilton provisional governor of Texas. Governor appointed D. Cleveland mayor of San Antonio on October 9.

On June 19, Maj. Gen. Gordon Granger landed in Galveston and announced an executive order declaring "all slaves are free." The event is celebrated annually in Texas as Emancipation Day, or "Juneteenth."

1870   The U. S. government acquired ninety-three acres of land northeast of the city for headquarters of the Chief Quartermaster, Department of Texas. Construction began in 1876. Post was renamed Fort Sam Houston on September 10, 1890.

1877   The first railroad reached San Antonio on February 19. Arrival of Galveston, Harrisburg and San Antonio Railway joined the city to the nation's railroad network.

1881   A second railroad, the International and Great Northern, reached San Antonio from the northeast. This brought an increase in settlers and manufactured building products that helped transform the appearance of the city to a more northeastern style, and that modernized it in other ways.

1889   Adina De Zavala (1861-1955) granddaughter of the vice president of interim government of the Republic of Texas, Lorenzo de Zavala, formed an organization to "keep green the memory of the heroes, founders, and pioneers of Texas" and began life-long organizational efforts to save and restore the Alamo, the missions, and the Spanish Governor's

Palace—and to place historical markers throughout the state to memorialize events.

1891   First Battle of Flowers Parade, celebrating San Jacinto Day—for the victory of Texas volunteers over Mexican forces at San Jacinto on April 21, 1836—was held on April 24. Later celebrations included remembrance of the Battle of the Alamo.

1910   On March 2 at Ft. Sam Houston, Lt. Benjamin D. Foulois, the U. S. Army's only officer assigned to flight duty, made four flights—including his first solo and first crackup. Later, he introduced the seatbelt and pilot use of radio.

1913   In June, Carl Kurz discovered oil while drilling a well near Somerset, fifteen miles southwest of San Antonio. An oil boom followed. The oilfield extended from Somerset to below Pleasanton and was the largest shallow oil field in the world known at the time. Two refineries in the field and a pipeline to San Antonio handled the high-gravity crude.

1915   Widening of Commerce Street from Main Plaza to Alamo Street was completed in May. Begun September 9, 1912, it was widened to sixty-five feet. Buildings on south side are moved fourteen feet or cut back. Entire five-story Alamo Bank building at corner of Commerce and Presa was lifted and moved back, and three more stories were added in 1916.

1917   The Chamber of Commerce offered the military a site for Kelly Field No. 5, near Berg's Mill. It was renamed Brooks Field on February 4, 1918.

1921   A cloudburst of seventeen-inch rainfall in Olmos Valley, north of the city, caused a flood on September 9-10 that took forty-nine lives in San Antonio, and left fourteen missing. It resulted in $8 million property loss.

1924   Destined to lead the community in preserving and restoring the enchanted city of Texas—and educating its residents about their inherited regional values and treasures

—the San Antonio Conservation Society was founded on March 22.

1926   To control flooding, Olmos Dam and Reservoir were completed at a cost of some $1.5 million, and work was begun for cutting an overflow channel of the river through Commerce, Market, and Dolorosa streets.

1930   Randolph Air Force Base, then the Army Air Corps Randolph Field, was dedicated on June 20 as a flying training center.

1941   Downtown river beautification project was completed on March 10, realizing architect Robert H. H. Hugman's River Walk plans and the dreams of conservationists and civic leaders that began in the 1920s.

1942   The War Department separated part of Kelly Field on June 26, for an aviation cadet training center, later renaming it for Brig. Gen. Frank D. Lackland.

1968   An international exposition, HemisFair '68, opened on April 6 and closed October 6 on 92.6 acres cleared of most homes and businesses, some of historic value. Today, HemisFair Park, German Heritage Park, and Tower of Americas mark a renewed city.

University of Texas Medical School at San Antonio was established. It became the foundation for Health Science Center, an international leader in the biosciences with a medical faculty of 4,300 persons.

1988   Sea World of Texas was opened as the world's largest marine life park, with 250 acres of shows, educational exhibits, water park, restaurants, and special attractions for children.

Rivercenter, shopping and entertainment complex, was opened on East Commerce not far from the Alamo, and the river was branched to become its focal point for colorful events.

1992   Fiesta Texas opened; the 200-acre family entertainment theme park celebrates the heritage of Texas through

music, food, rides, and other attractions in four areas—
Hispanic, German, Western, and 1950s. It became Six Flags
Fiesta Texas in 1995.

1993   After 112 years, the *San Antonio Light* published its last
issue on January 27, making San Antonio another "one-
daily-newspaper city." James P. Newcomb published the
pro-Union *Alamo Express* in 1860 and 1861 and the *Evening
Light* from 1881 to 1883. After he sold it, its name was
changed to the *San Antonio Light*.

Alamodome opened May 15, a pavilion with roof suspended from four 300-foot-high minaret-like towers. Seats
5,000 to 73,200; 65,000 for football; all seats with column-
free view. Two permanent Olympic-class ice rinks.

Hyatt Regency Hill Country Resort opened. A full-scale
destination resort on 200 tree-covered acres, with 500-room
hotel, championship golf course, restaurants, and ball-
rooms. Water park has pools and "river floating."

1994   On March 25, President Clinton designated San Antonio
as home of the North American Development Bank, making the city the financial center for environmental and
infrastrucure work along U.S.-Mexican border. This
involves border cleanup and community development for
border cities.

1995   U. S. government's Defense Base Closure and Realignment
Committee (BRAC) voted on June 22 to close Kelly Air Force
Base. Major programs were begun by the city to privatize
the production and service capabilities of the facility.

"State-of-the-art," $38 million, seven-floor Central Library
opened on May 20, as its "enchilada red" color and spectacular architecture plus computerized services and special Spanish language features drew national attention.

San Antonio Museum of Art announced the addition of a
Latin American Art Center to include one of the nation's
outstanding collections of Mexican folk art, as well as

pre-Columbian, Spanish Colonial, and contemporary Latin American art.

Historic HemisFair Arena, built during the world fair in 1968 and recent home of the Spurs basketball team, was demolished to make way for expanded convention space, as the city's visitor industry continued to grow.

1996   Mission San José Visitor Center opened. The 12,000-square-foot facility will enhance visitors' understanding and appreciation of all the missions, including the former Mission San Antonio de Valero, now known as the Alamo.

Nelson A. Rockefeller Center for Latin American Art, a new $11 million, three-story wing to the San Antonio Museum of Art, was dedicated on September 7 for completion in the fall of 1998. The 30,000-square-foot center will be the first facility in the nation dedicated to the study of and appreciation of Latin American art for the past 3,000 years.

1997   Alamo Wall of History dedicated at the Alamo.

Facts About San Antonio

Population in 1997

San Antonio --- 1,144,800
Bexar County --- 1,371,100
Metropolitan Statistical Area (MSA) --------------------- 1,537,900
(Includes Bexar, Comal, Guadalupe, and Wilson counties—New Braunfels has joined San Antonio as one of the MSA's two central cities.)

- San Antonio is 8th largest city in United States.
- Seven larger cities are: New York, Los Angeles, Chicago, Houston, Philadelphia, San Diego, and Phoenix.
- San Antonio's MSA is 29th in the country. (U.S. Bureau of Census estimate)
- Median age in the city is 29.8—lower than national.

Ethnic Composition

San Antonio
    Spanish language or surname—55.6%
    Anglo—35.9%
    African American—7.0%
    Other—1.5%

Metropolitan Statistical Area
    Spanish language or surname—46.9%
    Anglo—44.8%
    African American—6.7%
    Other—1.6%

Geography

San Antonio occupies 377.2 square miles.

Bexar County occupies 1,248 square miles.

Average city elevation is 701 feet above sea level.

Bexar County altitude is 500 to 1,900 feet.

Located between Hill Country and Gulf Coastal Plains.

Metropolitan Statistical Area occupies 3,338 square miles.

Global Position:

29 degrees 31 minutes 53 seconds north latitude.

98 degrees 29 minutes 45 seconds west longitude.

Weather

Average monthly temperature is 70.8 degrees.

Average rainfall is about twenty-eight inches—heaviest in May and September. Measurable snowfall once every three or four years.

Daily average maximum temperature during June, July and August is above 90 degrees, with minimums above 70.

Only about twenty days per year below freezing.

Education

Bexar County's sixteen independent public school districts had an average daily attendance of 224,961 students during the 1995-96 school year. In addition, fifty parochial schools and more than 100 private schools serve the city. San Antonio has seventeen colleges and universities.

Government

San Antonio

■ Council-manager government. Employs city manager.

■ Council members from ten districts elected for two-year terms; mayor, the 11th council member, is elected at large.

■ Four-member County Commission governs Bexar County.

■ Elected commissioners are headed by elected judge.

■ Special districts for water, sewer, and flood control.

Cities in Bexar County:
- Besides San Antonio, there are twenty-four suburban cities and special districts within the county. To newcomers, most of these appear to be neighborhoods inside San Antonio. Most of them are served by San Antonio telephone and utility services. Fire and police protection are provided by special arrangements with San Antonio or Bexar County where they are not provided by the incorporated community. Residents of the twenty-four communities do not pay San Antonio taxes, but may pay in their incorporated areas.
- In addition to San Antonio, the following incorporated cities are in Bexar County: Alamo Heights, Olmos Park, Terrell Hills, Castle Hills, Shavano Park, Windcrest, Grey Forest, Hill Country Village, Hollywood Park, China Grove, Balcones Heights, Lytle, Converse, Elmendorf, Helotes, Kirby, Live Oak, Leon Valley, St. Hedwig, Schertz, Selma, Somerset, Universal City, and Fair Oaks Ranch.

Alamo Area Council of Governments (AACOG): More than ninety local governments across twelve counties are brought together to coordinate plans and actions for advancement of the entire regional community. AACOG was established in 1967.

Thirteen Chambers of Commerce: Chambers of Commerce in the San Antonio area serve special community interests. These are: the Greater San Antonio Chamber of Commerce (organized in 1894); African-American Chamber of Commerce; Alamo Heights Chamber of Commerce; Alamo City Chamber of Commerce (oriented toward city's East Side); North San Antonio Chamber of Commerce; San Antonio Hispanic Chamber of Commerce (formerly Mexican Chamber of Commerce); Southside Chamber of Commerce; San Antonio Women's Chamber of Commerce; Westside Chamber of Commerce; Randolph Metrocom Chamber of Commerce; Helotes Area Chamber of Commerce, Taiwanese Chamber of Commerce, and San Antonio Junior Chamber of Commerce.

Getting the Facts BEFORE You Arrive:

You can order a free *Information Packet* containing a simple map of San Antonio plus information about attractions in the area, a calendar of events, and a lodging guide. The kit is available from San Antonio Convention and Visitors Bureau, P.O. Box 2277, San Antonio, Texas 78298. It also can be ordered by calling 1-800-447-3372. Internet address is: www.sanantoniocvb.com. Make reservations early for lodging and special events!

Another source of information about San Antonio and all of Texas is the free *Texas Travel Guide* and *Travel Map,* which you may request by calling 1-800-452-9292 any day between 8 A.M. and 6 P.M. Central Time, except on weekends, when hours are 8 A.M. to 5 P.M. The guide describes numerous Texas towns. Also available free upon request from the same source is the annual *Texas Accommodations Guide.*

The Guide to San Antonio is an exceptionally informative publication. It is updated twice a year by the Economic Research Department of Greater San Antonio Chamber of Commerce, P.O. Box 1628, San Antonio, Texas 78296. (210) 229-2104. This guide is especially useful to new residents and other persons planning to stay in San Antonio for an extended time. The sixty-page booklet, together with a detailed street map of the city, costs $12, including postage.

A good phone number to call if you're seeking lodging is the *Lodging Line*: (210) 227-6667 or 1-800-858-4303.

Getting the Facts AFTER You arrive

Once you arrive in San Antonio, you can find detailed information about entertainment and good places to eat from visitor guides such as the monthly *Fiesta* magazine, published by the *Express-News, Key* magazine, part of a national group, and *Rio,* the official River Walk magazine plus several local newspapers—especially the Friday issue of the *San Antonio Express-News*, (210) 250-3000. It contains the section titled "Weekender, etc.," which includes numerous events and places to visit in San Antonio, as well as activities in nearby towns. Also, on the last Monday of every month, the *Express-News* publishes "What's Happening," a community calendar.

Moreover, the *San Antonio Current*, published every Thursday, is an unusually lively publication that offers numerous suggestions for entertainment and recreation. Several monthly periodicals, such as *Visitors' Guide* and *S. A. Calendar*, are also distributed free.

Another informative source is listed under *"Fingertip Facts"* in the yellow-page telephone book (Swbyp's) published by Southwestern Bell. It contains maps of the city with key points marked—plus information on attractions, events, transportation, food and lodging, community services, and other data.

If you walk directly across from the Alamo, you can get a great deal of assistance from friendly experts at the *San Antonio Visitor Information Center* at 317 Alamo Plaza (San Antonio, Texas 78205). A number of advisers are there to show you how to find virtually any place in the area—for many miles around—and to help you enjoy your visit. A variety of free brochures are available at the center. It is open from 8:30 A.M. to 6:00 P.M., Monday through Friday, and 8:30 to 5:00 P.M., Saturday and Sunday.

During those same hours (Central Time), you can telephone (210) 270-8748 to get answers to your questions from advisers at the Visitor Information Center.

The specialists at the Information Center say that perhaps the most vital piece of advice they can give is *make reservations long before you arrive*—or, in their words, book early!

Another source of information: The Alamo Visitor Center, on Crockett Street south of the Alamo, provides a number of pamphlets and other information sources, as well as advice from visitor specialists.

Transportation. Getting around the city is quite simple and inexpensive. VIA, the city's Metropolitan Transit Authority, serves the entire metropolitan area. It operates daily from 5 A.M. to midnight. Fares are low. It offers discounts for senior citizens and students. Call 227-2020 for route information.

It costs only fifty cents to visit many key sites downtown if you ride on one of VIA's rubber-tired streetcars. The route includes stops at such places as the Alamo, Spanish Governor's Palace, Market Square (El Mercado), St. Paul Square, King William District, the Municipal Auditorium, Southwest Craft Center, and the Institute of Texan Cultures.

San Antonio is served by two municipal airports, six bus lines, four railroads, and forty-two common-carrier truck lines.

Your Own Walking Tour

The San Antonio Conservation Society has devised a walking tour of downtown historic sites called "The Texas Star Trail." The Society provides a map with descriptions of sites and routes to get to them. You can begin at any point along its 2.6-mile length. The route can also be abbreviated or walked in sections. Each of the locations numbered on the map is marked at the site with a large red and blue aluminum Texas Star plaque. Instructions for the walk are part of the map. The society also provides directions for a King William Walk. To obtain information from the San Antonio Conservation Society, phone (210) 224-6163, or write to the Society at 107 King William Street, San Antonio, Texas 78204. The fax number is (210) 224-6168.

Guided Tours

Among the best sources of information about various tours and specially trained guides is the city's official Visitor Information Center. To contact *certified* tour guides—experts on a wide area— you can write to the Professional Tour Guide Association of San Antonio, P.O. Box 17256, San Antonio, TX 78217. Their telephone number is (210) 228-5097. Trained riverboat guides can tell you about noteworthy sites on the river banks as you cruise around the downtown area beside the River Walk. Among other guided tours are those presented by Texas Trolley, San Antonio City Tours, Lone Star Trolley Tours, and Gray Line of San Antonio.

Acknowledgments

I want to thank Judyth Rigler, book editor for the *San Antonio Express-News*, who in 1990 encouraged me to use my articles published in San Antonio newspapers and in *Texas Highways* magazine as bases for a book. The project became a totally new undertaking in which portions of my published articles comprised only fragments of paragraphs here and there.

Without the rich lode of information made available to me by John Leal—until recently the Bexar County Archivist—the book would have had many fewer anecdotes. His careful review of my early manuscript was reassuring. John is a ninth-generation descendant of the first mayor of San Antonio, Juan Leal Goraz, who by general consensus became *alcalde* (mayor) in 1731—appointed to the office for life by a representative of the Spanish Crown.

You can thank John Igo, lifelong San Antonian with a prodigious memory, Professor of English Emeritus at San Antonio College, poet, theater historian, novelist, and book reviewer, for generously listing many specific comments to greatly enrich the final manuscript.

I thank Mrs. Ilse Griffith, former manager of the bookstore of the San Antonio Conservation Society, and later Chairman of the Society's Library/Archives standing committee. As a knowledgeable collector and student of Texas books and a kindly adviser on the mysteries of San Antonio life, this wonderful lady, born in 1900, shared with me her keen view of the wide Texas world. New Braunfels book dealer Fred White, Sr., opened his book-filled warehouse a number of times to me when he lived in Bryan, Texas, and for years has kept me informed of Texas books I could add to my library. Fred and his wife, Edith, long active as a Daughter of the Republic of Texas, have been both advisers and friends to me. San Antonio book appraiser and dealer Dr. Frank Kellel also has been very helpful.

The late J. John "Jack" Newman, former writer for the *San Antonio Light*, with experience as first chairman of the Texas Folklife Festival, director of international relations for HemisFair '68, and chairman of the San Antonio Bicentennial Committee, gave me valuable comments on the manuscript.

One of the most knowledgeable San Antonians about the history and lore of the city, Sue McDonald, a lifelong Texan from Victoria, has been lecturing and officially guiding visitors in the Enchanted City for more than ten years. A consultant for several destination management companies, Sue is past president of the Professional Tour Guide Association of San Antonio. Her comments on my manuscript were of extraordinary help. In a similar way, my friend Sandra Hodsdon Carr, veteran editor at the University of Texas Institute of Texan Cultures, provided keen appraisal by a scholar more aware than most Texans of the implications of San Antonio's unique confluence of cultures.

I thank local historians Mary Ann Noonan Guerra and Henry Guerra for advising me years ago to study the writings of the diarists who came with the Spanish authorities to the San Antonio area in the 1600s and 1700s. By reading the diarists, one learns, for example, that San Antonio was founded on San Pedro Creek, not on the San Antonio River.

Dr. Félix D. Almaráz, Jr., professor of history at the University of Texas at San Antonio, author, former *Express-News* columnist, fellow and 1995-1996 president of the Texas State Historical Association, and for many years an official in the Bexar County Historical Commission, has been extraordinarily helpful to me as a constant adviser and friend. Of priceless help to me also was Robert H. Thonhoff, friend, historian, author, fellow and 1994-1995 president of the Texas State Historical Association.

It was Susan Yerkes, columnist for the *San Antonio Light* in 1987 and now a *San Antonio Express-News* columnist, whose mention of my interest in having the city erect signs identifying historic San Pedro Creek prompted my deeper research into San

Antonio's origins. After reading her column, Cyndi Taylor Krier, then a State Senator and now the County Judge of the Bexar County Commissioners Court, asked me to apply for a Texas Historical Marker to be placed by the creek at Houston and Camaron streets. I thank both of them for inspiring me to delve into the enchanting history of San Antonio. I thank my friends Jake and Celia Flores for sparking my interest in the history of San Pedro Creek, Haymarket Plaza, and the chili queens, after Jake, a gifted metal sculptor—and now director general of Casa San Antonio in Guadalajara, Mexico—was elected president of El Mercado Merchants Association in 1987.

San Antonio's Historic Preservation Officer for nineteen years before retiring in 1992, Mrs. R. Jean Osborne, known to everyone as "Pat," was unusually helpful with advice. The city is dotted with architectural treasures she has heroically helped save from destruction.

I'm indebted to Dora Guerra, recently head of special collections and archives at the library of the University of Texas at San Antonio, for translating a significant but obscure eighteenth-century Spanish document for me—and for other advice and help.

Archaeologist Waynne Cox, Research Associate, Center for Archaeological Research at the University of Texas, San Antonio—and a longtime scholar of local history—reviewed my manuscript at an early stage and provided valuable insights then and later.

I also owe much to the kindly assistance of Cathy Herpich, former director, and Martha Utterback, Linda Edwards, Charles (Rusty) Gamez, Warren Stricker, Linda Koch, Jeannette Phinney, and others at the Daughters of the Republic of Texas Library at the Alamo, and to Mrs. Jo Myler and other librarians at the Central Library. Judy Zipp, librarian of the *Express-News* (now retired), assisted me in many ways. Experts at the University of Texas Institute of Texan Cultures at San Antonio, especially photo archivist Tom Shelton, Diane Bruce, and Claire Bass, gave me generously of their time and advice. Presidents and other officials at the San Antonio Conservation Society have helped me for a decade to better understand the city's history. At the Society library, Mrs. C. S. (Nellie Lee) Weincek, Mrs. Eva Milstead, and Kathy Bailey have helped me for years. Mendell Morgan, library director of the University of the Incarnate Word in San Antonio, and librarians at San Antonio's Trinity University, San Antonio College, and the Center for American History at the University of Texas in Austin shared with me their special knowledge and limited time.

In compiling data for a book dealing with more than three centuries of San Antonio and Texas history, I have sought the advice of a variety of experts, some of them possessing rarely found information and some in positions calling for special knowledge about the city. Adolph Herrera—a descendant of a signer of the Texas Republic's Declaration of Independence, José Francisco Ruíz, as well as of San Antonio's mayor in 1836, Francisco Antonio Ruíz—has been especially helpful. So has Kevin R. Young, historical consultant and a leading expert on authentic living-history presentations. Dr. Scott Baird, Associate Professor of Linguistics at Trinity University, gave me valuable insights on special ways that San Antonians pronounce certain words. Ernie Loeffler, Director of Public Relations, San Antonio Convention and Visitors Bureau, and Tina Rosales, researcher at the Greater San Antonio Chamber of Commerce, have provided essential information.

The dean of Texas historical illustrators, José Cisneros of El Paso, has most generously permitted me to use a number of his distinctive drawings of early-day Texas, as has Jack Jackson, noted illustrator of western history and a fellow in the Texas State Historical Association. Eric von Schmidt, whom I've known for decades, permitted me to use what I believe is the best researched and most spectacular painting of the Battle of the Alamo ever created. The beautifully executed original is ten feet high and twenty-three feet wide.

Throughout the book you see the illustrations of Fred Himes, a comic book illustrator, court illustrator, student of history, and friend over the years. Throughout the final stages of the production of this book, he advised me on art technicalities as well as creating unprecedented Texas action scenes.

I thank Alice Evett-Geron, among the most experienced book editors in Texas, who used her meticulous eye to detect inconsistencies in my manuscript, and who expertly excised all asides, commentaries, and quotations that could impede the textual flow.

I am profoundly grateful to Lynnell Burkett, Editorial Page Editor of the *Express-News,* who in July 1995 invited me to submit my manuscript for possible publication as a book. Her trust—and that of W. Lawrence Walker, Jr., Publisher and CEO of the *Express-News*—that I could provide readers with an interesting and informative view of San Antonio made this new publishing venture possible.

Most of all, I publicly thank Dr. Isabel Yumol Jennings, my wife, for her professional advice on languages, knowledge of computers, and complete support and encouragement during the years when this book sought to take center stage in our lives.

January 1, 1998
Frank W. Jennings
San Antonio, Texas

Index

About the author

A native of Montana, and for the past twenty years a resident of Texas, Frank W. Jennings worked for forty years as a civilian writer and editor of military policy and motivational communication with the U.S. Army in the Philippines, and Office of the Secretary of Defense and Office of the Secretary of the Air Force in Washington D.C. and in San Antonio. After attending the University of Nebraska, he was drafted by the Army, and commissioned an officer and later appointed civilian director of Information Services for the Philippine and Ryuku Islands (Okinawa). He served for five years as editor in chief in the Armed Forces Information and Education Division of the Office of the Secretary of Defense. For twenty-six years, until 1985, he was the writer-editor of the biweekly Air Force Policy Letter for Commanders ("the Blue Letter"), published by the Director of Public Affairs in the Office of the Secretary of the Air Force. He is a retired lieutenant colonel in the U.S. Air Force Reserve.

Jennings has written numerous articles on Texas historical topics in the *Texas Highways* monthly travel magazine, *San Antonio Express-News*, the former *San Antonio Light*, the *San Antonio Conservation Society News*, and *The Senior Sentinel*, a newspaper published monthly by the Senior Citizens Council of Bexar County. He is an active member of the Texas State Historical Association, the San Antonio Historical Association, the San Antonio Genealogical & Historical Society, the San Antonio Conservation Society, and the Vaqueros, the San Antonio corral of Westerners International.

Eric von Schmidt's painting of the Battle of the Alamo was completed in March 1986, as it hung on a wall in San Antonio's Witte Museum. He spent a month and a half adding final details—for example, placing statues (St. Francis and St. Dominic) in the upper niches of the former mission's facade. He had worked on the ten-foot by twenty-three-foot painting for more than three years, researching every aspect, even the exact types of the several kinds of weapons used by both the Mexican Government troops and Texian and Tejano defenders—and details of uniforms and clothing,

such as Davy Crockett's "peculiar cap" mentioned by Susanna Dickinson. As seen in this painting, Crockett's headgear has a visor. In an article in the March 1986 *Smithsonian*, von Schmidt described his research, including his analysis of the famous Alamo Battle paintings done in earlier years. The scene he captured was, he says, about fifteen or twenty minutes before the battle's end around 6:30 A.M. — "three days after the full moon on March 6, 1836." This was just before the Texas fighters in the open had withdrawn to the long barracks and the church. (Courtesy Eric von Schmidt)